THE ESSENTIAL HANDBOOK
OF INTERNAL AUDITING

THE ESSENTIAL HANDBOOK
OF INTERNAL AUDITING

K H Spencer Pickett

John Wiley & Sons, Ltd

Other Wiley Editorial Offices

John Wiley & Sons Inc., 111 River Street, Hoboken, NJ 07030, USA

Jossey-Bass, 989 Market Street, San Francisco, CA 94103-1741, USA

Wiley-VCH Verlag GmbH, Boschstr. 12, D-69469 Weinheim, Germany

John Wiley & Sons Australia Ltd, 33 Park Road, Milton, Queensland 4064, Australia

John Wiley & Sons (Asia) Pte Ltd, 2 Clementi Loop #02-01, Jin Xing Distripark, Singapore 129809

John Wiley & Sons Canada Ltd, 22 Worcester Road, Etobicoke, Ontario, Canada M9W 1L1

Wiley also publishes its books in a variety of electronic formats. Some content that appears
in print may not be available in electronic books.

Library of Congress Cataloging-in-Publication Data:

Pickett, K. H. Spencer.
   The essential handbook of internal auditing / K. H. Spencer Pickett.
        p. cm.
   Condensed version of: Internal auditing handbook. 2nd ed. c2003.
   Includes bibliographical references and index.
   ISBN-13 978-0-470-01316-8 (pbk. : alk. paper)
   ISBN-10 0-470-01316-8 (pbk. : alk. paper)
   1. Auditing, Internal.   I. Pickett, K. H. Spencer. Internal auditing
handbook. II. Title.
   HF5668.25.P53 2005
   657'.458—dc21
                                               2005004185

British Library Cataloguing in Publication Data

A catalogue record for this book is available from the British Library

ISBN-13 978-0-470-01316-8 (PB)
ISBN-10 0-470-01316-8 (PB)

Typeset in 9.5/12pt Gill Sans Light by Laserwords Private Limited, Chennai, India
Printed and bound in Great Britain by Antony Rowe Ltd, Chippenham, Wiltshire
This book is printed on acid-free paper responsibly manufactured from sustainable forestry
in which at least two trees are planted for each one used for paper production.

This book is dedicated to the memory
of my father, Harry Pickett

CONTENTS

LIST OF ABBREVIATIONS

AC	Audit Committee
ACCA	Association of Chartered Certified Accountants
AICPA	American Institute of Certified Public Accountants
AO	Accounting Officer
APA	Audit Policy and Advice
APB	Auditing Practices Board
BBC	British Broadcasting Corporation
BCCI	Bank of Credit and Commerce International
CBI	Confederation of British Industry
CCAB	Consultative Committee of Accounting Bodies
CCTV	Closed Circuit Television
CEO	Chief Executive Officer
CFO	Chief Finance Officer
CG	Corporate Governance
CICA	Canadian Institute of Chartered Accountants
CIMA	Chartered Institute of Management Accountants
CIPFA	Chartered Institute of Public Finance and Accountancy
CISA	Certified Information Systems Auditor
COBIT	Control Objectives for Information and Related Technology
CoCo	Criteria of Control
COSO	Committee of Sponsoring Organizations of the Treadway Commission
CPA	Certified Public Accountant
CRO	Chief Risk Officer
CRSA	Control Risk Self-Assessment
CSA	Control Self-Assessment
DA	District Audit
DF	Director of Finance
DTI	Department of Trade and Industry
EA	External Audit
FCO	Foreign and Commonwealth Office
GAAP	Generally Accepted Accounting Policies
HMT	Her Majesty's Treasury
HR	Human Resources
IA	Internal Audit
ICAEW	Institute of Chartered Accountants in England and Wales
IIA	Institute of Internal Auditors
IIA Inc.	Institute of Internal Auditors Incorporated (USA)
IIA.UK&Ireland	Institute of Internal Auditors in the United Kingdom and Ireland
IoD	Institute of Directors
IS	Information Systems

ISO	International Standards Organization
IT	Information Technology
KPI	Key Performance Indicators
LSE	London Stock Exchange
MIS	Management Information Systems
NAO	National Audit Office
NED	Non-Executive Director
NHS	National Health Service
PC	Personal Computer
PI	Performance Indicators
PPF	Professional Practices Framework
PR	Public Relations
PwC	PricewaterhouseCoopers
QA	Quality Assurance
RM	Risk Management
SE	Stock Exchange
SEC	Securities and Exchange Commission
SEE	Social, Ethical and Environmental
SIC	Statement on Internal Control
TI	Transparency International
UK	United Kingdom
USA	United States of America
VFM	Value for Money

Chapter 1

INTRODUCTION

Introduction

The second edition of the *Internal Auditing Handbook* was published in December 2003 and reflected the significant changes in the field of internal auditing over the last few years. This detailed handbook comprised over 700 pages of text covering all aspects of the work of the 'new look' internal auditors who carry the weight of a heightened expectation from society on their shoulders. *The Essential Handbook of Internal Auditing* is a slimmed down version of the original handbook and is aimed at students, auditors, managers and the growing army of people who need to know a little more about internal auditing. In this way, *The Essential Handbook* consists of extracts from the main handbook for those who need a less detailed account of the world and work of the internal auditor. Note that the term chief audit executive (CAE) is used throughout the handbook to describe the top position within an organization responsible for the internal audit activities.

1.1 Reasoning behind the Book

The new context for internal auditing is set firmly within the corporate governance arena. As a response, the Institute of Internal Auditors has designed a new definition of internal auditing:

> Internal auditing is an independent, objective assurance and consulting activity designed to add value and improve an organization's operations. It helps an organisation accomplish its objectives by bringing a systematic, disciplined approach to evaluate and improve the effectiveness of risk management, control and governance processes.[1]

The Essential Handbook of Internal Auditing contains the same format as the original handbook and includes chapters on Corporate Governance Perspectives, Managing Risk and Internal Controls. It is only after having addressed these three interrelated topics that we can really appreciate the internal audit role. There are chapters on professional standards, audit approaches, managing internal audit, planning, performing and reporting audit work and specialist areas such as consulting projects, fraud and information systems. The final chapter attempts to look towards the future. Note that there are several updates in this new book whenever it has been necessary to track important developments during 2004 and beyond.

1.2 The IIA Standards and Links to the Book

The Essential Handbook addresses many aspects of internal auditing that are documented in the Institute of Internal Auditors' (IIA) professional standards. The Attribute Standards outline what a good internal audit set-up should look like, while the Performance Standards set a benchmark for the audit task. Together with the Practice Advisories (and Professional Briefing Notes) and other reference material they constitute a professional framework for internal auditing.

1.3 How to Navigate around the Book

A brief synopsis of the Handbook should help the reader work through the material.

Chapter 1 — Introduction

This first chapter deals with the content of the Handbook. It is important to establish the role of internal audit at the start of the book to retain this focus throughout the next few chapters that cover corporate perspectives.

Chapter 2 — Corporate Governance Perspectives

Chapter 2 covers corporate governance in general in that it summarizes the topic from a business standpoint rather than focusing just on the internal audit provisions. The governance equation is quickly established, and then profiles of some of the well-known scandals are used to demonstrate how fragile the accountability frameworks are. New look models of corporate governance are detailed using extracts from various codes and guidance to form a challenge to business, government and not-for-profit sectors.

Chapter 3 — Managing Risk

Many writers argue that we are entering a new dimension of business, accounting and audit whereby risk-based strategies are essential to the continuing success of all organizations. Reference is made to various risk standards and policies and we comment on the need to formulate a risk management cycle as part of the response to threats and opportunities.

Chapter 4 — Internal Controls

Some noted writers argue that internal control is a most important concept for internal auditors to get to grips with. Others simply suggest that we need to understand where controls fit into the risk management equation. Whatever the case, it is important to address this topic before we can get into the detailed material on internal auditing.

Chapter 5 — The Internal Audit Role

This chapter moves into the front line of internal audit material. Having got through the reasoning behind the audit role (governance, risk management and control), we can turn to the actual role. The basic building blocks of the charter, independence, ethics and so on are all essential aspects of the Handbook.

Chapter 6 — Professionalism

The auditors' work will be determined by the needs of the organization and the experiences of senior auditors, and most audit shops arrive at a workable compromise. One feature of the upwards direction of the internal audit function is the growing importance of professional standards and this is dealt with in Chapter six.

Chapter 7—The Audit Approach

There is a wide range and variety of audit services that fall under the guise of internal auditing and a lot depends on the adopted approach. Rather than simply fall into one approach, it is much better to assess the available positions armed with a good knowledge of possible alternatives. Control Risk Self-Assessment (CRSA) is discussed along with other specialist audit work involving management consulting, fraud investigations and information systems auditing.

Chapter 8—Setting an Audit Strategy

One view is that formulating an internal audit strategy is one of the most important tasks for the chief audit executives and this is covered in Chapter eight.

Chapter 9—Audit Field Work

Audit field work covers the entire audit process, from planning the assignment to reporting the results, while interviewing is discussed as an important means of obtaining information for the audit.

Chapter 10—Meeting the Challenge

This short chapter attempts to track key developments that impact on internal auditing and includes comments from various sources on its future direction.

1.4 The Handbook as a Development Tool

The Essential Handbook of Internal Auditing contains a basic foundation of audit information that should be assimilated by the reader and there are various multi-choice questions at the end of each chapter that can be used to gauge the extent to which this assimilation is working (see Appendix A for a suggested answer guide). Answers to the multi-choice questions may be entered in the form that can be found at Appendix B. Where The Essential Handbook is being used as an educational tool by universities and colleges, the answer guide should be removed before the book is given out to students. Students may be given three minutes per question to tackle the multi-choice questions and asked to record their answers as Appendix B. There are some 100 questions and a score of 60% and above may suggest that the student or audit trainee has achieved an acceptable standard in acquiring a basic understanding of modern internal auditing.

1.5 The Development of Internal Auditing

Internal audit is now a fully developed profession. An individual employed in internal audit ten years ago would find an unrecognizable situation in terms of the audit role, services provided, and approach. For a full appreciation of internal auditing, it is necessary to trace these developments and extend trends into the future. It is a good idea to start with the late Lawrence Sawyer, known as the Godfather of internal audit, to open the debate on the audit role. Sawyer has said that audit has a long and noble history: 'Ancient Rome "hearing of accounts" one official compares records with another—oral verification gave rise to the term "audit" from the Latin "auditus"—a hearing.'[2]

The Evolution of the Audit Function

It is important to understand the roots of internal auditing and the way it has developed over the years.

1 Extension of external audit   Internal audit developed as an extension of the external audit role in testing the reliability of accounting records that contribute to published financial statements. The IIA.UK&Ireland have suggested this link between external and internal audit:

> The nineteenth century saw the proliferation of owners who delegated the day-to-day management of their businesses to others. These owners needed an independent assessment of the performance of their organizations. They were at greater risk of error, omissions or fraud in the business activities and in the reporting of the performance of these businesses than owner-managers. This first gave rise to the profession of external auditing. External auditors examine the accounting data and give owners an opinion on the accuracy and reliability of this data. More slowly the need for internal auditing of business activities was recognized. Initially this activity focused on the accounting records. Gradually it has evolved as an assurance and consulting activity focused on risk management, control and governance processes. Both external audit and internal audit exist because owners cannot directly satisfy themselves on the performance and reporting of their business and their managers cannot give an independent view.[3]

2 Internal check   The testing role progressed to cover non-financial areas, and this equated the internal audit function to a form of internal check. Vast numbers of transactions were double-checked to provide assurances that they were correct and properly authorized by laid-down procedures. The infamous 'audit stamp' reigned supreme indicating that a document was deemed correct and above board.

3 Probity work   Probity work arrived next as an adaptation of checking accounting records where the auditors would arrive unannounced at various locations and local offices, and perform a detailed series of tests according to a preconceived audit programme. Management was presented with a list of errors and queries that were uncovered by the auditors. The auditors either worked as a small team based in accountancy or had dual posts where they had special audit duties in addition to their general accounting role.

4 Non-financial systems   The shift in low-level checking arose when audit acquired a degree of separation from the accounting function with internal audit sections being purposely established. This allowed a level of audit management to develop which in turn raised the status of the audit function away from a complement of junior staff completing standardized audit programmes.

5 Chief auditors   Another thrust towards a high profile, professional audit department was provided through employing chief internal auditors (or chief audit executives) with high organizational status.

6 Audit committees   Audit committees bring about the concept of the audit function reporting to the highest levels and this had a positive impact on perceived status. Securing the attention of the board, chief executive, managing director, non-executive directors and senior management also provides an avenue for high-level audit work, able to tackle the most sensitive corporate issues.

7 Professionalism   The Institute of Internal Auditors (IIA) has some history going back over 50 years. *Brink's Modern Internal Auditing* has outlined the development of the IIA:

> In 1942, IIA was launched. Its first membership was started in New York City, with Chicago soon to follow. The IIA was formed by people who were given the title internal auditor by their organizations and wanted to both share experiences and gain knowledge with others in this new professional field. A profession was born that has undergone many changes over subsequent years.[4]

The Development of Internal Audit Services

The developmental process outlined above highlights the way the function has progressed in assuming a higher profile and a greater degree of professionalism, and these developments over the last 20 years may likewise be traced:

1 Internal check procedures   Internal audit was seen as an integral component of the internal checking procedures designed to double-check accounting transactions.

2 Transaction-based approach   The transactions approach came next, where a continuous programme of tests was used to isolate errors or frauds.

3 Statistical sampling   Statistical sampling was later applied to reduce the level of testing along with a move away from examining all available documents or book entries.

4 Probity-based work   Probity-based work developed next, again featuring the transaction approach where anything untoward was investigated.

5 Spot checks   It was then possible to reduce the level of probity visits by making unannounced spot checks so that the audit deterrent (the possibility of being audited) would reduce the risk of irregularity. Moreover, most internal auditors assumed a 'Gotha' mentality where their greatest achievements resided in the task of finding errors, abuse and/or neglect by managers and their staff.

6 Risk analysis   The transaction/probity approach could be restricted by applying a form of risk analysis to the defined audit areas so that only high risk ones would be visited. Each unit might then be ranked so that the high risk ones would be visited first and/or using greater resources.

7 Systems-based approach   Then came a move away from the regime of management by fear to a more helpful service. Systems-based audits (SBA) are used to advise management on the types of controls they should be using. Testing was directed more at the controls than to highlight errors for their own sake.

8 Operational audit   Attention to operational areas outside the financial arena provided an opportunity to perform work not done by the external auditor. The concepts of economy, efficiency and effectiveness were built into models that evaluated the value-for-money implications of an area under review.

9 Management audit   Management audit moves up a level to address control issues arising from managing an activity. It involves an appreciation of the finer points relating to the various managerial processes that move the organization towards its objectives.

10 Risk-based auditing   Many internal audit shops have now moved into risk-based auditing where the audit service is driven by the way the organization perceives and manages risk. Rather than start with set controls and whether they are being applied throughout the organization properly, the audit process starts with understanding the risks that need to be addressed by these systems of internal control.

This is no linear progression in audit services with many forces working to take the profession back to more traditional models of the audit role where compliance and fraud work (financial propriety) are the key services in demand.

Moving Internal Audit out of Accountancy

Many of the trends behind the development of internal audit point to the ultimate position where the audit function becomes a high profile autonomous department reporting at the highest level. This may depend on moving out audit functions currently based in accountancy. It is possible to establish internal audit as a separate profession so that one would employ internal auditors as opposed to accountants. This is a moot point in that there are those who feel that the auditor is above all an accountant. Not only is this view short-sighted but it is also steeped in the old version of the internal auditor as a poor cousin of the external auditor. The true audit professional is called upon to review complicated and varied systems even if the more complicated and sensitive ones may often be financially based. A multidisciplinary approach provides the flexibility required to deal with operational areas. Many organizations require internal auditors to hold an accounting qualification or have accountancy experience. A move outside the finance function allows staff to be employed without an accounting background. There are clear benefits in this move in terms of securing a firmer level of independence from the finance function:

- The traditional reporting line to the director of finance (DF) may have in the past created a potential barrier to audit objectivity.
- One might therefore give greater attention to the managerial aspects of providing financial systems and move away from merely checking the resulting transactions.
- The relationship with external audit may become better defined where the differing objectives are clarified.
- The audit approach may move from an emphasis on financial audits to the exciting prospect of reviewing the entire risk management process itself.
- The potential for establishing a powerful chief audit executive (CAE) may arise which might be compared to the previous position where the CAE merely acted as a go-between for the director of finance (DF) and the audit staff, giving them batches of projects that the DF wanted done.

In short we would need to be close to, but at the same time be some distance from, the DF. However, as we move into the era of the audit committee, and the stronger links between this forum and internal audit, things are changing. The trend is for more of a break between the finance link, as internal audit gets more and more involved in the actual business side of the organization. Again, this move is strengthened by the growing involvement in enterprise-wide risk management. The latest position is that there is normally no longer a clear logic to the chief audit executive to continue to hold a reporting line to the director of finance.

Influences on the Internal Audit Role

1 Contracting out internal audit   All internal auditing departments are under threat where the in-house unit may be deleted, downsized or replaced by an inspectorate, quality assurance or operational review service. All CAEs should have a number of key issues uppermost in their minds including:

- A formal strategy for meeting competition from internal and/or external sources.
- The audit budget and current charge-out rates for each auditor and how these figures compare to other audit departments.
- The pricing strategy for audit services will range between being cheap and cheerful to being extremely expensive.

The pricing strategy cannot be completed until marketing research has been carried out that establishes exactly what the client requires.

2 Globalization   The big picture of internal auditing must include that it is a discipline universally applicable throughout the world. The IIA's professional standards are applied in each member country with slight changes in terminology to accommodate local requirements, and there now exists a Global IIA with relevant representation from across the world.

3 Quality management   The continuing interest in quality management is derived from a desire to secure excellence in service/product delivery. This allows a top downwards review of existing practices. Internal auditors are well versed in the principles and practice of management, which is examined in IIA examinations.

4 The compliance role   There is some debate on the role of internal audit in compliance with procedure. The technical view argues we have moved away from detailed checking as the profession developed. One may now audit corporate systems of importance to the entire welfare of the organization. However, there are organizations such as banks and retail companies that make great play of compliance checks and have a need for an audit service that management knows and understands.

5 Independence   Much has been written on independence and it is no longer treated as an esoteric entity that is either held on to, or given up through greed or ignorance. A response to the threat of external competition from the big accountancy firms was that they could not be independent. This argument is insufficient. Independence is perceived more practically as the basic ability to do a good job.

6 The expectation gap   Audit services will have to be properly marketed, which is essentially based on defining and meeting client needs. This feature poses no problem as long as clients know what to expect from their internal auditors. It does, however, become a concern when this is not the case, and there is a clear gap in what is expected and what is provided.

7 *Legislation*   This is an important component in the development of internal auditing:

- It may alter the audit role by providing additional work.
- It may bring into the frame competitors for the current audit contract.
- It may impact the status of internal auditing, e.g. any moves towards mandatory audit committees or for that matter mandatory internal audit.

8 *Corporate governance, risk management and control*   As suggested by the new definition of internal auditing, these three concepts now form the framework for the design and provision of the internal audit service. This is why the next three chapters deal with these topics.

Summary and Conclusions

This first chapter of *The Essential Handbook* takes the reader through the structure of the book and highlights the pivotal role of the IIA standards. We have also provided a brief snapshot of the development of the internal audit role as an introduction to the subject. Many of the points mentioned above are dealt with in some detail in the main part of the book, although it is as well to keep in mind the basics of internal audit while reading more widely. The concept of internal audit is really quite simple—it is the task of putting the ideals into practice that proves more trying. We have featured Sawyer's views in this chapter, which is why we close with another quote on the wide range of benefits from a good internal audit team:

> IA can assist top management in:
>
> - monitoring activities top management cannot itself monitor;
> - identifying and minimizing risks;
> - validating reports to senior management;.
> - protecting senior management in technical analysis beyond its ken;
> - providing information for the decision-making process;
> - reviewing for the future as well as for the past;
> - helping line managers manage by pointing to violation of procedures and management principles.[5]

Whatever the new risk-centred jargon used to describe the audit role, many of the above benefits described by Sawyer remain constant. A worthwhile profession is based on clear principles, and not just fancy jargon.

Chapter 1: Multi-Choice Questions

Having worked through the chapter the following multi-choice questions may be attempted. (See Appendix A for suggested answer guide and Appendix B where you may record your score).

1. **Insert the missing word:**
   Internal auditing is an independent, ... assurance and consulting activity designed to add value and improve an organization's operations. It helps an organisation accomplish its objectives by bringing a systematic, disciplined approach to evaluate and improve the effectiveness of risk management, control and governance processes.

a. professional.
b. objective.
c. systematic.
d. reliable.

2. Which is the most appropriate sentence?
    a. The Implementation Standards outline what a good internal audit set-up should look like, while the Performance Standards set a benchmark for the audit task.
    b. The Attribute Standards outline what a good internal audit set-up should look like, while the Performance Standards set a benchmark for the audit structure.
    c. The Attribute Standards outline what a good internal audit set-up should look like, while the Performance Standards set a benchmark for the audit task.
    d. The Attribute Standards outline what a good internal audit set-up should do, while the Performance Standards set a benchmark for the audit task.

3. Insert the missing word:
Sawyer has said that audit has a long and noble history: 'Ancient Rome "hearing of accounts" one official compares records with another—oral verification gave rise to the term "audit" from the Latin "auditus"—. . . . .'.
    a. conference.
    b. verification.
    c. account.
    d. hearing.

4. Insert the missing word:
The infamous . . . . reigned supreme indicating that a document was deemed correct and above board.
    a. 'audit stamp'.
    b. 'audit approval'.
    c. 'audit nose'.
    d. 'sign-off'.

5. Which is the most appropriate sentence?
    a. Moreover, most internal auditors assumed a 'Gotha' mentality where their greatest achievements resided in the task of finding good performance by managers and their staff.
    b. Moreover, most internal auditors assumed a 'Gotha' mentality where their greatest fear resided in the task of finding errors, abuse and/or neglect by managers and their staff.
    c. Moreover, most internal auditors assumed a 'Gotha' mentality where their greatest achievements resided in the task of finding errors, abuse and/or neglect by managers and their staff.
    d. Moreover, most internal auditors assumed a 'partnership' mentality where their greatest achievements resided in the task of finding errors, abuse and/or neglect by managers and their staff.

References

1. IIA Professional Practices Framework.
2. Sawyer, Lawrence B. and Dittenhofer, Mortimer A., Assisted by Scheiner James H. (1996) *Sawyer's Internal Auditing*, 4th edition, Florida: The Institute of Internal Auditors, p. 8.

3. Internal Auditing (2002) *Distance Learning Module*, Institute of Internal Auditors UK&Ireland.
4. Moeller, Robert and Witt, Herbert (1999) *Brink's Modern Internal Auditing*, 5th edition, New York: John Wiley and Sons Inc.
5. Sawyer, Lawrence B. and Dittenhofer, Mortimer A., assisted by Scheiner James H. (1996) *Sawyer's Internal Auditing*, 4th edition, Florida: The Institute of Internal Auditors, p. 13.

Chapter 2

CORPORATE GOVERNANCE PERSPECTIVES

Introduction

Corporate governance is a term that, over the last two decades, has found its way into popular literature. It has been described by Sir Adrian Cadbury as the way organizations are directed and controlled. This simple statement contains many profound elements including the performance/conformance argument. An organization's main task is to achieve the level of performance that it was established for. But at the same time, an organization must adhere to all relevant standards, rules, laws, regulations, policies and expectations that form a framework within which this performance must be assessed. Which in turn may cause many difficulties in the real world. Corporate governance codes and policies have come to be relied on to re-establish the performance/conformance balance to ensure integrity, openness and accountability. The codes are supported by structures that promote these three ideals and the internal audit function is a key component of the structure. Internal audit has a further role in educating top management in the available solutions and to help develop tools and techniques in this respect. The internal auditor who has a sound grasp of corporate governance is best placed to play a major role in the drive to ensuring sustainability as well as success in all business and public service sectors. The sections covered in this chapter are:

2.1   The Agency Concept
2.2   Corporate Ethics and Accountability
2.3   International Scandals and their Impact
2.4   Models of Corporate Governance
2.5   Putting Governance into Practice
2.6   The External Audit
2.7   The Audit Committee
2.8   Internal Audit
2.9   The Link to Risk Management and Internal Control
2.10 Reporting on Internal Controls
       Summary and Conclusions
       Chapter 2: Multi-Choice Questions

2.1 The Agency Concept

The main driver for corporate governance is based on the agency concept. Here corporate bodies are overseen by directors who are appointed by the owners, i.e. the shareholders. The directors formulate a corporate strategy to achieve set objectives and meet market expectations, and in turn, employ managers and staff to implement this strategy. A simple model sets out this relationship in Figure 2.1.

Shareholders
Directors

Managers

Supervisors

Operational and front line staff

FIGURE 2.1   Corporate governance (1).

If everyone was totally competent and totally honest then the model in Figure 2.1 would work quite well. Directors oversee their managers while managers run the business through the other employees. To achieve published objectives the directors set targets for their management team, authorize a budget and then establish a mechanism for measuring performance. All business activity feeds into the accounting system and the directors report the results back to their shareholders in the annual report on performance and accompanying final accounts. Shareholders check the overall performance and financial results each year and ensure that their investment is intact. They have a right to any dividends and may well see a growth in the value of their investment through strong share prices. Meanwhile, the directors have a duty to take all reasonable steps to protect the business and account for their activities. The Stewardship concept means directors owe this responsibility to the parties who have a vested interest in the organization. They work for and on behalf of their masters, and need to demonstrate competence, which is not always easy.

There are two further mechanisms that need to be included in our model to reflect both the performance and accountability dimensions that are important in agency theory. This is a further aspect of the performance/conformance concept that has already been discussed, that is strategic performance measures and published accounts in Figure 2.2.

Shareholders

PERFORMANCE	Directors	ACCOUNTABILITY
Objectives		Directors' report
Policies	Managers	Performance review
Strategies		Final accounts
Plans	Supervisors	Profit and loss
Key PIs		Balance sheet
Procedures	Operational and front line staff	Accounting policies
Performance reports		Statutory disclosures

FIGURE 2.2   Corporate governance (2).

The standard performance accountability model needs three further refinements to ensure the proper running of the business. These are shown in Figure 2.3.

There is a raft of laws such as maximum working hours, minimum wage, anti-discrimination, consumer protection, anti-competition, insider trading, and health and safety along with company regulations set by the Department of Trade and Industry (DTI) and the Stock Exchange to guide

FIGURE 2.3   Corporate governance (3).

the way business is conducted and the way people are treated. Final accounts are checked by an external firm of accountants to ensure they show a true and fair view of the company's financial performance and position. Most organizations have a set of ethical standards that are made clear to employees and others which help define unacceptable conduct. In this way the growth, stability and demise of businesses is essentially dependent on the free flow of funds along with fair and open competition. The fittest companies survive while the less able must change, collapse or be consumed by stronger enterprises. The above model is straightforward and well understood as the proper basis for a capitalist system. The public sector is catered for by replacing the board with the accounting officer (for central government bodies) or chief executive for local authorities and other public service organizations. Not-for-profit organizations would have a similar responsible person at the helm. For public bodies, the owners are the taxpayers and the external auditors have an additional role in assessing performance and value for money (VFM) as well as verifying the financial statements. In this way public sector service strategies and performance measures are validated in the absence of the private sector profit motive. Again, a fairly simple model of corporate accountability. Unfortunately, there are certain flaws in this standard model, many of which hinder the degree of reliance that can be placed on the reports and representations published by large organizations. These potential problems include:

- Boards dominated by the chief executive officers (CEO) who manipulate the companies to their own personal agenda.
- Boards that are ineffectual and consist simply of a network of friends who fail to represent the shareholders to any real extent.
- Boards that are incompetent and meet on an irregular basis and simply rubber stamp the position set by the CEO or a small group of dominating board members.
- CEOs and chief finance officers (CFO) who conspire with other board members to distort the published results of the company for reasons of personal gain. Or because of a fear that a fall in the share price will strip the value of shares and options they hold in the company. Particularly where the market expects instant and large returns in rapid growth business sectors.
- Employees who are regularly able to abuse company systems and exploit loopholes again for personal gain.
- Significant business ventures, take-overs and development projects that involve huge shifts of resources and large returns for entrepreneurs but which involve major risks that have not been fully addressed.

- Short-term measures such as dumping waste, skipping important safety checks or exploiting third world labour and resources that reap significant returns but involve illicit hardship to third parties. Many of these acts then being concealed through misreporting or cover-ups.
- Organizations with great emphasis on success where bad news is not tolerated and losses, problems, errors or breach of procedure are either ignored or concealed.
- One-dimensional performance targets where operations are inappropriately skewed towards quick wins or figures that are massaged to produce predetermined results.
- Organizations where accountabilities have not been properly established and where a blame culture means certain employees are unfairly targeted.
- External audit routines that are designed to protect top management where the in-charge audit partner has a basic allegiance to the company directors, particularly the CFO—who in reality determines the auditor's employment prospects, fees and substantial amounts of additional consulting work.

Defining Stakeholders

The enhanced model in Figure 2.3 has changed the one-dimensional concept of *Shareholders* to the wider concept of *Stakeholders*. Most commentators argue that corporations need to acknowledge a wide range of people and groups affected by their operations and presence. Andrew Chambers has devised a 'Court of public opinion' as consisting of key figures including:

Customers	Regulators
Financiers	Business partners
Politicians	Shareholders
The media	Competitors
Employees	Government
Business leaders	Local communities[1]

Meanwhile, companies are now paying much more attention to the needs of their shareholders and as one commentator states:

> Twenty years ago management had scant if any regard for shareholders, unless they were part of the family! In the 1980s two things happened. Once management thought they had better start talking to investors because they could sack the board. Then we had firms being bid for and normally they weren't the ones which had achieved much. As they tried to defend what they had done, you heard the great cry of short-termism which really meant—we failed to perform for the last three years but don't worry, we will do for the next three. Suddenly the bulb went on in our brains that we had power and could influence management. Boards also recognised they had to talk to their shareholders. Today we do have sensible dialogues.[2]

2.2 Corporate Ethics and Accountability

The first question to ask is whether we need to establish corporate ethics within organizations? A survey by Management Today and KPMG Forensic Accounting of more than 800 directors, managers and partners illustrates why ethics needs to be considered in the working life:

- More than 2 out of 3 say that everyone lies to their boss on occasion.
- Less than half consider the people at the top to be strong ethical role models.

- Over 20% felt it was okay to surf the net for pleasure during work time.
- Around 25% would not say that favouring friends or family in awarding contracts was totally unacceptable.
- Some 7% agreed it was okay to artificially inflate profits so long as no money was stolen.
- Only 1 in 5 were prepared to say that charging personal entertainment to expenses was totally unacceptable—(less than 15% for board directors).
- People over 40, those in financial positions and those in the public sector take a more judgemental approach to ethical behaviour.
- A dishonest member of staff may receive a clean reference from 3 in 10 managers.
- Reasons for not reporting a fraud include—alienate myself, none of my business, jeopardize my job, everybody's doing it, it is fair game.
- Nearly 10% of board directors say it is acceptable to massage their profit figures as long as no money is stolen.[3]

The immediate impact of poor ethical standards is demonstrated in the following story of the demise of one small business owner: 'The garage owner who sold Britain's most expensive petrol during the fuel crisis has gone bust after being boycotted by his customers, it emerged yesterday.'[4]

Ethical Codes

There are many different codes that have been developed to suit various organizations. These codes cover items such as conduct, gifts, objectivity, and honesty.

The Nolan principles This is a set of standards that cover people in public life, be they ministers, civil servants or people working in the wider public sector. The short but powerful set of seven principles can be used as the basis for developing a more detailed code for public sector organizations. There are seven standards in the Nolan code:

1. **Selflessness**—Holders of public office should take decisions solely in terms of the public interest. They should not do so in order to gain financial or other material benefits for themselves, their family or their friends.
2. **Integrity**—Holders of public office should not place themselves under any financial or other obligation to outside individuals or organizations that might influence them in the performance of their duties.
3. **Objectivity**—In carrying out public business, including making public appointments, awarding contracts or recommending individuals for reward or benefits, holders of public office should make their choices on merit.
4. **Accountability**—Holders of public office are accountable for their decisions and action to the public and must submit themselves to whatever scrutiny is appropriate to their office.
5. **Openness**—Holders of public office should be as open as possible about all the decisions and actions that they take. They should give reasons for their decisions and restrict information only when the wider public interest clearly demands.
6. **Honesty**—Holders of public office have a duty to declare any private interests relating to their public interests and to take any steps to resolve any conflicts arising in a way that protects the public interest.
7. **Leadership**—Holders of public office should promote and support these principles by leadership and example.[5]

Implementing Ethics

Statements, codes and a recognition that corporate ethics underpins the value system of an organization are all good starters to ensuring business lives up to set standards. We need to go further in implementing suitable systems of corporate ethics so that the policies reach everyone in the organization (and those that are associated with it). The Institute of Directors (IoD) has developed the HUB programme to get ethics on the corporate agenda in a practical manner. The IoD say that:

> HUB is a long term programme to change the culture and attitude of both business and its stakeholders by benchmarking business reputation. We need to find out how our stakeholders experience our business conduct. Our reputation is founded on the perceptions our stakeholders have of our business. The IoD HUB initiative sets out to enhance the reputation of business in Britain... [6]

Ethical Reporting

The growth in Social, Ethical and Environmental (SEE) reporting has resulted in a code prepared by the Association of British Insurers on this topic, and extracts include that the board:

- takes regular account of the significance of SEE issues.
- identifies significant risks and opportunities arising from SEE issues.
- has adequate information and directors are trained in SEE issues.
- should ensure effective systems are in place to manage significant SEE risks. [7]

Some companies have taken a lead in ethical reporting. As an example there follows a quote from Anita Roddick, from the Body Shop, posted on the Body Shop website:

> I would love it if every shareholder of every company wrote a letter every time they received a company's annual report and accounts. I would like them to say something like 'Okay that's fine, very good. But where are the details of your environmental audit? Where are your details of accounting to the community? Where is your social audit?' [8]

Tesco, the retail company, have published their Corporate Social Responsibility Review (CSR) 2001/2002 on their website:

> The CSR strategy corresponds with the Tesco core Purpose and Values. We aim to set robust policies backed by a comprehensive programme and to communicate these effectively. We have a key accountability matrix which sets out the respective responsibilities of the departments and Directors for each area. We have divided our policies into three sections, Economic, Social and Environmental in accordance with GRI guidelines. Although we have divided our CSR policies into these categories, many of them, such as regeneration, straddle all three areas.
>
> 1. Economic Policies.
> 2. Corporate Governance.
> 3. Risk Management. [9]

Whistleblowing

The Public Interest Disclosure Act 1998 applies to England, Scotland and Wales. Disclosures relate to crimes, breaches of legal obligations, miscarriages of justice, dangers to health and safety or the environment and concealing information relating to these items. Protected disclosures should be made:

- In good faith.
- Not for personal gain.
- Only after all relevant internal processes have been utilized.

The burden of proof for the above rests with the employee. Internal procedures can only be avoided where:

- Employee believes s/he would be 'subject to a detriment' if disclosure made to the employer.
- Evidence would be concealed by employer.
- Employee has already made a disclosure of substantially the same information.

If internal procedures are unsafe then any official regulator should be informed (the prescribed body). Public sector employees' information classified say under the Official Secrets Act does not benefit from the Public Interest Disclosure Act's protection. Gagging clauses are probably void under the Act. Employees dismissed as a result of protected disclosure should make representation to the employment tribunal within seven days of the dismissal. Neil Baker has described the FSA's Guidance for firms' whistleblowing policies:

- A clear statement that the firms take failures seriously. Failures in this context means doing something that a worker might want to blow the whistle about.
- An indication of what is regarded as a failure.
- Respect for confidentiality of workers who raise concerns, if they wish this.
- An assurance that, where a protected disclosure has been made, the firm will take all reasonable steps to ensure that no person under its control engages in victimization.
- The opportunity to raise concerns outside the line management structure, such as with the compliance director, internal auditor or company secretary.
- Penalties for making false and malicious allegations.
- An indication of the proper way in which concerns may be raised outside the firm if necessary.
- Providing access to an external body such as an independent charity for advice.
- Making whistleblowing procedures accessible to staff of key contractors.
- Written procedures.[10]

2.3 International Scandals and their Impact

Some of the more famous cases where good governance ideals have not been met are mentioned below.

Guinness—1986

Ernest Saunders, the Chief Executive of Guinness, paid himself £3 million plus interest, and paid large sums to those who helped him rig shares in order to try and take over another drinks company, Distillers. He rigged the shares to beat Argyll, the company in competition with him to try and take over Distillers.

Barlow Clowes—1988

The Barlow Clowes business collapsed owing millions of pounds. The Joint Disciplinary Scheme (JDS) stated that there was in general inadequate planning of the Barlow Clowes audit work and that: 'in many respects the audit work was poorly controlled and inadequately focused to ensure that reliable audit opinions could be drawn'. Money was also moved between client accounts as and when the need arose and spent without any regard to the rights of investors.[11]

Polly Peck International — 1989

Asil Nadir was the head of Polly Peck International until its value dropped from £1 billion to less than half of that amount in 1989. The Stock Exchange had to suspend trading in Polly Peck International shares because of this fall in value. Asil Nadir was charged with false accounting and stealing a total of £31 million. There were also reports of insider trading. Asil Nadir fled to northern Cyprus in May 1993, shortly before his trial. Elizabeth Forsyth, Nadir's right-hand woman, however, was jailed for five years in March 1996 accused of laundering £400,000 Nadir allegedly stole from shareholders to pay off his debts.[12] Elizabeth Forsyth felt confident after fraud charges against former Polly Peck chief accountant John Turner were dropped because it was unfair to try him in Nadir's absence.[13]

BCCI (Bank of Credit and Commerce International) — 1991

BCCI, regarded as the world's biggest fraud, caused a bank operating in over 60 countries worldwide, and supposedly valued at $20 billion, to become worthless. The bank collapsed in 1991 owing $13 billion.[14]

Maxwell — 1991

Robert Maxwell, the founder and Chief Executive of the Maxwell publishing empire, manipulated funds to give the impression that the company was financially liquid, in order to disguise the fact that he had perpetrated a huge fraud, which came to light in 1991.[15]

Baring Futures (Singapore) — 1995

Baring Futures Singapore (BFS) was set up to enable the Baring Group to trade on the Singapore International Money Exchange (SIMEX). Nick Leeson, an inexperienced trader, was employed to manage both the dealing and settlement office (front and back office). Leeson was unable to trade in the UK due to a false statement made to the regulatory body for financial traders, the Securities and Futures Authority. On appointment by BFS, he opened an unauthorized account, which he used to cover up his large trading losses, which remained undiscovered until Barings collapsed in 1995.[16]

Metropolitan Police — 1995

Anthony Williams, Deputy Director of Finance for the Metropolitan Police, was exposed as a fraudster. He stole £5 million over a period of eight years between 1986 and 1994 from a secret bank account, set up as part of a highly sensitive operation against terrorists.[17]

Sumitomo Corporation — 1996

Yasuo Hamanaka was a copper trader working for Sumitomo Corporation, the world's biggest copper merchant. Yasuo Hamanaka was a rogue trader, who during ten years of double-dealing in Tokyo ran up losses of £1.2 billion. One senior manager said: 'This is probably the biggest loss you will ever see.'[18]

Daiwa Bank—1996

Between 1984 and 1995 Toshihide Iguchi made bad trades in the bond market at the Manhattan branch of Daiwa Bank. He covered up his bad trades by selling bonds from Daiwa's own accounts and forging documentation for the bank's files, to cover his tracks. He was in control of both the front and back offices of the bank, in a small understaffed branch, where his activities remained unmonitored for 11 years. [19]

Morgan Grenfell—1996

In 1996, it was revealed that Peter Young lost $600 million belonging to city bank Morgan Grenfell. Peter Young, as head of Morgan Grenfell's European Growth Unit Trust in 1995, a fund worth £788 million, became interested in buying shares in a company called Solv-Ex. Solv-Ex's US directors claimed to be able to extract oil from sand cheaply. Peter Young spent approximately £400 million of his company's money on Solv-Ex. He set up 'shell' companies in Luxembourg to buy Solv-Ex shares illegally. In 1996, Solv-Ex was under US federal investigation. By the time of his trial in 1998, Peter Young was declared mentally unfit. He attended court in women's clothing carrying a handbag.[20]

Inland Revenue—1997

Michael Allcock was group leader of the Inland Revenue's Special Office 2, investigating foreign businessmen's tax affairs between 1987 and 1992, when he was suspended from duty charged with fraud, accepting cash bribes, a lavish overseas holiday with his family, and the services of a prostitute, in exchange for information on cases. Allcock was jailed in 1997.[21]

Sellafield—2000

Process workers were to blame for the scandal that hit Sellafield nuclear power plant and led to cancelled orders and the resignation of the chief executive. Process workers at the Sellafield nuclear plant falsified records measuring batches of fuel pellets processed from reprocessed plutonium and uranium. Safety inspectors gave managers at the plant two months to present an action plan to address their failures.[22]

Alder Hey—2001

Police conducted an enquiry into Dutch pathologist Professor Dick Van Velzen, who worked at the Alder Hey Hospital in Liverpool between 1988 and 1995. The scandal came to light when a mother discovered that when her child, who died at three months, was buried in 1991, all of his organs were not intact. Eight years later organs belonging to him were discovered at Alder Hey Hospital in Liverpool, and she held a second funeral service. The Government's Chief Medical Officer Professor Liam Donaldson revealed that 10,000 hearts, brains and other organs were still being held at other hospitals across England, and that thousands of families remain unaware that the loved ones they buried have had organs illegally removed without their consent.[23]

Enron—2001

Enron, a multinational energy trading company based in Houston, Texas, collapsed when credit rating firms prepared to lower their assessments of the company's debt. Enron would have been compelled to repay loans gained on the basis of its loan rating, and faced weakened share price. Enron went from being worth $60 billion to bankruptcy and collapsed because of its complicated trading activities and financial manipulation.[24]

Just as the US economy was recovering from the Enron saga another huge scandal appeared in the form of WorldCom.

WorldCom—2002

WorldCom was valued at $180 billion in 1999. The company was originally a small local telecommunications agency that grew very quickly into one of the largest providers in the industry. There was a change of senior management at WorldCom in 2002, who asked the internal auditor to examine particular accounting transactions. The internal auditor discovered that corporate expenses were being treated as capital investments. That is, expenses were being set against long-term budgets, rather than being offset against profits immediately. This practice resulted in the inflation of WorldCom's profits and share value, creating the impression that the company was more valuable than it actually was.[25] WorldCom admitted co-ordinating one of the biggest accounting frauds in history in 2002 and inflating its profits by $3.8 billion (£2.5 billion) between January 2001 and March 2002. Six Enron directors associated with the fraud resigned in the US in December 2002. The Joint Disciplinary Scheme (JDS) will investigate the role of the now-defunct Andersen's London office in the shredding of documents.[26]

Allied Irish Bank (AIB) Allfirst (US Subsidiary)—2002

Allfirst, Allied Irish Bank's subsidiary, was based in Baltimore, Maryland, USA. In early 2002, AIB revealed that one of its traders, John Rusnak, had made transactions that resulted in a loss of almost $700 million (actual $691 million). Similarly to the Barings scandal, Rusnak had been allowed to trade unsupervised for almost five years before the scale of his losses was discovered.[27]

Xerox—2002

The Securities and Exchange Commission, the US financial regulator, filed a suit against Xerox in April 2002 for misstating its profits to the tune of almost $3 billion. Xerox reached a settlement with the SEC and agreed to pay a fine of $10 million, but neither denied or admitted any wrongdoing. The fine imposed by the Securities and Exchange Commission was the largest fine ever imposed on a publicly traded firm in relation to accounting misdeeds.[28]

Merrill Lynch—2002

The investment bank was fined by New York attorney general Eliot Spitzer to the tune of $10 million in 2002. The bank's analysts were suspected of advising investors to purchase worthless stocks, so the former could then secure investment banking business from the businesses concerned. The settlement imposed by Spitzer did not require Merrill Lynch to admit guilt for its actions.[29]

Credit Suisse First Boston (CSFB) — 2002

The Financial Services Authority (FSA), the UK's financial watchdog, fined CSFB, the US-based investment banking arm of Switzerland's Credit Suisse, £4 million ($6.4 million) for trying to mislead the Japanese tax and regulatory authorities in 2002.[30]

Over the last few years there has been a continuing stream of scandals relating to, for example, Jarvis, Railtrack, Parmalat, Equitable Life, endowment policies mis-selling, the United Nations' Iraqi oil-for-food scheme, Martha Stewart (who received a 5 months prison sentence), Goldman Sachs (theft of £3.4 m by a secretary), Bradford and Bingley (fined £650 k by the FSA), Lloyds TSB (mis-selling precipice bonds) — and other significant corporate concerns.

2.4 Models of Corporate Governance

We have established the classical model of corporate accountability and the ethical frameworks that are being used by organizations to promote sustainability. The last section provided a frightening insight into the fallout when things go wrong. The ripples caused by corporate scandals have recently become strong waves of discontent as the search has been made for workable and lasting solutions. Most solutions come in the guise of codes of practice that have been documented and appear as regulations or guidance for relevant organizations. Whatever the format and whatever the country, there is a growing trend towards corporate governance standards to be part of the way business and public services are conducted. We deal with some of the more well-known codes in this section of the chapter. The 1992 Cadbury Report described corporate governance:

> The country's economy depends on the drive and efficiency of its companies. Thus the effectiveness with which their boards discharge their responsibilities determines Britain's competitive position. They must be free to drive their companies forward, but exercise that freedom within a framework of effective accountability. This is the essence of any system of corporate governance. (Para. 1.1)

Cadbury went on to document the simple but now famous phrase: 'Corporate governance is the system by which companies are directed and controlled' (para. 2.5).[31]

Note that a synonym for governance is *controlling*. The globalization of governance processes is bringing the world closer in terms of commonality. Hand in hand with international accounting standards, we are approaching an era of closer comparability throughout the developed and developing world. One phrase that is often used by proponents of corporate government is that 'a one size fits all model will not work in practice'. Moreover, there is no point listing a set of rules that can be ticked off and filed under 'Job Done!' There needs to be a constant search for principles that set the right spirit of enterprise that has not been left to run wild. European Union regulations mean member states' listed companies have to adopt International Accounting Standards by 2005 and this has brought Europe closer to becoming a single equity market.

The UK Experience

Cadbury   The development of corporate governance in the United Kingdom provides a remarkable synopsis of the topic as it has evolved and adapted, slowly becoming immersed into the culture of the London business scene. The Code covers 19 main areas:

[1] The board should meet regularly, retain full and effective control over the company and monitor the executive management.

[2] There should be a clearly accepted division of responsibilities at the head of a company, which will ensure a balance of power and authority so that no one individual has unfettered powers of decision.

[3] The board should include non-executive directors of sufficient calibre and number for their views to carry significant weight.

[4] The board should have a formal schedule of matters specifically reserved to it for decision to ensure that the direction and control of the company are firmly in its hands.

[5] There should be an agreed procedure for directors, in the furtherance of their duties to take independent professional advice if necessary at the company's expense.

[6] All directors should have access to the advice and services of the company secretary, who is responsible to the board for ensuring that board procedures are followed and that applicable rules and regulations are complied with.

[7] Non-executive directors (NED) should bring an independent judgement to bear on issues of strategy, performance, resources, including key appointments and standards of conduct.

[8] The majority of NEDs should be independent of management and free from any business or other relationship which could materially interfere with the exercise of independent judgement, apart from their fees and shareholdings.

[9] NEDs should be appointed for specified terms and re-appointment should not be automatic.

[10] NEDs should be selected through a formal process and both this process and their appointment should be a matter for the board as a whole.

[11] Directors' service contracts should not exceed three years without shareholders' approval.

[12] There should be full disclosure of a director's total emoluments and those of the chairman and highest paid UK directors.

[13] Executive directors' pay should be subject to the recommendations of a remunerations committee made up wholly or mainly of NEDs.

[14] It is the board's duty to present a balanced and understandable assessment of the company's position.

[15] The board should ensure that an objective and professional relationship is maintained with the auditors.

[16] The board should establish an audit committee of at least three NEDs with written terms of reference which deal clearly with its authority and duties.

[17] The directors should explain their responsibility for preparing the accounts next to a statement by the auditors about their reporting responsibilities.

[18] The directors should report on the effectiveness of the company's system of internal control.

[19] The directors should report that the business is a going concern, with supporting assumptions or qualifications as necessary.

Cadbury went on to describe the underpinning principles behind the code:

1. **Openness**—on the part of the companies, within the limits set by the competitive position, is the basis for the confidence which needs to exist between business and all those who have a stake in its success. An open approach to the disclosure of information contributes to the efficient working of the market economy prompts boards to take effective action and allows shareholders and others to scrutinize companies more thoroughly.

2. **Integrity**—means both straightforward dealing and completeness. What is required of financial reporting is that it should be honest and that it should present a balanced picture of the state of the company's affairs. The integrity of reports depends on the integrity of those who prepare and present them.

3. **Accountability**—boards of directors are accountable to their shareholders and both have to play their part in making that accountability effective. Boards of directors need to do so through the quality of information which they provide to shareholders, and shareholders through their willingness to exercise their responsibilities as owners.[32]

Rutteman   The 1993 working party chaired by Paul Rutteman considered the way the Cadbury recommendations could be implemented. The draft report was issued in October 1993 and retained the view that listed companies should report on internal controls but limited this responsibility to internal financial controls.[33]

Nolan   Lord Nolan's 1994 standards in public life have been mentioned above. This forum was set up by the then Prime Minister to prepare codes for MPs, civil servants and people who are in public life, and reinforced the need to ensure a sound ethical base in the public sector, against the backdrop to allegations of sleaze and abuse that was a regular feature of the early 1990s. Also the new format of the civil service in the guise of departments, agencies, non-departmental public bodies (NDPBs) and other public bodies made it harder to ensure consistency in public behaviour. This committee was later chaired by Lord Neill and then Sir Nigel Wick and issues regular update reports to Parliament.

Greenbury   As government was beset with problems of fees, and cash paid to ministers by lobby groups and others, the City had a similar problem explaining why and how directors received what appeared to be excessive fees, bonuses and benefits (including options and special joining/leaving and pension arrangements). To address the mounting disquiet from stakeholders the Richard Greenbury Committee was set up by the Confederation of British Industry in 1995 to report independently on directors' earnings. The resultant report established a code of best practice in setting and disclosing directors' remuneration.[34]

Hampel   The committee chaired by Sir Ronnie Hampel was set up in 1995 by the London Stock Exchange, the CBI, the IoD, CCAB, National Association of Pension Funds and the Association of British Insurers. This committee was the main successor to Cadbury and had the task of updating further the corporate governance debate and ensured the stated intentions of Cadbury were being achieved. They decided that while directors should review the effectiveness of internal control they need not report on the effectiveness of these controls. Internal audit was supported but not mandatory, although the need for an internal audit function should be reviewed annually.

Combined code   The recommendations provided by Cadbury and the later reviews of corporate governance were consolidated into what was known as the Combined Code in 1998. This code became part of the Stock Exchange listing requirements but still left a gap as the guidance was simply a mix of the previous guides. It also became clear that the corporate governance provisions had some relevance to organizations beyond listed companies.

Turnbull committee   The ongoing saga of large company corporate governance was continued through the work of Sir Nigel Turnbull who prepared a short report in 1999. This working party was set up by the ICAEW in 1998 with support from the London Stock Exchange focusing on the internal control reporting provisions from the Combined Code. The final report in September 1999 was fairly brief and reinforced most of the sentiment from past work. The big leap confirmed the need to report across the business on statements of internal control (and not only the narrow financial controls), and linked this to the COSO control framework (see the chapter on internal control) and underpinning risk assessment as a lead into sound controls. This report provided the foundation for the rapid growth in enterprise-wide risk management (see the chapter on risk management). In the words of Turnbull the guidance is intended to:

- reflect sound business practice whereby internal control is embedded in the business processes by which a company pursues its objectives;
- remain relevant over time in the continually evolving business environment; and
- enable each company to apply it in a manner which takes account of its particular circumstances. (para. 8)

The guidance requires directors to exercise judgement in reviewing how the company has implemented the requirements of the Code relating to internal control and reporting to shareholders thereon. The guidance is based on the adoption by a company's board of a risk-based approach to establishing a sound system of internal control and reviewing its effectiveness. This should be incorporated by the company within its normal management and governance processes. It should not be treated as a separate exercise undertaken to meet regulatory requirements. (para. 9)

Selected extracts from the confirmed listed companies annual reporting requirements include the following:

- Principle D2: The board should maintain a sound system of internal control to safeguard shareholders' investment and the company's assets (para. 2)
- Principle D2.1: The directors should, at least annually, conduct a review of the effectiveness of the group's system of internal control and should report to shareholders that they have done so. The review should cover all controls, including financial, operational and compliance controls and risk management. (para. 3)
- Principle D.2.2: Companies which do not have an internal audit function should from time to time review the need for one. (para. 4)
- A narrative statement of how it has applied the principles set out in Section 1 of the Combined Code, providing explanation which enables its shareholders to evaluate how the principles have been applied. (para. 5.a)
- A statement as to whether or not it has complied throughout the accounting period with the Code provisions set out in Section 1 of the Combined Code. (para. 5.b)
- The intention is that companies should have a free hand to explain their governance policies in the light of the principles, including any special circumstances which have led to them adopting a particular approach. (para. 6)[35]

The saga continues and we expect to see further codes appear in the UK and abroad as the search for practical, workable and acceptable concepts goes on. In fact the Financial Reporting, which is responsible for the combined code, is reviewing the current guidance to ensure that it is effective and proportionate. The Flint review on corporate governance has issued a draft report in 2004 that asks a number of fundamental questions to drive the debate forward and get the material in published codes into the spirit of corporate behaviour[36]. These questions are designed to find out how companies are responding to governance requirements and where improvements can be made:

1. Has the Turnbull guidance succeeded in its objectives?
2. Are companies behaving differently as a result of the guidance? In particular, has the guidance had an impact on:
   - the understanding of risks and controls (a) at board level; and (b) more widely within companies and groups?
   - the way boards have approached business risk and strategy?

- the risk appetite of the board?
- improving the quality of risk management and internal control within companies?

3. What difficulties, if any, have organizations had in implementing the Turnbull guidance?
4. Should the guidance continue to retain a high level and risk-based approach to internal control rather than move to a more prescriptive approach?
5. Should the guidance continue to cover all controls?
6. Are there parts of the guidance on internal control that are (a) out of date or now unnecessary; (b) unclear; or (c) lacking in sufficient detail? If so, please identify them.
7. If additions are needed to the guidance, what form should they take, what should they cover and why would they be useful? Examples might include:
   - additional questions in the current appendix;
   - indicators to help boards and board committees identify where there may be potential cause for concern, for example of fraud or aggressive earnings management; or
   - more examples of the types of risks that boards should consider, for example business continuity risk.
8. Do you have any other suggestions for changes to the guidance that are not covered by questions 6 and 7 above?
9. How useful to investors and companies are the existing disclosures on internal control? What value is placed on such disclosures by investors when making investment decisions?
10. Would a different or extended form of disclosure facilitate better decision making? If so, how?
11. What distinctions or linkages should be made between the business risk-related disclosures to be made in the Operating and Financial Review and the disclosures made as a result of the Turnbull guidance?
12. What are the advantages and disadvantages of turning the board's private assessment of effectiveness into a public statement of their conclusion on effectiveness?
13. Would boards and investors wish to see additional disclosures on the outcomes of the boards' review of effectiveness and actions taken following that review? If so, what information would be appropriate?
14. What benefit does the existing work performed by external auditors on internal control, and the subsequent dialogue with the board, provide to: (a) the board of a company; and (b) investors?
15. What are the advantages and disadvantages of extending the external auditors' remit beyond the existing requirements? If you consider that any change should be made to the existing remit, what might this be and why?
16. What impact, if any, might an extended role for the external auditor have on the relationship and dialogue between the external auditor and the board and its committees?
17. Are there any other matters that should be brought to the attention of the Review Group?

Global Governance

Corporate governance is a concept that has affected most developed and developing countries. The Organisation for Economic Cooperation and Development has prepared an inclusive set of corporate governance principles that seeks to take on board the kept elements of this topic. This is particularly important in emerging democracies where the concept of registered companies may be less developed. The principles are as follows:

1. The corporate governance framework should promote transparent and efficient markets, be consistent with the rule of law and clearly articulate the division of responsibilities among different supervisory, regulatory and enforcement authorities.

2. The corporate governance framework should protect and facilitate the exercise of shareholders' rights.
3. The corporate governance framework should ensure the equitable treatment of all shareholders, including minority and foreign shareholders. All shareholders should have the opportunity to obtain effective redress for violation of their rights.
4. The corporate governance framework should recognize the rights of stakeholders established by law or through mutual agreements and encourage active co-operation between corporations and stakeholders in creating wealth, jobs and the sustainability of financially sound enterprises.
5. The corporate governance framework should ensure that timely and accurate disclosure is made on all material matters regarding the corporation, including the financial situation, performance, ownership, and governance of the company.
6. The corporate governance framework should ensure the strategic guidance of the company, the effective monitoring of management by the board and the board's accountability to the company and the shareholders.[37]

The Toronto Stock Exchange believes that good disclosures gives investors a solid understanding of how decisions are made that may affect their investment. With this in mind they have addressed the Canadian governance context by issuing 14 guidelines that cover:

1. **Stewardship of the company**   Which covers the strategic planning process, management of principal risks, succession planning, communications policy, integrity of internal controls.
2. **Board independence**   Where the majority of directors should be independent.
3. **Individual unrelated directors**   Where the concept of unrelated directors is addressed.
4. **Nominating committee**   For nominating and assessing directors.
5. **Assessing the board's effectiveness**   This is normally carried out by the nominating committee.
6. **Orientation and education of directors**   For new recruits to the board.
7. **Effective board size**   The adopted size should ensure effective decision making.
8. **Compensation of directors**   Compensation should reflect responsibilities and risks involved in being a director.
9. **Committee of outside directors**   These should normally consist of outside directors.
10. **Approach to corporate governance**   Every board director is responsible for developing the approach having considered these guidelines.
11. **Position description**   Corporate objectives for the CEO should also be developed.
12. **Board independence**   Where board structures and chairing arrangements should promote independence.
13. **Audit committee**   Comprised only of outside directors with oversight of internal control and direct links with internal and external audit.
14. **Outside advisors**   These should be engaged where appropriate.[38]

Over in Australia, the Australian Stock Exchange issued guidance through its Corporate Governance Council in 2003 to maintain an informed and efficient market and preserve investor confidence. The guidance is based around ten principles:

1. Lay solid foundations for management and oversight.
2. Structure the board to add value.
3. Promote ethical and responsible decision-making.
4. Safeguard integrity in financial reporting.
5. Make timely and balanced disclosures.
6. Respect the rights of shareholders.
7. Recognize and manage risk.

8. Encourage enhanced performance.

9. Remunerate fairly and responsibly.

10. Recognize the legitimate interests of stakeholders.

Principle seven means the company should establish a sound system of risk oversight and management and internal control.[39]

The United States has been at the forefront in setting standards for regulating registered companies. The now famous Sarbanes-Oxley Act of 2002 set the benchmark for the new rules issued by the Securities and Exchange Commission (SEC). Registered companies have to comply with many provisions regarding independent directors, audit committee, nominations/governance committees, compensation committees, codes of business conduct and various governance disclosures regarding the board and the company directors. Not least is the need for companies registered on the New York Stock Exchange to have an internal audit function, and that the audit committee must provide oversight of internal audit and meet separately with the internal auditor. Chief Executive Officers and Chief Finance Officers have to respond to a whole new raft of rules, including the need to certify that:

- The financial statements and other financial information in the report on the condition and results of the company are presented fairly in all material respects.
- They have taken responsibility for the design and maintenance of disclosure controls and evaluated their effectiveness, presenting details of corrective actions they have taken.
- They have disclosed to the audit committee and external auditors all significant deficiencies in the design or operation of internal financial controls, and any fraudulent acts.

While the rigors of Section 404, require companies to report on their internal controls and provide:

- A statement of management's responsibility for establishing and maintaining adequate internal control over financial reporting.
- A statement identifying the framework used by management to evaluate the effectiveness of the company's internal control over financial reporting.
- Management's assessment of, and a statement on, the effectiveness of the company's internal control over financial reporting as of the end of the company's most recent fiscal year.
- A statement that the auditors have issued an attestation report on management's assessment.

This means that the external auditors have to issue an attestation report on management's assessment of internal controls and procedures for financial reporting using standards established by the Public Company Oversight Board. The US experience has provided sound links between governance disclosures, risk management and internal controls. This is because Section 404 disclosures include the control framework in use that is established by an authoritative body and which has been released for public comment. Meanwhile, any investigation by the SEC of a registered company will start with an examination of the risk management process in use and in turn the type of control framework that is being applied by the company. Note that the UK's Turnbull report has been accepted as a control framework for the purposes of section 404, where UK companies are listed on the New York Stock Exchange.

2.5 Putting Governance into Practice

As a start we need to consider the ways corporate governance can be made to work in practice. Andrew Chambers' book on corporate governance provides a simple list of what he calls the ten 'principia' of effective corporate governance as follows:

1. Stakeholder control of the business.

2. Maximum and reliable public reporting.
3. Avoidance of excessive power at the top of the business.
4. A balanced board composition.
5. A strong involved board of directors.
6. A strong, independent element on the board.
7. Effective monitoring of management by the board.
8. Competence and commitment.
9. Risk assessment and control.
10. A strong audit presence. [40]

The Board and Directors

The board is responsible for reporting on their corporate governance arrangements. The IIA has provided a definition of the board: 'A board of directors, audit committee of such boards, heads of an agency or legislative body to whom internal auditors report, board of governors or trustees of a non profit organisation, or any other designated governing bodies of organisations.'[41]

The UK's Institute of Directors (IoD) has produced standards and guidelines for boards and directors and suggest that the boards should focus on four key areas:

1. establishing vision, mission and values;
2. setting strategy and structure;
3. delegating to management;
4. exercising accountability to shareholders and being responsible to relevant stakeholders.

While the responsibilities of individual company directors have been documented by the Institute of Directors:

- determining the company's strategic objectives;
- monitoring progress towards achieving the objectives and policies;
- appointing senior management;
- accounting for the company's activities to relevant parties, e.g. shareholders.

Statutory duties:

- a director must not put himself in a position where the interests of the company conflicts with his personal interest or his duty to a third party.
- a director must not make a personal profit out of his position as a director unless he/she is permitted to do so by the company.
- a director must act in what he/she considers is in the interests of the company as a whole, and not for any collateral purpose.

Directors are responsible for making sure the company fulfils its statutory duties (generally through the company secretary)... the main duty is the preparation of the accounts and report.

Directors are expected to display a certain amount of skill and exercise reasonable care in the performance of their work. In certain circumstances directors can be disqualified—e.g. wrongful trading (when insolvent) and fraudulent trading (defrauding the creditors).[42]

In the eyes of many officials charged with drafting corporate governance codes, the non-executive director represents the key to the future of corporate accountability. This all-seeing, all-knowing individual will examine the accounts, test the external auditor, watch over the board, align with the internal auditor, appraise the corporate strategy and ensure that enterprise-wide risk management is effectively imbedded within all parts of the organization. And at the same time be independent of the executive board members and protect the interests of all major stakeholders. No mean feat. The IoD have noted the contribution of NEDs:

> There is no legal distinction between executive and non executive directors. Essentially the NED's role is to provide a creative contribution to the board by providing objective criticism... they bring to the board:
>
> - independence
> - impartiality
> - wide experience
> - special knowledge
> - personal qualities
>
> Responsibilities of NEDs:
>
> - strategic direction—with a clearer and wider perspective
> - monitoring performance of executive management
> - communication—using outside contacts and opinions
> - audit—it is the duty of the whole board to ensure that the company accounts properly to its shareholders by presenting a true and fair reflection of its actions and financial performance and that the necessary internal control systems are put in place and monitored regularly and rigorously
> - remuneration of executive directors
> - appointing directors
>
> The demands of the NED role call for courage, integrity, common sense, good judgement, tenacity and to communicate with clarity, objectivity and brevity... business acumen... numeracy and the ability to gain an adequate understanding of the company's finance...
>
> The contribution of NEDs can help to raise the level of discussion and improve the quality of decision-making on the board, thus increasing the chances of the company acting in the best interests of its long term security and prosperity.[43]

Meanwhile, the NEDs are seen by many as important components of corporate governance by institutional investors as they strive to ensure their investments are being handled properly:

> Non-executive directors should not just be talking to the board directors. They should be spending part of their time visiting plants, talking to people at all levels and building up a picture of how the company is running.[44]

2.6 The External Audit

External audit fits into the corporate governance jigsaw by providing a report on the final accounts prepared by the board. They check that these accounts show a true and fair view of the financial performance of the company and its assets and liabilities at the end of the accounting year. The corporate governance model can be further developed to include an additional layer of accountability through the external audit process in Figure 2.4.

FIGURE 2.4 Corporate governance (4).

The Different Objectives

The starting place is to clearly set out the different objectives of internal and external audit:

The external auditor   The external auditor seeks to test the underlying transactions that form the basis of the financial statements.

The internal auditor   The internal auditor, on the other hand, seeks to advise management on whether its major operations have sound systems of risk management and internal controls.

Background to External Audit

There are features of the private sector external auditor's role that may be noted to help understand the relationship between internal and external audit:

- External auditors are generally members of CCAB professional accountancy bodies and are employed under the companies legislation to audit the accounts of registered companies.
- They are appointed annually at the annual general meeting by their clients, the shareholders.
- Their remuneration is fixed at general meeting.
- They have a right to attend general meetings to discuss any audit-related matters.
- They have a right of access to all books, information and explanations pertaining to the financial statements.
- In a limited company they can be removed by ordinary resolution with special notice.
- They cannot be officers, corporations or partners or employees of officers.
- In the event of their resignation they have to provide a statement of circumstances to the new incoming auditor that will document any specific problems with the audit cover.
- Where there is a problem with the accounts the auditor will fashion a suitable report to reflect the nature of the problem.

External audit will arrive at an opinion using the criteria in Figure 2.5.

In this way the external auditor will form an opinion on the accounts based on the adopted position. Note that the public sector and not-for-profit organizations will also be subject to external audits.

	EFFECT ON THE ACCOUNTS	
AUDITOR'S VIEW	**MATERIAL**	**FUNDAMENTAL**
UNCERTAINTY	'subject to'	'disclaimer'
DISAGREEMENT	'except for'	'adverse'

FIGURE 2.5 External audit report format.

The Main Similarities

The main similarities between internal and external audit are as follows:

- Both the external and internal auditor carry out testing routines and this may involve examining and analysing many transactions.
- Both the internal auditor and the external auditor will be worried if procedures were very poor and/or there was a basic ignorance of the importance of adhering to them.
- Both tend to be deeply involved in information systems since this is a major element of managerial control as well as being fundamental to the financial reporting process.
- Both are based in a professional discipline and operate to professional standards.
- Both seek active co-operation between the two functions.
- Both are intimately tied up with the organization's systems of internal control.
- Both are concerned with the occurrence and effect of errors and misstatement that affect the final accounts.
- Both produce formal audit reports on their activities.

The Main Differences

There are, however, many key differences between internal and external audit and these are matters of basic principle that should be fully recognized:

- The external auditor is an external contractor and not an employee of the organization as is the internal auditor. Note, however, that there is an increasing number of contracted-out internal audit functions where the internal audit service is provided by an external body.
- The external auditor seeks to provide an opinion on whether the accounts show a true and fair view, whereas internal audit forms an opinion on the adequacy and effectiveness of systems of risk management and internal control, many of which fall outside the main accounting systems. It is important to get this concept clearly in mind and the illustration in Figure 2.6 may assist.

The three key elements of this model are:

1. Financial systems may be considered by the external auditor as a short-cut to verifying all the figures in the accounts to complete the audit process. The internal auditor will also cover these systems as part of the audit plan.
2. Overall risk management arrangements are the main preoccupation of the internal auditor who is concerned with all those controls fundamental to the achievement of organizational objectives.

FIGURE 2.6   Auditing controls versus accounts.

3. The final accounts are the main preoccupation of the external auditor who is concerned that the data presented in the accounts present a true and fair view of the financial affairs of the organization.

- It should be clear that the external audit role is really much removed from the considerations of the internal auditor both in terms of objectives and scope of work.
- External audit is a legal requirement for limited companies and most public bodies, while internal audit is not essential for private companies and is only legally required in parts of the public sector.
- Internal audit may be charged with investigating frauds and, although the external auditors will want to see them resolved, they are mainly concerned with those that materially affect the final accounts.
- Internal auditors cover all the organization's operations whereas external auditors work primarily with those financial systems that have a bearing on the final accounts.
- Internal audit may be charged with developing value-for-money initiatives that provide savings and/or increased efficiencies within the organization. This applies to some external auditors in the public sector (e.g. Audit Commission and National Audit Office).
- The internal auditor reviews systems of internal control in contrast to the external auditor who considers whether the state of controls will allow a reduced amount of testing.
- Internal audit works for and on behalf of the organization whereas the external auditor is technically employed by and works for a third party, the shareholders.
- The internal audit cover is continuous throughout the year but the external audit tends to be a year-end process even though some testing may be carried out during the year.

It is possible to outline the key differences in Table 2.1.

IIA Performance Standard 2050 covers the co-ordination of internal and external audit and contains the following requirement: 'the CAE should share information and coordinate activities with other internal and external providers of relevant assurance and consulting services to ensure proper coverage and minimise duplication of efforts'. We can now discuss some of the ways that may be used to foster greater co-operation, which include:

A common audit methodology   A close co-operation can result from adopting a common approach to audit work.

Joint training programmes   Fully integrated training programmes, as an ideal, are not possible due to the different nature of the two audit functions. A policy of joint training can nonetheless be applied so long as this is limited to general audit techniques.

TABLE 2.1   Internal versus external audit.

Factor	Internal audit	External audit
Objectives	sound risk management and controls	accounts = true and fair view
Scope of work	overall systems: VFM, fraud, MIS and compliance	accounts, Profit and Loss a/c, balance sheet, annual report and financial systems
Independence	from operations by professionalism and status	from company via statutory rights and APB codes
Structure	varies: CAE, managers, seniors and assistants	partners, managers, seniors and trainees
Staff	competent persons trained in internal auditing	qualified and part qualified accountants
Methodology	risk-based systems-based audits, assurances and consulting work	vouching and verification and some use of risk-based systems approach
Reports	comprehensive structured reports to management and the audit committee and brief executive summaries	brief standardized published reports to shareholders and users of accounts
Standards	IIA and/or other	various APB requirements
Legislation	generally not mandatory apart from parts of public sector, but encouraged in most sectors	companies legislation and various public sector statutes
Size	only larger organizations	all registered companies and public sector (small companies may have exemptions)

Joint planning of audit work   This is the single most useful policy in terms of co-ordinating internal and external audit. Harmonization of the planning task is fundamental in this respect.

There are several levels to which audit planning may be interfaced as Figure 2.7 suggests.

STAGE ONE

copies of plans exchanged when complete

STAGE TWO

a joint meeting where plans are discussed

and harmonized—issued separately

STAGE THREE

regular meetings where fully integrated

plans are issued as ône composite document

FIGURE 2.7   Interfaced audit planning.

The stages move from one through to three to reflect an increasingly greater degree of interface between internal and external audit. At the extreme it can result in one planning document being prepared for the organization.

Direct assistance with each other's projects   A swap of resources creates further co-operation as the available audit skills base is added to as and when required.

Exchanging reports   This is a simple method of keeping each side informed, although it is more relevant within a public sector environment. Unfortunately what at first appears straightforward may involve an amount of political manoeuvring where each side applies special rules for confidential reports or reports that have not reached final report status.

Things have moved on and, like all business professionals, external audit has been swept up into the *risk tide*. The ICAEW Audit and Assurance Faculty has a clear view on this:

> The external audit approach has moved from 'audit risk' to 'business risk'—that is the business risks that the client faces in areas such as business environment, operations and control processes—and auditors spend more time in considering the broader aspects of risks as well as the related management controls. Move from audit to business assurance service.[45]

IIA Practice Advisory 2050-1

The guidance from 2050-1 covers the co-ordination of internal and external audit activities and key points extracted from this practice advisory include the following:

- Internal and external auditing work should be coordinated to ensure adequate audit coverage and to minimize duplicate efforts.
- Oversight of the work of external auditors, including coordination with the internal audit activity, is generally the responsibility of the board.
- The CAE may agree to perform work for the external auditor in connection with their annual audit of the financial statements.
- The CAE should make regular evaluations of the coordination between internal and external auditors.
- In exercising its oversight role, the board may request the CAE to assess the performance of external auditors . . . on coordination with internal audit and other issues such as—professional knowledge and experience, knowledge of the industry, independence, specialist services, responsiveness, continuity of key personnel, working relations, contract commitments, delivering overall value.
- EA may communicate issues to the board such as—independence, significant control weaknesses, errors and irregularities, illegal acts, accounting estimates, audit adjustments, disagreement with management and difficulties with the audit—CAE should have a good understanding of these issues.
- Coordination—audit coverage, access to programs and work papers, exchange of audit report and management letters, common understanding of audit techniques, methods and terminology.
- It may be more efficient for internal and external auditors to use similar techniques, methods, and terminology to effectively coordinate their work and to rely on the work of one another.

Financial Reporting and Independence

The final accounts that are prepared by limited companies represent the main vehicle through which the company communicates with the outside world. The importance of an effective dialogue between corporate bodies and external stakeholders has become a key concern in the business community and there is a growing interest in seeking to improve this communication. This is fine in practice but where the company has misrepresented its financial position there can be tremendous implications for banks, shareholders, suppliers, customers, the tax authorities, its auditors, investment advisors, insurance companies, employees, regulators, managers and all those other stakeholders who are affected by the activities of big corporations. The WorldCom and Enron examples show the fallout where the misstatements hit the billions mark. In economies where large, short-term returns are expected as the norm and huge bonuses and share options depend on income figures, then all pressures focus on performance targets and financial results. Complex technical conjuring tricks can be used to achieve the right results and stay within the rules, or to achieve the right results and 'appear' to stay within the rules. This is where the external audit comes into play—to independently check that what appears to be true is in fact true. This task becomes increasingly difficult where the control environment is poor and the following factors are involved:

- Performance targets are extremely challenging.
- The environment throws up unexpected developments.
- Executives have an aggressive approach to earnings management.
- There is high turnover of technical personnel, particularly in accounting and financial management.
- There is an abundance of complicated inter-company transfers and schemes and third party transactions.
- The board is dominated by a small in-group revolving around the chief executive officer and chief finance officer. The appointed chair has no authority (or inclination) to redress this imbalance.
- Recruitment of senior people is based on personal recommendation.
- The board adopt a high risk strategy without checking with the auditors.
- One main criterion for new projects is that they are passed by an army of corporate lawyers.
- There are many adjustments and journal transfers made in the accounts and directors are able to override the financial procedures with little documentation.
- The audit committee has little or no financial expertise and has a history of rubber-stamping key decisions.
- The control environment and ethical climate encourages a disregard for regulators, auditors and stakeholders. There is little open communication between the board and with managers and employees.
- There is a blame culture in place as well as a 'no bad news' attitude where failure to meet targets is generally unacceptable.
- The staff disciplinary code stresses loyalty to the company and to the management and whistleblowing is not encouraged at all. Here many of what would be considered *red flags* are simply ignored by everyone.
- Where there are poor financial controls and an ineffectual internal audit function this means transactions can be posted with no real probability of detection.
- And finally—the external auditors are given large amounts of extra work and consulting projects. Moreover, where the auditor asked too many questions, they are simply replaced. (Many company shareholders simply follow the board's recommendations on auditor selection.)

The external auditor will perform audit tests that provide a reasonable expectation of uncovering fraud that has a material affect on the financial statements, although it is not their prime objective to uncover fraud. Many problems are caused by differing perceptions by external audit and users of financial statements audited by the external auditors. This is commonly known as the 'Expectations gap'. Many users (including institutional and other shareholders) feel that the external auditor has verified the accounts to ensure they are correct. They expect the auditor to perform a 100% examination of the underlying transactions that go to produce the resultant figures—an unqualified audit opinion meaning that the accounts are reliable and the financial statements show a true and fair view, and that there are no major frauds in the company. The true position is that the external auditor uses samples for testing and the external audit can only provide a reasonable expectation that frauds, errors, insolvency, abuse and problems that have a material affect on the accounts may be uncovered.

National Audit Office

In the UK, the Exchequer and Audit Departments Act 1866 created the position of Comptroller and Auditor General and an Exchequer and Audit Department. The National Audit Act 1983 resulted in the Comptroller and Auditor General (C&AG) becoming an officer of the House of Commons, reporting to Parliament on value for money within government bodies. The C&AG is appointed by the Queen on address jointly proposed by the Prime Minister and the Chair of the PAC (and approved by the House of Commons) and is an officer of the House of Commons. The Public Accounts Committee (PAC) consists of a team of 15 Members of Parliament and is chaired by a member of the opposition.

The Audit Commission

The Audit Commission is the other big independent government external auditor and covers local authorities and NHS bodies, in contrast to central government organizations. Like the NAO it also has responsibility to promote improvement in value for money in public services. The Audit Commission produced a new Code of Practice in March 2002 building on the Audit Commission Act 1998 and the Local Government Act 1999 which addressed the statutory responsibilities and powers of appointed auditors. The Audit Commission is responsible for the appointment of auditors (from private firms and its own agency, the district audit) to local government and health authorities and NHS trusts. The Audit Commission is based on the premise that it supports local democracy by helping to ensure that the members and officers of elected local authorities are accountable to the communities they serve and by providing assurances that public money has been properly spent.

Current Issues

The WorldCom, Enron and other major cases of financial misreporting have put great pressure on the external audit community to ensure there is no conflict of interest in the way it furnishes its opinion on the accounts. There is an ongoing review of auditor independence and the issue of non-audit fees and whether they should be further restricted. Rotation of senior audit partners is another measure that should increase independence and there are moves to decrease the timeframe for such rotations (currently from seven to five years). Another high profile issue relates to periodic re-tendering for the external audit contract and whether there should be compulsory rules for such measures. The prime objective is to ensure the external auditor focuses on the final accounts, and has no distractions that impair the external auditor from delivering an objective and challenging review of the final accounts through the adoption of a healthy degree of professional scepticism. We are in a state of continuous review as report after report analyses the rules and practices that promote better auditor independence, or help improve the perceived state of independence of the external audit process.

The Department of Trade and Industry (DTI) review has focused on many related developments on company law, the adoption of international accounting standards, statutory operating and financial review and the role of executives and non-executive directors. The question of NEDs' independence is also a developing issue as is the much vexed matter of increasing external auditor independence. There are calls to strengthen the external audit and retain a higher degree of credibility by measures such as:

- Stopping external auditors from providing any non-audit services and promoting the growth of accounting firms that specialize in only providing external audit and no consulting services at all. Note that during 2003, no ban was provided over non-audit fees, although accounting firms were required to make more disclosure of earnings.
- Getting the audit committee to appoint, monitor and terminate the external audit using a carefully prepared specification that stresses independence and professionalism. At least one member of the audit committee should be a qualified accountant.
- Re-tendering the external audit contract periodically to instil competition. Although some argue that the incoming auditor will be new and may not be able to cope with complicated financial arrangements.
- Rotation of the senior partner on the audit so that there is less chance of excessive familiarity between the partner and the company executives.
- Better clarification of the role of the external auditor in terms of the degree of reliance that can be placed by users of published financial statements on the audit report.
- Interim audit accounts and audit coverage extended to statements and information released by the company.
- More robust quality assurance regimes with scrutiny from the professional bodies.

2.7 The Audit Committee

The topic of audit committees has an interesting background. The audit committee (AC) is a standing committee of the main board and tends to consist of a minimum of three non-executive directors (NEDs). Most audit committees meet quarterly and they are now found in all business and government sectors for larger organizations. The format is normally that the NEDs sit on the audit committee and the CFO, external audit, CEO and CAE attend whenever required. The committee will have delegated authority to act in accordance with its set terms of reference and also investigate areas that again fit with their agenda. The CAE will present reports to most regular committee meetings and will prepare an annual report to cover each financial year in question. We would hope that the audit committee is now providing another layer of stakeholder comfort in the search for good corporate governance and allows us to add to our growing model in Figure 2.8.

Groundbreaking work was performed in the US by the Blue Ribbon Committee in 1998 who prepared ten key recommendations on improving the effectiveness of audit committees:

1. NYSE and NASD adopt a definition of independent directors—not employed by (last 5 years) associate, family contact, partner, consultant, executive on company whose executives serve on the Remuneration committee etc. No relationship with the company that will impair independence.
2. NYSE and NASD listed companies with market capitalization over $200m have an AC of only NEDs.
3. NYSE and NASD listed companies with market capitalization over $200m have an AC minimum of 3 directors each of whom is financially literate and at least one member has accounting or related financial management expertise.
4. NYSE and NASD listed companies have an AC charter reviewed annually. Details of the charter disclosed in the companies proxy statement to annual shareholders' meeting.

FIGURE 2.8 Corporate governance (5).

5. SEC rules—statement that AC has satisfied its responsibilities under its charter.
6. NYSE and NASD charters of listed companies specify that external audit is accountable to the board and AC who have the ultimate authority to select, evaluate and replace the external auditor.
7. NYSE and NASD AC charter requires that the AC receive a formal statement detailing relationship between external audit and company, the AC should discuss EA independence and take or recommend to the board action to ensure independence of the external auditor.
8. GAAP revised to require external audit to discuss the auditor's judgement about the quality of accounting principles and financial reporting with the AC.
9. SEC adopt rules that the AC make a Form 10-K Annual Report covering: management has discussed quality of accounting principles, discussions with EA, discussed by AC members, AC believes financial statements are fairly presented and conform with GAAP.
10. SEC adopt rules that external audit conduct a SAS 71 Interim Financial Review before filing Form 10-Q and discuss the financial statements with the AC before filing the Form.

Staying with the US, each audit committee for companies listed on the NYSE, Nasdaq and AMEX must have a charter that shows:

- The scope of the AC responsibilities and how it carries them out.
- Ultimate accountability of the independent auditor to the board and AC.
- Ultimate authority of the board and AC to select, evaluate, and replace the independent auditors.
- The AC responsibilities re the independent auditor's independence.

The role of the audit committee is now firmly entrenched in business culture and they are mandatory for most international stock exchanges including London and New York. Even in smaller companies, their presence is recommended by many businesses—which some see as a substitute for an internal audit function.

The Role of the Audit Committee

An audit committee will be established by the main board to perform those duties that the board decides should be properly allocated to this specialist forum. The role of the audit committee may therefore incorporate some the following components in its terms of reference:

1. The external audit process   To review the external audit process and make recommendations to the board where appropriate.

2. The final accounts   To consider the annual accounts and the external audit report that attaches to these accounts.

3. Systems of internal control   To consider the adequacy of systems of internal controls. The current move to require directors to report on their systems of internal control means that this is starting to assume a higher profile.

4. Internal audit   Involvement in the appointment of the internal auditors and ensuring that the internal audit function operates to professional standards, performs well and discharges its responsibilities under the audit plan and strategy.

5. Risk management   The audit committee will ensure that there is an effective system of risk management within the organization and that this system supports the controls which, in turn, provide a reasonable expectation of achieving organizational objectives.

6. Compliance and propriety   An oversight of systems and procedures is in place to ensure compliance with regulations, policies, laws and procedures and the organization's code of conduct. Also ensure that the organization is able to prevent, detect and respond to fraud and allegations of fraud.

7. Financial management   To consider the finances and expenditure of the organization and ensure that there is a good financial reporting and budgeting system in place and that this feeds properly into the process for preparing the annual accounts.

8. Special investigations   The audit committee may request special investigation from the internal audit, compliance officer, external auditor and external specialists where there is a need to probe into sensitive problems that fall within its remit.

Audit Committees and Internal Audit

The developing significance of the audit committee has gone hand in hand with more reliance on internal auditing as a key aspect of the corporate governance solution. In 2002, the NYSE Rules made it clear that 'each listed company must have an internal audit function'. In the UK internal audit, while strongly encouraged, is not mandatory (although audit committees are required). The internal auditor needs to have regard to their audit committee and appreciate that this group forms a key customer. One key area that internal audit has a dominating expertise is in applying control models to an organization, and it is here that the CAE may help the audit committee understand the use and design of control models through which to base any view of internal controls that they might recommend to the main board. Many internal audit shops have a dotted line responsibility to the audit committee. While bearing this in mind, the internal auditor should also ensure there is a clear relationship between the CAE and the executive board, with reference to IIA Performance Standard 2060 on Reporting to the Board and Senior Management:

> The CAE should report periodically to the board and senior management on the internal audit activity's purpose, authority, responsibility, and performance relative to its plan. Reporting should

also include significant risk exposures and control issues, corporate governance issues, and other matters needed or requested by the board and senior management.

Meanwhile, the IIA definition of internal auditing takes the CAE into the heart of the audit committee's role and provides a platform to launch assurance and consulting work on *risk management, control and governance processes.* This is pretty much the language of the NEDs as well as the executives on the board members. The audit committee will want to know about internal audit's work but the CAE must be very careful not to turn this committee into a venue for second guessing top management. The IIA has posted material on its website on Internal Auditing and the Audit Committee: Working Together Toward Common Goals, which concluded that:

> The tasks, responsibilities, and goals of audit committees and internal auditing are closely intertwined in many ways. Certainly, as the magnitude of the 'corporate accountability' issue increases, so does the significance of the internal auditing/audit committee relationship. The audit committee has a major responsibility in assuring that the mechanisms for corporate accountability are in place functioning. Clearly, one of these mechanisms is a solid, well-orchestrated, co-operative relationship with internal auditing. The Institute of Internal Auditor's Position on Audit Committees is a step toward promoting that type of relationship—helping audit committees and internal auditing work together toward common goals.[46]

The Smith Report

The report by Sir Robert Smith was submitted to the Financial Reporting Council and contained various recommendations for changes to the code of practice for listed companies as follows:

D.3 Audit Committee and Auditors
Principle   The board should establish formal and transparent arrangements for considering how they should apply the financial reporting and internal control principles and for maintaining an appropriate relationship with the company's auditors.

Code provisions
D.3.1   The board should establish an audit committee of at least three members, who should all be independent non-executive directors. At least one member of the audit committee should have significant, recent and relevant financial experience.

D.3.2   The main role and responsibilities should be set out in written terms of reference and should include:

(a) to monitor the integrity of the financial statements of the company, reviewing significant financial reporting issues and judgements contained in them;
(b) to review the company's internal financial control system and, unless expressly addressed by a separate risk committee or by the board itself, risk management systems;
(c) to monitor and review the effectiveness of the company's internal audit function;
(d) to make recommendations to the board in relation to the appointment of the external auditor and to approve the remuneration and terms of engagement of the external auditor;
(e) to monitor and review the external auditor's independence, objectivity and effectiveness, taking into consideration relevant UK professional and regulatory requirements;
(f) to develop and implement policy on the engagement of the external auditor to supply non-audit services, taking into account relevant ethical guidance regarding the provision of non-audit services by the external audit firm.

D.3.3   The audit committee should be provided with sufficient resources to undertake its duties.

D.3.4   The directors' report should contain a separate section that describes the role and responsibilities of the committee and the actions taken by the committee to discharge those responsibilities.

D.3.5   The chairman of the audit committee should be present at the AGM to answer questions, through the chairman of the board.

2.8 Internal Audit

The Essential Handbook of Internal Auditing is primarily about the role, responsibilities and performance of the internal audit function. This section simply provides a brief account of where internal audit fits into the corporate governance jigsaw. The IIA have prepared performance standard 2130 on this issue which says: 'The internal audit activity should assess and make appropriate recommendations for improving the governance process in its accomplishment of the following objectives (1) Promoting appropriate ethics and values within the organization, (2) Ensuring effective organizational performance, (3) Effectively communicating risk and control information in appropriate areas of the organization, (4) Effectively coordinating the activities of and communicating information among the board, external audit and internal auditors and management.' This enables us to place internal audit into our corporate governance model in Figure 2.9.

FIGURE 2.9   Corporate governance (6).

There is much guidance to turn to for help in reinforcing the internal audit position. Gill Bolton has provided advice for auditors about implementing the Turnbull provisions on corporate governance:

Working with the board, the audit committee and the risk committee (where it exists) to embed risk management and internal control into the organisation as a whole, internal audit is likely to be the only function within an organisation that has deep understanding of risk and control:

• Providing risk management and control advice to relevant staff across the organisation.

- Providing independent and objective assurance to the board about the adequacy and effectiveness of key controls and other risk management activities across the organisation.
- Acting as risk and control educators across the organisation.[47]

While most parts of the public sector have adopted codes that require the existence of internal audit, some parts have enshrined the role of internal audit in legislation, and not only best practice guides. Under the Local Government Act 1972, section 151, every local authority shall make arrangements for the proper administration of their financial affairs and shall secure that one of the officers has responsibility for the administration of those affairs. This meant that the officer, e.g. finance officer, had to maintain an internal audit function. The Accounts and Audit Regulations of 1983 required the responsible financial officer to maintain an adequate and effective internal audit of the accounts of the body. Of late, the 1996 regulations meant that the head of finance need not now have direct control over the internal auditing function of the council, while larger organizations—universities, housing associations, health trusts, or other not-for-profit bodies—all have codes that require internal audit and it is becoming hard to find any organization of size that does not have internal audit.[48]

Turnbull on Internal Audit

This report provides more support for the internal audit function and paragraphs 42 to 47 contain the following provision on internal audit:

- Provision D.2.2 of the Code states that companies which do not have an internal audit function should from time to time review the need for one. (para. 42)
- The need for an internal audit function will vary depending on company-specific factors including the scale, diversity and complexity of the company's activities and the number of employees, as well as cost/benefit considerations. Senior management and the board may desire objective assurance and advice on risk and control. An adequately resourced internal audit function (or its equivalent where, for example, a third party is contracted to perform some or all of the work concerned) may provide such assurance and advice. There may be other functions within the company that also provide assurance and advice covering specialist areas such as health and safety, regulatory and legal compliance and environmental issues. (para. 43)
- In the absence of an internal audit function, management needs to apply other monitoring processes in order to assure itself and the board that the system of internal control is functioning as intended. In these circumstances, the board will need to assess whether such processes provide sufficient and objective assurance. (para. 44)
- When undertaking its assessment of the need for an internal audit function, the board should also consider whether there are any trends or current factors relevant to the company's activities, markets or other aspects of its external environment, that have increased, or are expected to increase, the risks faced by the company. Such an increase in risk may also arise from internal factors such as organizational restructuring or from changes in reporting processes or underlying information systems. Other matters to be taken into account may include adverse trends evident from the monitoring of internal control systems or an increased incidence of unexpected occurrences. (para. 45)
- The board of a company that does not have an internal audit function should assess the need for such a function annually having regard to the factors referred to in paragraphs 43 and 45 above. Where there is an internal audit function, the board should annually review its scope of work, authority and resources, again having regard to those factors. (para. 46)

- If the company does not have an internal audit function and the board has not reviewed the need for one, the Listing Rules require the board to disclose these facts. (para. 47)

We have referred to just a few of the codes and provisions for internal audit in the wake of moves to further the development of stronger corporate governance. The door has been opened for the once low profile audit teams that they may enter through and access the boardroom agenda. Moreover the internal auditor can be the best friend of the audit committee and perhaps one of the few parties that can be relied on to give impartial and reliable advice and information. This growing expectation represents a major opportunity to staff up the audit team with people who can provide sound strategic level judgements to senior officials in a move away from the desk-based and detailed analysis that was typically provided to junior management.

2.9 The Link to Risk Management and Internal Control

We have said that the role of internal auditing incorporates coverage of risk management, control and governance processes. It is a good idea to briefly establish the links between these three ideas so that while each chapter deals with each of the three concepts, they can be appreciated both separately and together. Figure 2.10 may help explain the links.

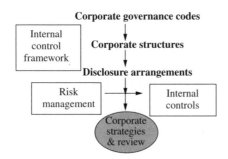

FIGURE 2.10   Linking RM to internal control.

Looking at each part of the model in turn:

1. Corporate governance codes: These are essentially the codes, guides, regulations and standards that, apart from family-run concerns, cover most larger organizations.

2. Corporate structures: The governance structures and processes include all those arrangements to ensure compliance with the governance codes. This includes, boardroom arrangements, splitting the CEO's and chair's roles, codes of conduct, audit committees, NEDs, internal and external audit and so on.

3. Disclosure arrangements: The matters that have to be included in the annual report including the audited accounts, external audit report, notes to the accounts, directors' report and operational review. This also includes disclosures on compliance with corporate governance codes, risk management arrangements and a statement on internal control.

4. Internal control framework: We deal with internal control in Chapter 4. For our model, we argue that all large organizations should adopt a control framework that sets out its vision of control. This provides a road map regarding the control environment, how people relate to each other and communicate, corporate structures and governance processes mentioned above.

5. Risk management: Within the context of the control framework, the organization should employ a process for identifying, assessing and managing risk. Note that risk management is covered in Chapter 3.

6. Internal controls: After having assessed key risk, they will need to be managed in line with a defined risk management strategy. One major component of this strategy is appropriately derived internal controls that seek to mitigate unacceptable levels of risk. Each control will address a defined risk or be part of a regulatory requirement that in turn addresses the risk of breaching law, procedures and rules.

7. Corporate strategies and review: The strategy for managing risk and ensuring controls do the job in hand should then be incorporated into an overall strategy that drives the organization towards the achievement of its objectives. The entire process should be directed, assessed, reviewed and improved in conjunction with a formal performance measurement system.

By considering the above components, we can see how corporate governance is the umbrella concept that drives a control and reporting framework, which in turn depends on risk management and an efficient system of internal control. The three big parts—governance, risk management and control—form an entire system that provides for effective performance and stakeholder accountability.

2.10 Reporting on Internal Controls

Sir Adrian Cadbury has said that corporate governance is about the way an organization is directed and controlled. If the board is in control of their business and they are adhering to all appropriate standards then stakeholders can take comfort in this fact. Meanwhile, being in control means that all foreseeable risks to the success of the business have been anticipated and addressed, as efficiently as possible. This alone does not guarantee success, but it does mean that there is a reasonable chance that the organization will maintain, if not exceed, market expectations. To underline the need to be in control, the published annual report for companies listed on the stock exchange and most public sector or bodies should include a statement of internal control. This statement is a bottom line item, which is derived from the complicated arrangement of systems, processes and relationships established within the organization. If these controls drive the organization forward and also tackle all known risks that threaten this positive direction, then there is a good system of internal control in place. A well-governed organization must have good controls and the statement of internal control represents a crucial vote of confidence from the board to the shareholders and other stakeholders. The Turnbull report includes a set of questions that the board may wish to discuss with management when considering reporting on internal control and carrying out its annual assessment. The list is based around the COSO model of control (see Chapter 4) and covers the following areas:

- Control environment.
- Risk assessment.
- Control activities.
- Information and communication.
- Monitoring.

It is clear that the board can secure information on the functioning of internal controls from sources within the organization, with much of this coming from the risk management and assurance reporting process that has been established. The internal and external auditors also provide a major input as does the audit committee. Some organizations require their top managers to provide assurance statements where they confirm that suitable controls are in place, that they have been reviewed and improved (where appropriate) and that they are designed to help manage all material risks to the achievement of objectives. Moreover, the statements may also incorporate a consideration of whether the controls are being applied as intended and that they are reliable. Internal audit is a big player in this field on control reporting and most audit teams have sharpened their focus to feed into the board's attestations (or chief executive for public sector organizations). The fully built model of corporate governance that we have been developing in this chapter is set out in Figure 2.11.

FIGURE 2.11   Corporate governance (7).

Many of the components of our model have already been referred to, but for completeness we can list them all and spend a little more time on the new additions:

- **Stakeholders**   Should understand the role of the organization and what they get from it, and be discerning in demanding information on the system of corporate governance in place.
- **Legislation, rules and regulations**   These should all contribute to protecting people and groups who have invested in the organization or who have a direct interest in either the services or products provided or any partnering arrangements. The regulatory framework should also ensure a level playing field for competitors and inspire substance over form.
- **Final accounts**   The annual report and accounts should contain all the information that is required by users and be presented in a true and fair manner (in conjunction with international accounting standards). It should act as a window between the outside world and the organization so that interested users can peer through this window and get a clear view of the way management behave and their performance, with no chance of skeletons being hidden in the closet.

- **External audit**   There should be a truly independent, competent and rigorous review of the final accounts before they are published, without the distraction of the need to attract large amounts of non-audit fees from the company in question.
- **The board**   The board should be a mix of executives and non-executives balanced so as to represent the interests of the shareholders in a professional and responsible manner, chaired by a respected NED. Their responsibilities should be fully defined and assessment criteria should be in place, that ensure fair rewards are available for effective performance (via a remunerations committee).
- **Audit committee**   This committee of non-executives should provide an oversight of the corporate governance process and have a direct line to the shareholders via a separate report in the annual report. The committee should also seek to ensure management are equipped to install effective risk management and controls in the organization. Competent and experienced people should sit on the committee and ensure they are able to commit sufficient time and effort to the task of guiding and monitoring the accounting, audit, accountability, ethical values and governance arrangements, with no conflicts of interest—real or perceived.
- **Performance, conformance and accountability**   These three concepts should form a framework for corporate behaviour where the spirit of the ideals are embraced (as part of organizational culture) in contrast to a list of rules that are studied by legal and accounting technicians with a view to 'getting around'.
- **KPIs**   Organizational effort should be formed around a clear mission, vision and set of values that fall into a balanced range of performance measures that ensure risks to effective performance are understood and properly managed.
- **Internal audit**   Should be professional, independent and resourced to perform to the professional standards enshrined in the new focus on risk management, control and governance; with a good balance of assurance and consulting effort.
- **Risk management**   There should be a robust system of risk management in place that is embedded into the organizational systems and processes and which feeds into an assurance reporting system (normally based on risk registers).
- **Managers, supervisors and operational and front line staff**   Should all understand the corporate governance framework and live up to the demands of their defined responsibilities (for performance, conformance and accountability) in this respect.
- **Systems of internal control**   Should exist throughout the organization and be updated to take account of all material risks that have been assessed, and should be owned and reviewed by the people who are closest to the associated operations. The published annual report should comment on the systems of internal control in place to manage internal and external risk.
- **Performance management**   The response to corporate governance ideals should be fully integrated into the way people are set targets and assessed in respect of their performance against these targets. Performance should be measured and managed in a balanced and meaningful manner.
- **Ethical standards**   Should form the platform for all organizational activities and should be given priority for all important decisions that are made. They should also underpin the human resource management systems (e.g. selection, training, appraisal, disciplinary, etc.) and be part of clear and consistent messages and values from top management. All employees should be encouraged to report all actual and potential risks to the business, customers and stakeholders, and positive action should be taken by management as a result.
- **Commitment and capability**   Are two further concepts that have been added to performance, conformance and accountability. Commitment is the embodiment of corporate governance values into the hearts and minds of everyone connected with the organization.

Capability relates to the training, budgets, time and understanding that are needed to make any new arrangements, such as control self-assessment, work. There are many organizations who send bold statements on the need for, say, better risk management but then fail to provide training, resources or space to enable people to do something about any gaps. Performance, conformance, accountability, commitment and capability are the key drivers for ensuring an enthusiastic response to corporate governance.

Companies are now being asked to prepare Operating and Finance Reviews that will provide investors with more information about business opportunities, significant risk and prospects. The need to maintain public confidence in the corporate sector and credibility in government and not-for-profit sectors has never been stronger. There are calls from all quarters to maintain this pressure to improve, develop and progress corporate governance arrangements as far as possible.

Summary and Conclusions

The corporate governance debate is ongoing. The various codes and guidance that have been prepared throughout the world tend to build on what is already available. New codes have the advantage of recent information on what is working well and where there are still problems matching the theory with real life. As soon as we present the latest position on codes of practice, they are overtaken by a new version which is more inclusive and generally more comprehensive. International codes are coming together to form a common understanding of how corporate, commercial and public life should be conducted. The tremendous pressures inherent in environmental groups and global activists place the conduct of large organizations in the spotlight where people are beginning to define acceptable and unacceptable corporate behaviours.

Chapter 2: Multi-Choice Questions

Having worked through the chapter the following multi-choice questions may be attempted. (See Appendix A for suggested answer guide and Appendix B where you may record your score).

1. **Insert the missing words:**
   The main driver for corporate governance is based on the . . . . Here corporate bodies are overseen by directors who are appointed by the owners, i.e. the shareholders.
   a. accountability regime.
   b. agency concept.
   c. friendship network.
   d. representation concept.

2. **Which item is the least appropriate?**
   There are seven standards in the Nolan code of public conduct:
   a. Selflessness and integrity.
   b. Objectivity and accountability.
   c. Openness and honesty.
   d. Leadership and acumen.

3. **Insert the missing words:**
   Cadbury went on to document the simple but now famous phrase: 'Corporate governance is the system by which companies are . . . .'

   a. directed and controlled.
   b. designed and administered.
   c. directed and managed.
   d. managed and developed.

4. Which item is the least appropriate?
Cadbury went on to describe the underpinning principles behind the code:
   a. Openness.
   b. Integrity.
   c. Accountability.
   d. Motivation.

5. Which is the most appropriate sentence?
The Organisation for Economic Cooperation and Development has prepared an inclusive set of corporate governance principles. Principle number one:
   a. The corporate governance framework should promote transparent and efficient markets, be consistent with the rule of law and clearly articulate the division of responsibilities among different supervisory, regulatory and police authorities.
   b. The corporate governance framework should promote transparent and efficient markets, be consistent with management theory and clearly articulate the division of responsibilities among different supervisory, regulatory and enforcement authorities.
   c. The corporate governance framework should promote transparent and efficient markets, be consistent with the rule of law and clearly articulate the division of responsibilities among different supervisory, regulatory and enforcement authorities.
   d. The corporate governance framework should promote transparent and failsafe markets, be consistent with the rule of law and clearly articulate the division of responsibilities among different supervisory, regulatory and enforcement authorities.

6. Insert the missing words:
The Toronto Stock Exchange believes that good disclosures gives investors a solid under-standing of how . . . . are made that may affect their investment.
   a. investments.
   b. decisions.
   c. appointments.
   d. losses.

7. Which is the most appropriate sentence?
   a. Over in Australia, the Australian Stock Exchange issued legislation through its Corporate Governance Council in 2003 to maintain an informed and efficient market and preserve investor confidence.
   b. Over in Australia, the Australian Stock Exchange issued guidance through its Corporate Governance Council in 2003 to maintain an informed and efficient market and preserve government confidence.
   c. Over in Australia, the Australian Stock Exchange issued guidance through its Risk Management Council in 2003 to maintain an informed and efficient market and preserve investor confidence.
   d. Over in Australia, the Australian Stock Exchange issued guidance through its Corporate Governance Council in 2003 to maintain an informed and efficient market and preserve investor confidence.

8. Which is the odd one out?

The United States has been at the forefront in setting standards for regulating registered companies. The now famous Sarbanes-Oxley Act of 2002 set the benchmark for the new rules issued by the Securities and Exchange Commission (SEC). Chief Executive Officers and Chief Finance Officers have to respond to a whole new raft of rules, including the need to certify that:

   a. the financial statements and other financial information in the report on the condition and results of the company are presented fairly in all material respects.

   b. they have taken responsibility for the design and maintenance of disclosure controls and evaluated their effectiveness, presenting details of corrective actions they have taken.

   c. they have disclosed to the audit committee and external auditors all significant deficiencies in the design or operation of internal financial controls, and any fraudulent acts.

   d. they have listed all those failed projects that indicate poor internal control.

9. Which is the most appropriate sentence?

   a. External audit fits into the corporate governance jigsaw by providing a report on the performance reports prepared by the board. They check that these accounts show a true and fair view of the financial performance of the company and its assets and liabilities at the end of the accounting year.

   b. External audit fits into the corporate governance jigsaw by providing a report on the final accounts prepared by the board. They check that these accounts show a true and fair view of the financial performance of the company and its assets and liabilities at the end of the accounting year.

   c. External audit fits into the corporate governance jigsaw by providing a report on the final accounts prepared by the board. They check that these accounts show a true and fair view of the financial performance of the company and its assets and staff at the end of the accounting year.

   d. External audit fits into the corporate governance jigsaw by providing a report on the final accounts prepared by the auditors. They check that these accounts show a true and fair view of the financial performance of the company and its assets and liabilities at the end of the accounting year.

10. Insert the missing words:

Many internal audit shops have a dotted line responsibility to the . . . . While bearing this in mind, the internal auditor should also ensure there is a clear relationship between the CAE and the executive board.

   a. audit committee.

   b. chief executive officer.

   c. director of finance.

   d. board.

References

1. Chambers, Andrew (2002) 'Stakeholders—the court of public opinion' in *Corporate Governance Handbook*, Tolley's, Reed Elsevier (UK) Ltd, p. 627.
2. *Daily Mail*, 17 Jan. 2002, p. 75, 'Tough guy rough is a hard act to follow' (David Rough), City and Finance, The City Interview by Cliff Feltham.
3. Weait, Mathew 'The workplace ethic—is it a crime'. *Management Today*, Jan. 2001, pp. 53–55.
4. *Daily Mail*, Tuesday 23 Jan. 2001, p. 7, 'Customers' revenge', Tozer James.

5. The Nolan Code (www.public-standards.gov.uk).

6. Harpur, Oonagh Mary, warningChief Executive of the Institute of Directors, 'Promoting enterprise with integrity'. *Internal Auditing*, Feb 2000, p. 6.

7. Internal Auditing and Business Risk, Governance Responsibility Reporting, Moon, Chris Feb. 2002, pp. 36–37, Association of British Insurers Guidelines on Social, Ethical and Environmental (SEE) Issues—Investing in Social Responsibility—Oct. 2001.

8. www.bodyshop.com.

9. www.tesco.co.uk.

10. Baker, Neil, 'Ready to blow'. *Internal Auditing and Business Risk*, June 2002-09-24, pp. 23–25.

11. Baker, Neil and Lea, Robert, 'A fraud waiting to be detected'. *Accountancy Age*, 27 April 1995, p. 10.

12. 'Corporate governance failures and their impact: in the Institute of Internal Auditors—UK and Ireland Study Text'. *Corporate Governance and Risk Management*, Oct. 2002, p. 18.

13. *Daily Mail*, Saturday 7 April 1996, p. 17, 'Five years jail for fugitive Nadir's Miss Moneypenny'.

14. www.guardian.co.uk/Archive/Article, visited 15/12/2002.

15. 'Corporate governance failures and their impact: in the Institute of Internal Auditors—UK and Ireland Study Text'. *Corporate Governance and Risk Management*, Oct. 2002, p. 18.

16. 'Corporate governance failures and their impact: in the Institute of Internal Auditors—UK and Ireland Study Text'. *Corporate Governance and Risk Management*, Oct. 2002, p. 18.

17. Weekes, Tim, 'The £5m lesson in swindling'. *Accountancy Age*, 22 June 1995.

18. *Daily Mail*, Saturday 15 June 1996, p. 19, 'Fall of King Copper', Burt Jason.

19. www.guardian.co.uk/business, visited 15/12/2002.

20. www.guardian.co.uk/business, visited 15/12/2002.

21. *Financial Mail on Sunday*, 18 Oct. 1998, p. 15, 'Inland Revenue "failures" in corruption case prompt call for whistleblowers' charter—taxman under fire over bribes scandal'.

22. Cooper, Cathy, 'Management blasted at nuclear plant'. *People Management*, 16 March 2000, p. 16.

23. *Daily Mail*, Wednesday 31 Jan. 2001, p. 2, 'Agony of parents in babies scandal' William David and Jenny Hope.

24. 'Corporate governance failures and their impact: in the Institute of Internal Auditors—UK and Ireland Study Text'. *Corporate Governance and Risk Management*, Oct. 2002, p. 19.

25. 'Corporate governance failures and their impact: in the Institute of Internal Auditors—UK and Ireland Study Text' *Corporate Governance and Risk Management*, Oct. 2002, p. 19.

26. www.news.bbc.co.uk, visited 15/12/2002.

27. 'Corporate governance failures and their impact: in the Institute of Internal Auditors—UK and Ireland Study Text' *Corporate Governance and Risk Management*, Oct. 2002, p. 19.

28. www.news.bbc.co.uk/1/hi/business, visited 15/12/2002.

29. www.news.bbc.co.uk/1/hi/business, visited 15/12/2002.

30. www.news.ft.com/servlet, visited 15/12/2002.

31. Cadbury Report, Report of the Committee on the Financial Aspects of Corporate Governance, 1992, para. 2.5.

32. Cadbury Report, Report of the Committee on the Financial Aspects of Corporate Governance, 1992.

33. Rutteman Report, Internal Control and Financial Reporting: Guidance for Directors of Listed Companies Registered in the UK, 1994.

34. The Greenbury Report, Directors' Remuneration: Report of A Study Group Chaired by Sir Richard Greenbury, 1995.

35. Turnbull Report, Guidance for Directors on the Combined Code, 1999.

36. Review of the Turnbull Guidance on Internal Control, Evidence Gathering Phase, Consultation Paper, Financial Reporting Council, Turnbull Review Group December 2004, pp. 14 and 15.

37. OECD Principles of Corporate Governance

38. Corporate Governance, A guide to good disclosure, Toronto Stock Exchange, 2004

39. Australian Stock Exchange, Principles of Good Corporate Governance and Best Practice Recommendations, March 2003

40. Chambers Andrew (2002) 'Stakeholders—the court of public opinion' in *Corporate Governance Handbook*, Tolley's, Reed Elsevier (UK) Ltd. p. 12.

41. IIA Glossary of Terms.

42. IoD Factsheets, 8 July 2002, 'What are the responsibilities and liabilities of the directors?' (www.iod.co.uk).

43. IoD Factsheets, 8 July 2002, 'What is the role of the NED?' (www.iod.co.uk).
44. *Daily Mail*, City and Finance, 25 April 2002, p. 69, 'Pension champion who is scourge of fat cats', Ruth Sunderland interviewing Alan Rubenstein.
45. 'ICAEW audit and assurance faculty'. *Internal Auditing and Business Risk*, Oct. 2000, p. 21.
46. www.the iia.org, visited 6 Dec 2002
47. Bolton, Gill, 'Implementing Turnbull'. *Internal Auditing*, June 2000 (UK), p. 36.
48. IIA. Uk&Ireland—Local Government Auditing In England and Wales, 1998.

Chapter 3

MANAGING RISK

Introduction

The formal definition of internal auditing is repeated here as follows:

> Internal auditing is an independent, objective assurance and consulting activity designed to add value and improve an organization's operations. It helps an organization accomplish its objectives by bringing a systematic, disciplined approach to evaluate and improve the effectiveness of risk management, control and governance processes.

We need to understand risk and we need to appreciate the importance of risk management to an organization. Good corporate governance codes require the board to install a system of risk management and tell their shareholders about this system. This chapter addresses the concept of risk. We consider some of the material that has been written about risk and introduce the risk cycle as a way of understanding how risk management works. We touch on important aspects of the risk management system relating to risk policies and concepts such as enterprise-wide risk management and control self-assessment. The breakthrough into risk has impacted the internal auditor's work and an important account of this move into a new phase of internal auditing was provided in 1998 by David McNamee and Georges Selim, who defined three stages in the development of internal auditing:

1. counting and observing;
2. systems of internal control;
3. auditing the business process through a focus on risk.

They go on to describe the paradigm shift that enables this leap from stage two to stage three, and argue that:

> The implications of this paradigm shift are enormous. It turns the focus of the audit away from the past and present and toward the present and future. Focusing on controls over transactions buried the internal auditor in the details of the past, limiting the value from any information derived. By focusing on business risks to present and future transactions, the auditor is working at a level above the details and dealing with the obstacles for organisation success. The information derived from such exploration has great value to the management governance team.[1]

The emphasis on risk management now drives many larger organizations, not as a reporting requirement, but as a powerful business tool that, used properly, improves performance. In an attempt to get behind risk management we cover the following ground in this chapter:

3.1   What is Risk?
3.2   The Risk Challenge
3.3   Risk Management and Residual Risk
3.4   Mitigation through Controls
3.5   Risk Registers and Appetites

3.1 What is Risk?

We need go no further than the work of Peter L. Bernstein to get an insight into the quality of risk:

> The word 'risk' derives from the early Italian risicare, which means 'to dare'. In this sense, risk is a choice rather than a fate. The actions we dare to take, which depend on how free we are to make choices, are what the story of risk is all about. And that story helps define what it means to be a human being.[2]

This immediately introduces the concept of choice when it comes to risk. Not simply being subject to risks as a part of life, but being in charge of one's destiny as there is much that we can control if we have the time and inclination to do so. The stewardship concept underpinning corporate governance forces management to seek out risks to the business and address them, where appropriate. Peter L. Bernstein goes on to suggest: 'The capacity to manage risk, and with it the appetite to take risk and make forward-looking choices, are the key elements of energy that drives the economic systems forward.'[3]

Throughout the chapter we will develop a model to consider risk and risk management. The first part of our first model appears as shown in Figure 3.1.

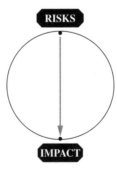

FIGURE 3.1   Risk management (1).

3.2 The Risk Challenge

The popular press is full of stories where things have gone terribly wrong. It seems that the mere act of walking out one's door, or getting into a car, or jumping into a swimming pool can mean disaster, injury or even death. We have said that controls are ways of minimizing risk and uncertainty and turning once again to Bernstein we can obtain a perspective of this concept of control: 'But if men and women were not at the mercy of impersonal deities and random chance, they could no longer remain passive in the face of an unknown future. They had no choice but to begin making decisions over a far wider range of circumstances and over far longer periods of time than ever before.'[4]

We arrive now at the view that risk represents a series of challenges that need to be met. Also, the key feature of this challenge is that it appears when a major decision has to be made. Risk has no real form unless we relate it to our own direction, that is what we are trying to achieve. It is the risks to achieving objectives that affect us in that they detract from the focus on success and stop us getting to the intended result. We may add to the risk model and incorporate this feature into the existing dimensions in Figure 3.2.

FIGURE 3.2 Risk management (2).

In this way the impacts become the effect the risks have on the objectives in hand. Good systems of risk management keep the business objectives firmly in mind when thinking about risk. Poor systems hide the objectives outside the model or as something that is considered peripheral to the task of assessing the impact of the risks. In reality it is not as simple as this. The act of setting objectives in itself is based on real and perceived risks, that is some uncertainty about the future. In recognition of this, we can adjust slightly our risk model to make the risk component interactive—in that the objectives are themselves set by reference to the uncertainty inherent in organizational climate in Figure 3.3.

FIGURE 3.3 Risk management (3).

The other concept that needs to be considered is that risk, in the context of achieving objectives, has both an upside and an downside. In our model we call these threats and opportunities. That is, it can relate to forces that have a negative impact on objectives, in that they pose a threat. Upside risk on the other hand represents opportunities that are attainable but may be missed or ignored, and so mean we do not exceed expectations. This is why risk management is not really about building bunkers around the team to protect them from the outside world. It is more about moving outside of familiar areas and knowing when and where to take risks. This is quite important in that if we view controls as means of reducing risk, we can now also view them as obstacles to grasping opportunities. So risk management is partly about getting in improved controls where needed and getting rid of excessive controls where they slow proceedings down too much. In other words, making sure controls are focused, worth it and make sense. We can turn once more to Peter Bernstein for a view of where opportunity fits into the equation: 'all of them (past writers) have transformed the perception of risk from chance of loss into opportunity for gain, from FATE and ORIGINAL DESIGN to sophisticated, probability-based forecasts of the future, and from helplessness to choice.'[5]

The South African King report on corporate governance also acknowledges the two sides of risk by suggesting: 'risk should not only be viewed from a negative perspective. The review process may identify areas of opportunity, such as where effective risk management can be turned to competitive advantage.' The next point to address is the basic two dimensions of measuring risk. That is, as well as defining the impact of the risk, we need also to think about the extent to which the risk is likely to materialize. To incorporate this feature into our risk model we need to add a separate box that provides a grid of likelihood and impact considerations regarding the effect of the risk on the set objectives in Figure 3.4.

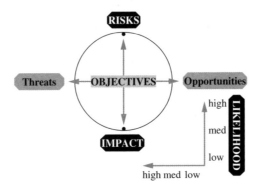

FIGURE 3.4   Risk management (4).

Having established the two aspects of risk, we can start to think about which risks are not only material, in that they result in big hits against us, but also whether they are just around the corner or kept at bay. Since risk is based on uncertainty, it is also based on perceptions of this uncertainty and whether we have enough information to hand. Where the uncertainty is caused by a lack of information then the question turns to whether it is worth securing more information or examining the reliability of the existing information. Uncertainty based on a lack of information that is in fact readily available points to failings in the person most responsible for dealing with the uncertainty. There is much that we can control, if we have time to think about it and the capacity to digest the consequences.

3.3 Risk Management and Residual Risk

Risk management is a dynamic process for taking all reasonable steps to find out and deal with risks that impact on our objectives. Organizational resources and processes are aligned to handle risk wherever it has been identified. We are close to preparing the risk management cycle and incorporating this into our original risk model. Before we get there we can turn to project management standards for guidance on the benefits of systematic risk management which include:

- More realistic business and project planning.
- Actions implemented in time to be effective.
- Greater certainty of achieving business goals and project objectives.
- Appreciation of, and readiness to exploit, all beneficial opportunities.
- Improved loss control.
- Improved control of project and business costs.
- Increased flexibility as a result of understanding all options and associated risks.
- Fewer costly surprises through effective and transparent contingency planning.[6]

Before we can delve into risk management we need to make a further point, that is that risk management is mainly dependent on establishing the risk owner, or the person most responsible for taking action in response to a defined risk, or type of risk, or risk that affects a particular process or project. The Turnbull report (see Chapter 2) on corporate governance for listed companies contains the following provisions regarding risk management:

> The reports from management to the board should, in relation to the areas covered by them, provide a balanced assessment of the significant risks and the effectiveness of the system of internal control in managing those risks. Any significant control failings or weaknesses identified should be discussed in the reports, including the impact that they have had, could have had, or may have, on the company and the actions being taken to rectify them. It is essential that there be openness of communication by management with the board on matters relating to risk and control. (para. 30)

> When reviewing reports during the year, the board should:
>
> - consider what are the significant risks and assess how they have been identified, evaluated and managed;
> - assess the effectiveness of the related system of internal control in managing the significant risks, having regard, in particular, to any significant failings or weaknesses in internal control that have been reported;
> - consider whether necessary actions are being taken promptly to remedy any significant failings or weaknesses; and
> - consider whether the findings indicate a need for more extensive monitoring of the system of internal control. (para. 31)

The government position is found in the HM Treasury guidance on strategic risk management which says: 'The embedding of risk management is in turn critical to its success; it should become an intrinsic part of the way the organisation works, at the core of the management approach; not something separated from the day to day activities.' (para. 9.1)

To summarize the risk management process we can turn again to the risk model in Figure 3.5. The stages of risk management are commonly known as:

Identification   The risk management process starts with a method for identifying all risks that face an organization. This should involve all parties who have expertise, responsibility and influence over the area affected by the risks in question. All imaginable risks should be identified and recorded. Business risk is really about these types of issues, and not just the more well-known disasters, acts of God or risks to personal safety.

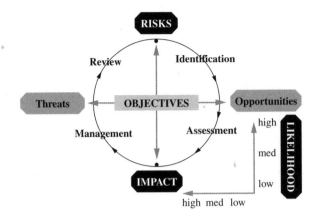

FIGURE 3.5   Risk management (5).

Assessment   The next stage is to assess the significance of the risks that have been identified. This should revolve around the two-dimensional Impact, Likelihood considerations that we have already described earlier.

Management   Armed with the knowledge of what risks are significant and which are less so, the process requires the development of strategies for managing high impact, high likelihood risks. This ensures that all key risks are tackled and that resources are channelled into areas of most concern, which have been identified through a structured methodology.

Review   The entire risk management process and outputs should be reviewed and revisited on a continual basis. This should involve updating the risk management strategy and reviewing the validity of the process that is being applied across the organization.

   The above cycle is simple and logical and means clear decisions can be made on the types of controls that should be in place and how risk may be kept to an acceptable level, notwithstanding the uncertainty inherent in the nature of external and internal risks to the organization. In practice, the application of this basic cycle does cause many difficulties. Most arise because we impose a logical formula on an organization of people, structures and systems that can be complicated, unpredictable, vaguely defined and perceived, emotive and in a state of constant change. Most risk management systems fail because the process is implemented by going through the above stages with no regard to the reality of organizational life. Managers tick the box that states the stages have been gone through and eventually the board receives reports back that state risk management has been done in all parts of the organization. Our risk models will have to be further developed to take on board the many intricacies that have to be tackled to get a robust and integrated system of risk management properly in place.

3.4 Mitigation through Controls

We have suggested that risk management is an important part of the risk cycle, as it allows an organization to establish and review their internal controls, and report back to the shareholders that these controls are sound. The internal control framework consists of all those arrangements, and specific control routines and processes that drive an organization towards achieving objectives. In terms of risk management we need to add to our risk model to set out the types of response

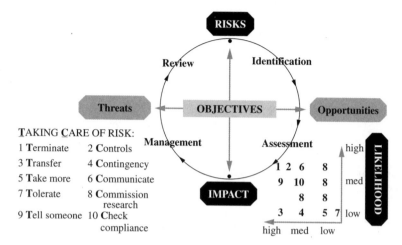

FIGURE 3.6   Risk management (6).

to risk that ensure we can remain in control. Borrowing from the thinking of Peter Drucker, these responses consist of specific controls over processes and overall control over the delivery of the agreed strategy. Our latest risk model becomes Figure 3.6.

We have developed ten measures for addressing risks that have already been assessed for impact and likelihood, in the bottom left box of our model. Each of the ten responses (5Ts and 5Cs) are numbered and can be located within the appropriate part of the Impact Likelihood Grid in the bottom right of the risk model. For example, where we have assessed a risk as high impact but low likelihood, we may want to transfer (or spread) some of this risk, to an insurer as a suitable response (in this case number 3). The responses are further described:

1. Terminate   Here, where the risk is great and either cannot be contained at all or the costs of such containment are prohibitive.

2. Controls   One of the principal weapons for tackling risks is better controls. Note that this is the subject of the next chapter.

3. Transfer   Where the risks are assessed as high impact but low likelihood, we may wish to adopt a strategy of spreading risk, wherever possible.

4. Contingencies   A useful response to risk that is again high impact, low likelihood is based around making contingency arrangements in the event the risk materializes.

5. Take more   One dimension of the risk management strategy is derived from the upside risk viewpoint. Where the impact, likelihood rating shows operations located down at low/low for both factors, this does not necessarily mean all is well. Risk management is about knowing where to spend precious time and knowing where to spend precious resources. Low/low areas are ripe for further investment (for commercial concerns) or ripe for further innovative development (for public sector services).

6. Communicate   One aspect of risk management that is often missed relates to high impact and either medium or high likelihood, where controls may not address the risk to an acceptable level, that is a strategy to communicate this risk to stakeholders and make them aware that this impairs the organization's ability to be sure of success (at all times).

7. Tolerate   The low/low risks that come out of our assessment will pose no threat and as such can be tolerated.

8. Commission research   More developed risk management systems will allow some thinking time, where one decision may be to go and find out more about the risk, its impact and whether it will probably materialize—that is to commission further research.

9. Tell someone   Some high/high risks create a blockage in that they can only really be resolved by parties outside of those participating in the risk management exercise.

10. Check compliance   The final weapon in the arsenal of risk responses is often overlooked. This is to focus on areas where controls are crucial to mitigating significant risks, and to ensure that they are actually working as intended.

The 5Ts and 5Cs model provides a wide range of techniques for developing a suitable risk management strategy in the bottom right corner of Figure 3.6.

3.5 Risk Registers and Appetites

The basic risk model has to be made more dynamic to incorporate the next risk tool, that is the risk register in Figure 3.7.

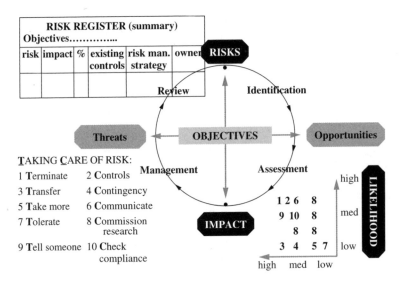

FIGURE 3.7   Risk management (7).

The subject of risk registers has a very interesting past. Project managers have used them for a long time as they assess risks at an early stage in a large project and enter the details in a formal record which is inspected by the sponsors. The insurance industry again is well used to documenting assumptions about risk and using this to form judgements on where to offer insurance cover and what aspects of an operation are included in this cover. More recently, they have come to the fore as an important part of general business risk management. Risk registers act as a vehicle for capturing all the assessment and decisions made in respect of identified risks. Moreover, the registers may form part of the assurance process where they can be used as evidence of risk containment activity, which supports the statement of internal control. We have suggested that risk management is simply the task of defining risk, identifying risks, assessing this risk for impact and materiality and then devising suitable ways of dealing with more significant risks. Risk registers can be attached to this process to record the above stages and end up with both a record and action plan. The register in our model in Figure 3.7 is a basic version that details the key objectives in question, the risks that have been identified by those closest to the action, their impact and likelihood and then a set of actions required to reflect the adopted strategy, which is then the responsibility of the risk owner. The register should be updated to reflect changes in the objectives, external and internal risks and controls, all of which in turn happens because of changes in the environment within which we operate. What goes in the register and what we document as significant as opposed to immaterial risk depends on the perception of risk, that is the risk appetite, or what some call the risk tolerance. An elementary diagram forms the basis for a consideration of risk appetite in Figure 3.8.

FIGURE 3.8   Risk appetites.

The risk appetite defines how we see residual risk, after we have dealt with it through an appropriate strategy, and whether it is acceptable or not, that is, is the risk acceptable as it stands or do we need to do more to contain it, or perhaps exploit areas where risk is too low? We need to turn once again to Peter Bernstein for an authoritative view on risk appetites. In short, it all depends: 'Few people feel the same about risk every day of their lives. As we grow older, wiser, richer, or poorer, our perception of risk and our aversion to taking risk will shift, sometimes in one direction, sometimes in the other.'[7]

The concept of risk appetite (or tolerance) is very tricky to get around. The contrasting positions are that the board sets a clear level of tolerance and tells everyone inside the organization; or that people are empowered to derive their own levels based around set accountabilities. These accountabilities mean defined people are responsible for getting things right and also must explain where this has not happened and things are going wrong.

While authoritative writers have argued that: 'risk like beauty is in the eye of the beholder. Although many people associate risk with loss of assets, the concept is viewed by the auditor as much broader.'[8]

If an organization gets the risk tolerance wrong then key stakeholders may well misunderstand the extent to which their investment is insecure, and conversely, where corporate risk tolerance is low, returns on investment may be likewise restrained. Funds will move in accordance with the level of risk that they are attracted to, so long as this level has been properly communicated to all interested parties. Risk appetite varies between organizations, between departments, between section, teams and more importantly between individuals.

If risk tolerance throughout an organization hovers at different levels with no rational explanation, then we may well experience problems. Key performance indicators need to be set to take on board acceptable risk tolerances so that the organization is pulled in a clear direction and not subject to fits and starts as different parts of the organization slow things down while others are trying to speed them up. Where the entire organization has a high risk tolerance, then it will tend not to install too many controls, particularly where these controls are expensive.

One model used to assess risk appetite uses the scale in Figure 3.9.

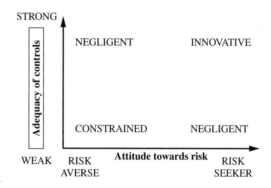

FIGURE 3.9   Risk attitudes and controls.

Here we balance the extent to which an organization's management seeks risk with the degree to which there are effective controls in place. Some people are active risk seekers as is clear from one article which describes how a gambling addict who ran up a £33,000 credit card bill has been jailed for a year and ordered to pay back the money. 'In his three month spending spree, he never won more than a fiver.'[9]

When considering risk tolerance, we need to build the control factor into the equation. Risk taking is fine so long as we can anticipate problems and work out how to counter them. Much confusion results from mixing gross and net risk. Risk, before we have put in measures to deal with it, is gross, or what we have called inherent risk. Risk that has been contained, so far as is practicable, is net, or what we have called residual risk. A high risk occupation such as an astronaut may in practice be relatively safe because of the abundance of controls in place for each journey. The risk tolerance for space exploration agencies may be near on zero, with a focus on controls and quality assurance routines and numerous tests of these controls.

Attitudes to risk tolerance become even more important when we consider the responsibilities of an organization to its stakeholders. The board members have a fiduciary duty to act in a reasonable manner and shareholders have a right to receive any announced dividends and to have their investment managed adequately. But, they will also need to understand the way the organization behaves towards risks.

While companies need to work out their view on risk, it is much the same for government bodies. The NAO has reviewed risk management in government bodies along with the need to support innovation. They recognize that the civil service culture has: 'values, ethos, ethics and training underpinning the department's management approach—has traditionally been risk averse'. And found that some 42% of departments regarded themselves as risk averse rather than risk taking. This may inhibit innovation in the way government services are designed, resourced and delivered. The NAO went on to document the now famous phrase that: *'the external auditor of government departments, the NAO, support well managed risk taking that is intended to result in tangible benefits for taxpayers'*. (para. 8)[10]

Accountability arrangements that are manipulated at one level in an organization to cover poor strategies or failures to implement or monitor strategy at a more senior level are a feature of blame-based organizational cultures. It is in this type of environment that it becomes hard to develop consistent messages about risk tolerance. The Turnbull report contains a reminder that board expectations must be made clear throughout the company. The section covering risk assessment includes questions that Turnbull states that each company should ask itself:

- Are the significant internal and external operational, financial, compliance and other risks identified and assessed on an ongoing basis? (Significant risks may, for example, include those related to market, credit, liquidity, technological, legal, health, safety and environmental, reputation, and business probity issues.)
- Is there a clear understanding by management and others within the company of what risks are acceptable to the board?

A focused board with a well-considered strategy that is properly implemented, reviewed and further developed is the foundation for establishing risk tolerances that actually make sense to all managers and employees. Without these prerequisites there will always be problems where the concepts of accountability and blame become confused. One dynamic method of developing corporate risk appetites is to start with the board. If the board carry out a risk assessment to isolate their top ten risks then this reasoning may form the basis for categorizing risks throughout the organization which could then form the basis for developing risk registers at senior and middle level management. For each of the categories, top-down messages can be sent on what is acceptable and what may not be, depending on the type of operational risk and where it fits with the top ten board risks.

3.6 The Risk Policy

Our risk model has taken a clear form with many components that form the basis of effective risk management. In some organizations, risk assessment workshops are set up for key teams as a response to the trend towards CRSA programmes, often on the back of recommendations from the auditors or an external consultant. Teams get together, talk about risk and how it is being managed in their outfit and come out with a risk register that is filed and action points given to nominated managers. This annual exercise appears to be enough to satisfy the auditors and someone within the organization attempts to place the risk registers onto a database and eventually prepares summary reports for top management and the board. Better models use a key to highlight high impact, high likelihood (perhaps indicated in red), which then triggers a rapid response from the board who will want to know that action is being taken to handle key exposures. The board then reports that it has reviewed the system of internal control, partly through the use of the risk management process as described. This fairly typical arrangement has a number of shortcomings:

- Many staff do not know why they are engaged in the workshops and simply see it as a one-off exercise for the auditors.

- Many managers are reluctant to spend time on the workshops as they are busy doing 'real work'.
- Many workshops operate completely outside the important strategic realignment, restructuring and other change initiatives that are a feature of most large organizations.
- Many workshops are seen as clumsy devices for getting more work out of fewer staff.
- Many of the programme workshops result in masses of information that are impossible to co-ordinate or make into a whole.
- A lot of the action points that come out of the workshops are superseded by subsequent events and new developments.
- Most workshops are developed outside of the performance management system and there is little incentive to take on additional tasks that do not hit any KPIs.
- Many see control self-assessment as relating only to the financial aspects of operations.
- Many workshop participants have already carried out risk assessment in their specialist fields of health and safety, security, project management, legal compliance, and other areas of the business.
- Often the workshop facilitator introduces the event as a discrete exercise with no links to the organization's strategic direction.
- Many participants suffer the fallout from initiative overload and have spent much time in teambuilding events, performance review meetings, change programmes, budget reduction exercises, diversity training, e-business projects and so on.
- Many participants have experienced a culture where good ideas from staff never go anywhere and motivation levels are fairly low.

We could go on, where risk workshops or risk reviews based on survey or interviews are derived from an incomplete model of the risk management system. As a result, we have developed our risk model to incorporate further dimensions that seek to counter the negatives listed above, as Figure 3.10 demonstrates. The amended model has built in three new factors (based around the risk policy), that is: the board sponsor, people buy-in, and a chief risk officer (CRO). Each one is discussed briefly below:

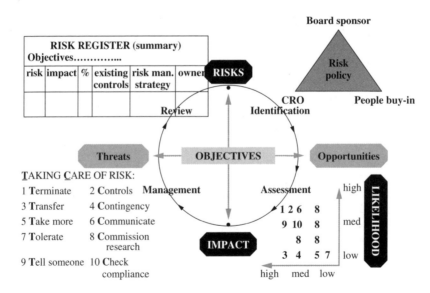

FIGURE 3.10   Risk management (8).

Board Sponsor

Where there is no board member driving the risk management process it will tend to fail. The board make a statement on the systems of internal control in the annual report and it is the board that reports that this system has been reviewed. The King report (from South Africa) makes this point crystal clear:

> The board is responsible for the total process of risk management, as well as for forming its own opinion on the effectiveness of the process. Management is accountable to the board for designing, implementing and monitoring the process of risk management and integrating it into the day-to-day activities of the company. (para. 3.1.1) The board should set the risk strategy policies in liaison with the executive directors and senior management. These policies should be clearly communicated to all employees to ensure that the risk strategy is incorporated into the language and culture of the company. (para. 3.1.1)

The Turnbull report contains guidance on the board's statement on internal control and states in paragraph 35 that:

> In its narrative statement of how the company has applied Code principle D.2 (reporting on internal controls), the board should, as a minimum, disclose that there is an ongoing process for identifying, evaluating and managing the significant risks faced by the company, that it has been in place for the year under review and up to the date of approval of the annual report and accounts, that it is regularly reviewed by the board and accords with the guidance in this document.

Turnbull represents aspirations that may not always be matched in practice.

> We are engaged in a continual search for better business practice. Meanwhile, the first cornerstone of the risk management policy rightly sits at the board, as the highest part of the organization. The board may in turn establish a risk management committee or look to the audit committee for advice and support, in respect of ensuring there is a reliable system for managing risks, or the audit committee may be more inclined to provide an independent oversight of the risk management and whether the arrangements are robust and focused. Regardless of the set-up, the board remains responsible for ensuring management have implemented proper risk management. Some organizations have gone all the way and appointed a director of risk management, particularly in sectors such as banking, where the risk agenda is also driven by regulators. The board sponsor will direct the risk management activity and ensure that it is happening and makes sense. One way of mobilizing the board and audit committee is to get them to participate in a facilitated risk assessment around the corporate strategy. Many risk consultants suggest that the board arrive at the top ten or so risks to achieving the corporate strategy and make this information known to the management.

The board come back into the frame when reviewing the risk management process and ensuring it stands up to scrutiny. They would also consider the reports that come back from their management teams that isolate key risks and whether these are being contained adequately.

People Buy-In

Another problem with many risk management systems is that they do not mean anything to the people below middle management level. They are seen as another management initiative that is 'done' to employees along with the multitude of other tools and techniques for improving performance and driving down costs. At worst, the employees are squeezed in between performance and costs in an attempt to work harder for less or the same recompense. In one risk management policy the organization had prepared a detailed diagram covering roles, responsibilities and relationships in the risk management system with committees, boards, risk manager, facilitators, auditors and stakeholder analysis. At the bottom of the diagram is the word 'individuals' with no further detail. The impression is that the risk management process is something that happens to them. The individual is really the foundation of risk management, since it is what people do and how they behave that determines whether an organization succeeds or fails. It would have been more apt to start with the individual and work through how they fit into the risk management process, or better still, how risk management can be made part of the way they work in future. This point has not been lost on the people who prepare guides to risk management and several extracts demonstrate the significance of 'people buy-in' for successful risk management.

Chief Risk Officer

The final leg of the risk policy stool relates to the need for a person responsible for co-ordinating risk effort around the organization. This person proactively directs the effort and sets up systems that embed the risk policy into everyday activities. A version of a job advertisement for a business risk manager illustrates the importance of the new role:

> Reporting directly to the Audit Committee and Group Finance this role is a rare opportunity to join an exciting company and continue the development of the overall Risk Management framework for the business on a global basis. Skills include:
>
> - Sound knowledge of risk management techniques, corporate governance and audit assurance.
> - Highly developed communications and presentation skills.
> - The ability to ask the right questions and remain independent.
> - The ability to make the right practical decisions.
> - A dedicated, energetic and enthusiastic approach, and be a true team player.

Proponents of the role of chief risk officer (CRO), such as Tim Leech, recognize the need for someone to pull the risk jigsaw together and make sense of it all for the board and senior management. They argue that we need to put right the silo reports on risks that are a feature of most big organizations. Still others, such as Terry Cunnington, have described arrangements where a risk assurance service provides enterprise risk management, internal audit and risk consultancy from one integrated team. There needs to be an in-house expert who can drive through the risk policy and make it work in practice. Their role may include:

- Translating the board's vision on risk management.
- Helping to develop and implement the corporate risk policy.
- Ensuring the people buy-in mentioned earlier.
- Providing training and awareness events where appropriate.
- Helping respond to requirements from regulators that impact on risk management systems.
- Establishing a strategic approach to risk management across the organization with programmes, the appropriate approaches, tools and reporting arrangements.
- Ensuring that the business is responding properly to changes and challenges that create new risks on a continuous basis.

- Establishing a risk reporting system from managers in the organization that can be used to provide assurances that support the board review of internal control.
- Helping facilitate risk management exercises and programmes.
- Becoming a centre of excellence on risk management and going on to develop an on-line support infrastructure, based on the latest technology that can be used by all parts of the organization.
- Helping co-ordinate risk management activities such as health and safety, security, insurance, product quality, environmental matters, disaster recovery, compliance teams and projects and procurement.
- Providing advice on sensitive issues such as perceptions of risk tolerance and the consistency of messages in different parts of the organization.
- Seeking to implement enterprise-wide risk management as an integrated part of existing processes such as decision making, accountability and performance management.

We could go on and there is a short-cut to defining the role of the CRO—it is to make good all aspects of our risk model and ensure that together they provide an effective system of risk management that is owned by all employees and integrated into the way the organization works. No risk policy will work without a commitment to resource the necessary process and ensure there is someone who can help managers translate board ideals into working practices.

Risk Policy

We have defined the main aspects that support the risk policy as board sponsorship, people buy-in and a source of expertise and assistance (the CRO). To close, it is possible to list the items that may appear in the published risk policy and strategy itself:

1. Define risk and state the overall mission in respect of risk management.
2. Define risk management and the difference between upside and downside risk.
3. Make clear the objectives of the risk policy—mention why we need a defined position on risk management.
4. Stakeholders and where they fit in—and the need to communicate a clear and reliable message.
5. Background to regulators and their requirements for risk management (and note on corporate governance code).
6. Position on appetite and whether the aim is risk avoidance, risk seeking or a measured balance.
7. Why bother?—list of benefits behind risk management; better controls and better performance and better accountability—impact on corporate reputation.
8. Background to the RM process (the risk cycle) and how it is integrated into decision making and planning, and performance management.
9. Risk responses and strategies leading to better certainty of achieving goals.
10. Internal controls—what this means with brief examples. The right control means putting in controls where risk is evident and getting rid of them where they are not required.
11. Training and seminars—importance and use.
12. Roles and responsibilities of all staff and specialist people such as board, CRO, internal audit, external audit and technical risk-based functions. Importance of the business unit manager.
13. Structures including board, audit committee, any risk committee and links to the CRO, quality teams and auditors.
14. Risk classifications or categories used in the risk management process.

15. Tools and techniques—guidance on the intranet including a short guide to CRSA workshop (method, tools and principles involved).
16. Links to the overall internal control model that is applied with particular reference to the need for a good control environment to underpin the risk process.
17. Links to established risk assessment practices built into projects, security, contingency planning and so on.
18. Assurance reporting—giving overall responsibilities, review points, validation of reports and the use of risk registers—including regular updates.
19. Need for integration into existing management systems such as performance management.
20. Glossary of terms.
21. Where to go to for help.

The policy may be a brief document that gives an overview of the organization's position of risk management with clear messages from the board. The risk strategy will go into more detail and develop more guidance on how to put the policy into action.

3.7 Enterprise-Wide Risk Management

Enterprise-wide risk management or enterprise risk management (ERM) is simply the extension of risk management across the organization in an integrated fashion. This is in contrast to the old approach where specialist pockets of dedicated processes such as contingency planning were risk assessed but only at a local level for the process in question. Before we delve into ERM further there is a related point to clarify with the risk model we have been using throughout this chapter. The new risk model is amended in Figure 3.11. In the middle box we have added **strategy** and **KPIs** to the original factor, **objectives**. We started with objectives as the driver for risk management and this viewpoint stands. What we are working towards is for risk management to be part of the strategic planning process and therefore integrated within the performance measurement system. This can be best illustrated with another model (Figure 3.12) that considers the role of risk assessment and where it fits into the organization's strategic analysis:

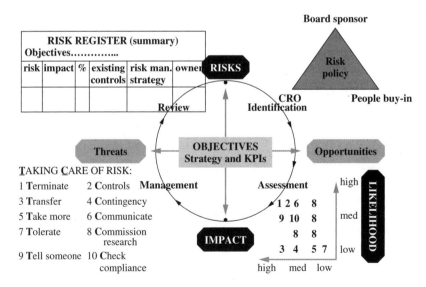

FIGURE 3.11   Risk management (9).

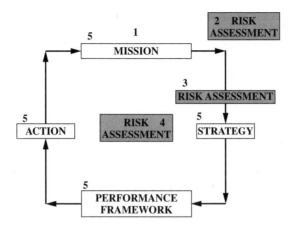

FIGURE 3.12   Stages of risk management.

The model is based on a simple management cycle with a mission that is translated into a strategy, which when implemented relates to performance measures that are used to monitor the progress of the adopted strategy and action taken to review and adjust. There are five development phases for risk assessment within the cycle as just described. Each of the five phases is noted as follows:

1. No risk assessment is carried out and the strategic management cycle (the four white boxes in Figure 3.12) takes no account of a formal identification and assessment of risk. There are very few organizations still at this stage. The policy may run along the following lines: 'many of our specialists people are already doing their own risk assessment anyway!'
2. Here risk assessment is an annual event that is a separate exercise which is removed from the corporate strategy. It may be done once and then left, or carried out each year, mainly for the disclosure requirements where the organization reports that it has a risk management system in place. Again, there is a minority of large organizations that take a mechanical view towards risk. The policy may run along the following lines: 'risk assessment is an annual exercise that is reported back to the board!'
3. Phase three places risk assessment inside the strategic management cycle. So that as strategy is revisited during the year or whenever there is a major change in direction, the assessment of key risks is also addressed. Many organizations are at this phase, where risk assessment is a separate but component aspect of developing strategy. The policy may run along the following lines: 'risk assessment is built into our strategic analysis, and as strategy changes so do the risk management responses!'
4. This phase locates risk assessment right inside an organization's corporate heart. It drives the way objectives are set, the strategic framework, performance issues and monitoring and decision making. It involves a culture shift towards formally addressing risk as part of business life. Here, all key decisions, change programmes and underpinning projects and resource shifts derive from a consideration of upside and downside risks. Organizations that claim an ERM system is in place will have arrived at phase four. The policy may run along the following lines: 'risk assessment is at the core of our activities and drives setting objectives, strategy and performance reviews!'
5. The final phase drops the term 'risk' and it disappears altogether. Risk assessment is so immersed into the culture of an organization that it becomes an implicit part of the corporate and personal value system for everyone involved with the organization. There is no longer a

need to talk about risk management and risk registers since it happens implicitly. The policy may run along the following lines: 'we no longer call it risk management, our values simply say that our people are taking good care of the business on behalf of our stakeholders!'

The key feature of the above model is that some organizations in high risk businesses such as derivatives are already at phase five. But for corporate governance reporting purposes they have to formalize their arrangements by designing a risk management system, demonstrating that it works well and then slowly place it back into the infrastructure, like a ship's engine, quietly throbbing unseen in the background as it drives the ship forward. One landmark development that consolidated current thinking on ERM was the COSO ERM. COSO stands for the Committee of Sponsoring Organizations. COSO consists of five major professional associations in the US and was formed in 1985 to sponsor the National Commission on Fraudulent Financial Reporting. The COSO ERM model was launched in September 2004 and consists of three dimensions. The first is four categories of management objectives:

a. Strategic.
b.. Operations.
c. Reporting.
d. Compliance.

These objectives are aligned to eight main components of ERM:

1. Internal environment.
2. Objective setting.
3. Event identification.
4. Risk assessment.
5. Risk response.
6. Control activities.
7. Information and communication.
8. Monitoring.

And these eight components, in pursuit of the four main objectives, run across the entire organization at various levels, which are described as:

- Entity-level.
- Division.
- Business unit.
- Subsidiary.

COSO has developed its own definition of ERM:

Enterprise risk management is a process, effected by an entity's board of directors, management and other personnel, applied in strategy setting and across the enterprise, designed to identify potential events that may affect the entity, and manage risk to be within its risk appetite, to provide reasonable assurance regarding the achievement of entity objectives.

In summing up COSO ERM, it is important to keep in mind the concepts behind the framework, in that it:

- Is a process.
- Is affected by people.
- Is applied in strategy setting.
- Is applied across the enterprise.

- Is designed to identify potential events.
- Manages risk so that it falls within risk appetite.
- Can only provide reasonable assurance.
- Supports the achievement of key objectives.

Note that COSO ERM makes reference to the role of internal audit and suggests that: 'Internal auditors play a key role in evaluating the effectiveness of—and recommending improvements to—enterprise risk management'.[11]

The final aspect of ERM relates to risk standards. The Australian/New Zealand Risk Management Standards was republished in 2004. This standard is built around seven main elements:

- **Communicate and consult** Communicate and consult with internal and external stakeholders as appropriate at each stage of the risk management process and concerning the process as a whole.
- **Establish the context** Establish the external, internal and risk management context in which the rest of the process will take place. Criteria against which risk will be evaluated should be established and the structure of the analysis defined.
- **Identify risks** Identify where, when, why and how events could prevent, degrade delay or enhance the achievement of the objectives.
- **Analyse risks** Identify and evaluate existing controls. Determine consequences and likelihood and hence the level of risk. This analysis should consider the range of potential consequences and how these could occur.
- **Evaluate risks** Compare estimated levels of risk against the pre-established criteria and consider the balance between potential benefits and adverse outcomes. This enables decisions to be made about the extent and nature of treatments required and about priorities.
- **Treat risks** Develop and implement specific cost-effective strategies and action plans for increasing potential benefits and reducing potential costs.
- **Monitor and review** It is necessary to monitor the effectiveness of all steps of the risk management process. This is important for continuous improvement. Risks and the effectiveness of treatment measures need to be monitored to ensure changing circumstances do not alter priorities.[12]

Interestingly enough, the Australian/New Zealand Risk Management Standard is built into the corporate governance context as it is referred to in the guideline issued by the Australian Stock Exchange (see chapter two). The Australian/New Zealand guide devotes a 43 page document to the use of risk management within the internal audit process, and this makes the point that:

> Internal auditing is an organizational function, established by top management to monitor the organization's risk management and control processes. By review of the critical control systems and risk management processes, the internal auditor can provide important assistance to organizational management.

The UK has not been slow to prepare a risk standard and Institute of Risk Management, The Association of Insurance and Risk Managers and The National Forum for Risk Managers in the Public Sector (collectively known as AIRMIC, ALARM, IRM) prepared a risk management standard in 2002. They felt that some form of standard is needed to ensure that there is an agreed:

- terminology related to the words used;
- process by which risk management can be carried out;
- organization structure for risk management; and
- objectives for risk management.

The Risk Management Standard set out a process that consists of:

- The organization's strategic objectives.
- Risk assessment:
  —Risk analysis—risk identification, description and estimation.
  —Risk evaluation.
- Risk reporting.
- Decisions.
- Risk treatment.
- Residual risk reporting.
- Monitoring.

This is set with a modification and audit process that runs across each of these elements. In fact there is a section dedicated to the role of internal audit which suggests that this may include some or all of the following:

- Focusing the internal audit work on the significant risks, as identified by management, and auditing the risk management processes across an organization.
- Providing assurance on the management of risk.
- Providing active support and involvement in the risk management process.
- Facilitating risk identification/assessment and educating line staff in risk management and internal control.
- Co-ordinating risk reporting to the board, audit committee, etc.

The standard goes on to suggest that in defining their role internal audit should ensure that the professional requirements for independence and objectivity are not breached. [13]

Integrating Risks

In the past, risks were considered in isolation but ERM seeks to have risks considered across the entire organization along with a determination of how they fit together. This big picture really does use the entire organization as the canvas for risk management. In keeping with this analogy, we might suggest that the canvas is painted Red, Amber and Green for high, medium and low risk areas, which can be reviewed at board level as in Figure 3.13.

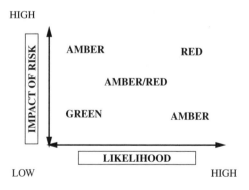

FIGURE 3.13   Risk scoring.

Each part of the organization will undertake risk assessment and compile risk registers containing the agreed risk management strategy. Reports from each section will be aggregated to form a

TABLE 3.1   Risk reports.

Dept.	Activity and date reviewed	Risk: Red, Amber Green and risk category code	Action plan	KPIs and review	Risk owner

summary version that gives the activities, risk rating, code (Red, Amber, Green), owner and action required, using a suitable reporting tool in Table 3.1.

The risk management policy should fit into the policy on performance management and each risk status should prompt different types of actions as a response to the risk exposure identified along, for example, the following lines:

High risk exposure—urgent board level reports and ongoing monitoring.

Major risk exposure—director involvement—rapid review.

Significant risk exposure—manager intervention and summary briefing to director.

Moderate risk exposure—basic management practice applied.

Low risk exposure—no special action.

Trivial—review whether able to remove resources away from monitoring.

In this way the board and top management may have a view on risk across the organization and how it is being handled. See the section above on risk appetite as this will impact on the way risks are reviewed and prioritized. There may be need for a validation procedure to ensure that each risk register is valid and this is something that the CRO would address. Note that there are some internal auditors who consider this validation of risk management practices a useful way of applying the audit resource.

Risk Categories

Each organization will have its own interpretation of risk. And this interpretation will fit the market, culture and mission of the organization in question. To help align the risk management process with the organization's systems and procedures many organizations capture risk in a structured manner, via a set of categories that suit them. We can review some of the well-known published risk guides and consider the prompts they contain on categorization. The King report suggests several general headings as a start to addressing the company's exposure to at least the following: physical and operational risks, human resource risks, business continuity and disaster recovery, credit and market risks and compliance risks. The UK Government Treasury's guide to the management of risk isolates three main categories of risk:

- **External** Arising from the external environment, not wholly within the organizations' controls, but where action can be taken to mitigate the risk. Comprising political, economic, socio-cultural, technological, legal/regulatory and environmental risks.

- **Operational**   Relating to existing operations—both current delivery and building and maintaining capacity and capability. Comprising delivery, service/product failure, project delivery, capacity and capability, resources, relationships, operations, reputation, risk management performance and capability, governance, scanning, resilience and security.
- **Change**   Risks created by decisions to pursue new endeavours beyond current capability. Comprising targets, change programmes, new projects and new policies.

3.8 Control Self-Assessment

The success of enterprise-wide risk management depends on an integrated process for ensuring that risks are assessed and managed across an organization in a dynamic and meaningful way. There are many techniques for reaching all parts of an organization so that self-assessment by front line staff becomes the norm. Some argue the widespread use of questionnaires that are completed by key employees as a way of assessing whether there are operations that are at risk and whether controls are addressing these risk areas properly. Another technique is the use of interviews with managers in particular business units to gauge whether the area is under control or not. A further approach is to commission comprehensive reviews of risk in high profile parts of the organization normally by the use of external consultants, who would report back on any problems found. These three techniques are fairly straightforward in that they involve a process superimposed on the normal business operations and support services. Unfortunately they reinforce the ad-hoc silo approach and appear as one-off exercises carried out by a special purpose head office team. A more popular approach is the use of control self assessment workshops, or what some call control and risk self-assessment (CRSA) workshops. The UK's CRSA Forum consists of a network of CSRA practitioners and interested persons who have formed a group that meets every quarter. Their mission is: 'Sharing, progressing and promoting best practices in self assessment of control and risk in all organisations.' At each meeting there are normally a couple of presentations by group members on the way CRSA is operated in the organization in question. Proponents of CRSA are convinced that the only way to get risk management into the heart and minds of the organization is to get everyone involved in a participative manner. CRSA may be called many different things in different organizations. In some companies the terms *risk* and *control* do not inspire people and other more friendly terms are applied to the workshops. Note that the technique is dealt with in Chapter 7 on the audit approaches. Here we simply mention the key principles relating to CRSA as part of the risk management system. An article by Paul Makosz in *CSA Sentinel* outlined the development of the CRSA approach:

> While I was at Gulf Canada Resources, we began to recognize that the heart of many problems lies in a corporate culture that could directly affect the bottom line; but we unfortunately had no tools to help us in identifying major risks before they became problems. Bruce McCuaig, my predecessor at Gulf Canada Resources, originated the CSA idea. He had been studying Watergate related issues at the parent company, Gulf Corp. About the same time, a serious management fraud had been discovered in a Gulf Canada subsidiary, although the internal auditors had been there only recently. Bruce kept asking, 'What's the point of auditing the little things if the culture is wrong-headed?' Gulf was going through some team productivity exercises at the time, so Bruce wanted to teach teams about internal control and have them self-assess their position. The rest is history. Bruce and I wrote about it in 'Ripe for Renaissance,' an article that appeared in the December 1990 edition of *Internal Auditor*.[14]

The important point to note in this section is the need to blend the CRSA technique into the risk management process generally. A staged approach can be applied to this end as illustrated in Figure 3.14.

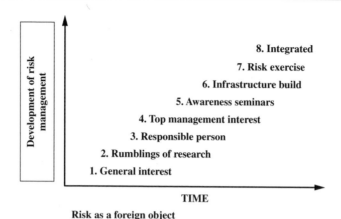

FIGURE 3.14 A staged approach to risk.

Stage one—general interest: build on the interest and focus it into a pro-organizational drive to get different specialist teams talking about their approach to risk management.

Stage two—rumblings of research: develop a database of best practice guidance and find out what others in the business sector are doing. Construct a checklist of matters to be addressed in formulating and implementing a corporate risk policy.

Stage three—responsible person: define respective roles and responsibilities, in particular a champion for the cause who can set a direction for the organization.

Stage four—top management interest: secure a sponsor on the board who can ensure risk management sits firmly on the corporate agenda. One way is to get the board (and audit committee) to carry out their own assessment to arrive at their top ten risks to start the process.

Stage five—awareness seminars: it is most important to get key players around the organization together in a series of events to provide understanding, promote buy-in and ensure each manager accepts that they have a clear and direct responsibility for managing risks in their areas of responsibility.

Stage six—infrastructure build: much of this will revolve around building a suitable information system that categorizes and captures risk activities into a formal assurance reporting format. Also, the risk activities will have to be decided on and whether this will happen throughout the organization or just in high profile areas.

Stage seven—risk exercises: here the organization will need to conduct surveys and/or facilitated workshops in a way that best suits the structure and culture of the business.

Stage eight—integrated: much of this will be based on defining the role and competencies of a chief risk officer or equivalent and ensuring that the risk assessment process is revisited and updated both regularly and whenever changes impact various risk profiles.

The problem facing some organizations is that they start the eight-stage process with no clear understanding of the stage development and targets. As a result, many get stuck at an early stage and write the entire thing off as a false start. CRSA only really works where the organization has arrived at stage seven.

3.9 Embedded Risk Management

We now arrive at the pinnacle of risk management best practice. The much-sought-after 'embedded risk management'. Again, like much of the theory of risk management, it sounds simple as an ideal and Turnbull includes among the criteria to assess the internal control framework (monitoring arrangements) the following question:

> Are there ongoing processes embedded within the company's overall business operations, and addressed by senior management, which monitor the effective application of the policies, processes and activities related to internal control risk management? (Such processes may include control self-assessment, confirmation by personnel of compliance with policies and codes of conduct, internal audit reviews or other management reviews.)

Most risk standards, guides, aids and commentary contain the phrase (or an equivalent term) *embedded risk management*. Gordon Hill warns about trying to do too much too quickly:

> Integration with existing process is as important but presents different challenges purely because the process will be operational. You could embark on a programme of reviewing all processes for risk. However, I would guard against this approach on the basis of 'if it ain't broke don't fix it'. Wait until there is a problem within a process that suggests changes are needed; this is the time to introduce risk assessment and this will ensure the greatest value is delivered. If benefit is provided then staff will understand the value of risk intervention. . . Attacking everything at once is not a practical solution. Organizations need a way of deciding where to integrate and when. Using a properly prioritized risk register to focus on the biggest issues is the most effective way of targeting effort. This way the organisation will achieve the fastest payback and the greatest commitment and will have in its grasp a route map to the managed risk culture.[15]

Meanwhile we can complete our risk model by putting in the remaining component of effective risk management, with a view to tackling the need to get risk firmly inside the organization's processes. By adding several factors consisting of three black boxes (ERM/CRSA, SIC and Stakeholders) and four grey boxes (time, cost, values, embed) we can achieve a fully developed model of effective risk management in Figure 3.15.

Starting with the black boxes first, these additions are explained below:

ERM/CRSA   As discussed above, there should be a process that ensures risk is understood, identified and managed at grassroots level ideally through a form of control risk self-assessment programmes. Meanwhile, there should be a further process for ensuring risk assessment is undertaken throughout key parts, if not all, of the organization and that it is driven from the top and runs down, across and throughout all levels of management. The chief risk officer (CRO) would help co-ordinate these efforts.

SIC   The risk efforts and ensuring controls should feed into the statement of internal control (SIC) that each larger organization should formally publish. The inputs to the annual SIC should

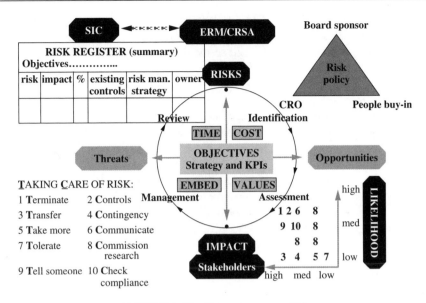

FIGURE 3.15   Risk management (10).

arrive from a suitable assurance reporting systems (perhaps revolving around local and aggregated risk registers).

Stakeholders   The organization should have a formal process for communicating with stakeholders the efforts of the risk management system and any information that gives value to various interested parties. The risk management system should address the concept of risk tolerance and make clear what areas are likely to pose a threat to the organization, or the general public where appropriate and the extent to which strategies and performance targets are likely to be fully achieved. Much use can be made of the Internet website to communicate risk publicly.

Time   The risk model is based on doing more to research, analyse and address risks that impact the organization. And ensuring there is transparency and competence in the way these risks are addressed.

Cost   This factor is linked to time. It does cost money to implement new ideas even where we are building these ideas into our existing systems.

Values   The best way to establish risk management is to avoid just delivering a set of regulations in the form of things that must be done to satisfy the policy requirements.

Embed   The final part of the model falls out of all the other components and consists of the bottom line concept of embedding risk management into and inside the organization.

3.10 The Internal Audit Role in Risk Management

This chapter has so far provided a brief introduction to risk management—the growing trend towards recognizing risk as a key driver for all the systems that underpin a successful organization.

We now have to touch on the way internal audit fits into the risk equation. As a start the IIA Implementation Standard 1220.A3 states that internal auditors must have regard to key risks and that 'the internal auditor should be alert to the significant risks that might affect objectives, operations, or resources. However assurance procedures alone, even when performed with due professional care, do not guarantee that all significant risks will be identified.'

Performance Standard 2100 argues that 'the internal audit activity should evaluate and contribute to the improvement of risk management, control and governance processes by using a systematic and disciplined approach.' While Implementation Standard 2110.A1 makes it clear that 'the internal audit activity should monitor and evaluate the effectiveness of the organisation's risk management system.'

This viewpoint represents an important challenge for the internal auditor who has been asked to champion the risk movement while retaining the independent assurance role. Models are available to help in the key decisions underpinning the new look internal audit role. Practice Advisory 2100-3 addresses Internal Audit's Role in the Risk Management Process; although reinforcing the point that risk management is a key responsibility of management, it goes on to suggest that internal audit's role may be found at some point along a continuum that ranges from stage 1 through to stage 4:

1. No role.
2. Auditing the risk management (RM) process.
3. Active continuous support in RM (oversight committees, status reporting).
4. Managing and coordinating RM process.

The briefing note closes with a view that, ultimately, it is the role of executive management and the audit committee to determine the role of internal audit in the RM process. Where there is no risk management system in place another Practice Advisory (2100-4) says that the absence of a risk management process should be brought to management's attention by internal audit, along with suggestions for establishing such a process if requested. Internal auditors can play a proactive role in assisting with the initial establishment of such a process but they should not 'own' or be responsible for the management of risks identified. There is another Practice Advisory (2110-1) that explains how internal audit should assess the adequacy of the risk management processes. This advisory argues that the risk management process should ensure:

1. Risks arising from business strategies and activities are identified and prioritized.
2. Management and the board have determined the level of risks acceptable to the organization.
3. Risk mitigation activities are designed and implemented to reduce, or otherwise manage, risk at levels that were determined to be acceptable to management and the board.
4. Ongoing monitoring activities are conducted to periodically reassess risk and the effectiveness of controls to manage risk.
5. The board and management receive periodic reports of the results of the RM process.

Internal auditors must add value to an organization and IIA Performance Standards 2000 state quite clearly that 'the CAE should effectively manage the internal audit activity to ensure it adds value to the organisation.' While the IIA's Implementation Standard 2010.C1 builds on this need to add value and get involved with promoting risk management as it states that 'the CAE should consider accepting proposed consulting engagements based on the engagement's potential to improve management of risks, add value, and improve the organisation's operations. Those engagements that have been accepted should be included in the plan.'

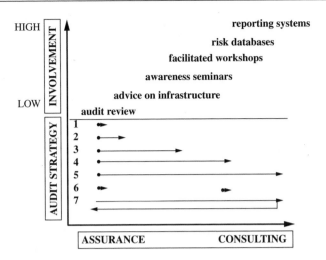

FIGURE 3.16 Assurance and consulting services.

It is possible to sum up the audit role in risk management by using a new model in Figure 3.16.

Before we go through the Assurance and Consulting Services model two key points needs to be made. First, reviews are more reliable where the reviewer is impartial. Second, value add means contributing specialist expertise to promote corporate success. When an organization needs to get a risk management system up and running, and looks to the auditor for help setting up, it is hard for the same auditor to then give an impartial assurance on this same system. At first sight the two concepts are incompatible. There are, however, various ways that this apparent inconsistency can be managed. The model we are using has seven approaches:

1. The standard audit review approach is adopted. Here the internal audit team monitor the way systematic business risk management is established and implemented, and then go on to review whether it is reliable, robust and meets the needs of the organization. In turn, internal audit is able to furnish independent assurances to the board on the state of risk management.
2. This is similar to approach one, with the addition of ad-hoc advice and guidance provided on request. Internal audit may make presentations to the board and turn up to meetings or workshops where risk management is being discussed and decided on, and make contributions as required.
3. Approach three takes things a step further and the internal auditors start to get involved in raising awareness. The main feature here is that internal audit would lead various seminars and events that promote corporate governance, risk management and control.
4. The next level is where internal audit facilitates CSA workshops and takes the risk message to the grassroots across the organization. Auditors bone up on facilitation skills and lead work teams, projects teams or process-based work groups and help the teams prepare suitable risk registers to reflect their prioritized risks and action plans.
5. Level five goes all the way. Here internal audit compiles the corporate risks database from all the risk-based activities that are happening in the organization. Audit will go on to develop a reporting system that provides aggregated and disaggregated reports at appropriate levels in the organization. The assumed role is akin to that of the so-called organization's chief risk officer.
6. The level six approach is based on establishing two separate strands to the internal audit service. The first focuses on the main assurance and review role, although this now likely to be

risk based, concentrating on operational risks that have been identified. The second performs a consulting role in facilitating CRSA events.

7. The final approach is to play a full role in starting and developing systematic risk management across the organization to get the process going. Then, having helped set up the process, internal audit moves away from the consulting service and back to the main assurance role. In this way the full responsibility to make risk management work is given back to the line.

The above basic strategies can be used as a platform to fit the internal audit service into the development of risk management throughout the organization. The approach and style selected will be whatever suits the organization and the audit team in question. A final word on the new role of internal auditors in enterprise risk management has been provided by the IIA UK and Ireland in their 2004 position statement on this topic. This guidance makes clear the core audit assurance role which is noted as:

- Giving assurances on the risk management process.
- Giving assurances that risks are correctly evaluated.
- Evaluating risk management processes.
- Evaluating the reporting of key risks.
- Reviewing the management of key risks.

Moving through this range of audit services, the next set of roles is described as acceptable, as long as there are suitable safeguards in place to protect the integrity of the core audit role:

- Facilitating identification and evaluation of risks.
- Coaching management in responding to risks.
- Co-ordinating ERM activities.
- Consolidated reporting on risks.
- Maintaining and developing the ERM framework.
- Championing establishment of ERM.
- Developing risk management strategy for board approval.

The necessary safeguards that mean the consulting role does not conflict with the assurance role is noted below:

- It should be clear that management remains responsible for risk management.
- The nature of internal audit's responsibilities should be documented in the audit charter and approved by the Audit Committee.
- Internal audit should not manage any of the risks on behalf of management.
- Internal audit should provide advice, challenge and support to management's decision making, as opposed to taking risk management decisions themselves.
- Internal audit cannot also give objective assurance on any part of the ERM framework for which it is responsible. Such assurance should be provided by other suitably qualified parties.
- Any work beyond the assurance activities should be recognized as a consulting engagement and the implementation standards related to such engagements should be followed.

To complete the circle, the guidance makes clear that there are certain roles that really do not fit with the audit role and should therefore not be undertaken by a professional audit function:

- Setting the risk appetite.
- Imposing risk management processes.
- Management assurances on risks.

- Taking decisions on risk responses.
- Implementing risk responses on management's behalf.
- Accountability for risk management.[16]

Summary and Conclusions

Risk management is not really a management fad. It provides a platform for corporate governance by giving comfort to shareholders and other stakeholders that the risks to their investment (or services) are understood by their representatives, the board and systematically addressed by the management. True risk management is about changing the culture of the organization to get people to embrace their responsibilities, knowing that this tool will help them get around problems and drive the business forward in a considered manner. The internal auditor is faced with a major challenge in defining where it fits in with the developing risk management processes and luckily there is much professional guidance that assists this task. Our final word comes from a speech by James Lam: 'Let me leave you with a final thought. Over the longer term, the only alternative to risk management is crisis management, and crisis management is much more embarrassing, expensive and time-consuming.'[17]

Chapter 3: Multi-Choice Questions

Having worked through the chapter the following multi-choice questions may be attempted. (See Appendix A for suggested answer guide and Appendix B where you may record your score.)

1. **Insert the missing words:**
   The other concept that needs to be considered is that risk, in the context of achieving objectives, has both an upside and an downside. In our model we call these . . . .
   a. threats and disasters.
   b. opportunities and challenges.
   c. threats and opportunities.
   d. threats and near misses.

2. **Which is the least appropriate sentence?**
   The benefits of systematic project risk management include:
   a. More realistic business and project planning and actions implemented in time to be effective.
   b. Complete certainty of achieving business goals and project objectives.
   c. Appreciation of, and readiness to exploit, all beneficial opportunities and fewer costly surprises through effective and transparent contingency planning.
   d. Improved loss control and improved control of project and business costs along with increased flexibility as a result of understanding all options and associated risks.

3. **Insert the missing words:**
   The subject of . . . . has a very interesting past. Project managers have used them for a long time as they assess risks at an early stage in a large project and enter the details in a formal record which is inspected by the sponsors. The insurance industry again is well used to documenting assumptions about risk and using this to form judgements on where to offer

insurance cover and what aspects of an operation are included in this cover. More recently, they have come to the fore as an important part of general business risk management.
a. risk identification.
b. data analysis.
c. control charts.
d. risk registers.

4. Insert the missing words:
The . . . . defines how we see residual risk, after we have dealt with it through an appropriate strategy, and whether it is acceptable or not, that is, is the risk acceptable as it stands or do we need to do more to contain it, or perhaps exploit areas where risk is too low?
a. risk appetite.
b. strategic development.
c. performance management.
d. control oversight.

5. Insert the missing words:
Where there is no . . . . driving the risk management process it will tend to fail.
a. external party.
b. internal auditor.
c. board member.
d. audit committee member.

6. Which is the most appropriate sentence?
a. Control compliance is really the foundation of risk management, since it is what people do and how they behave that determines whether an organization succeeds or fails.
b. The risk response is really the foundation of risk management, since it is what people do and how they behave that determines whether an organization succeeds or fails.
c. The auditor is really the foundation of risk management, since it is what auditors do and how they behave that determines whether an organization succeeds or fails.
d. Performance targets is really the foundation of risk management, since it is what people do and how they behave that determines whether an organization succeeds or fails.

7. Which item is wrong?
The COSO ERM model consists of three dimensions. The first is four categories of management objectives:
a. Strategic.
b. Operations.
c. Behavioural.
d. Compliance.

8. Which item is wrong?
These objectives are aligned to eight main components of COSO ERM which include:
a. Internal Environment and Objective Setting.
b. Event Identification and Risk Assessment.
c. Risk Appetite and Control Activities.
d. Information and Communication and Monitoring.

9. Which item is wrong?

And these eight components, in pursuit of the four main objectives run across the entire organization at various levels which are described as:

a. Entity-Level.

b. Work-team.

c. Business Unit.

d. Subsidiary.

10. Which item is wrong?

Practice Advisory 2100-3 addresses Internal Audit's Role in the Risk Management Process, although reinforcing the point that risk management is a key responsibility of management, it goes on to suggest that internal audit's role may be found at some point along a continuum that ranges from stage 1 through to stage 4:

a. stage 1: Chief Risk Officer role.

b. stage 2: Auditing the risk management (RM) process.

c. stage 3: Active continuous support in RM (oversight committees, status reporting).

d. stage 4: Managing and coordinating RM process.

References

1. McNamee, David and Selim, Georges, IIA Research Foundation, 'Risk management: changing the internal auditor's paradigm'. *Internal Auditing*, Dec. 1998 pp. 6–9.
2. Bernstein, Peter L. (1996) *Against the Gods*, New York: John Wiley and Sons Inc., p. 8.
3. Bernstein, Peter L. (1996) *Against the Gods*, New York: John Wiley and Sons Inc., p. 3.
4. Bernstein, Peter L. (1996) *Against the Gods*, New York: John Wiley and Sons Inc., p. 20.
5. Bernstein, Peter L. (1996) *Against the Gods*, New York: John Wiley and Sons Inc., p. 337.
6. BS6079-3:2000 Project Management Part 3—Guide to the Management of Business Risk.
7. Bernstein, Peter L. (1996) *Against the Gods*, New York: John Wiley and Sons Inc., p. 263.
8. Flesher, Dale (1996) *Internal Auditing: A One-Semester Course*, Florida: The Institute of Internal Auditors, p. 122.
9. *Daily Mail*, 2 Nov. 1999.
10. NAO, Supporting Innovation: Managing Risk In Government Departments, 26 July 2000.
11. (Committee of Sponsoring Organizations, Enterprise Risk Management, September 2004, Page 88)
12. (Australian/New Zealand Standard: Risk Management Guidelines AS/NZS 4360:2004, Pages 7 to 8)
13. (AIRMIC, ALARM, IRM Risk Management Standard, 2002).
14. Makosz, Paul, *Sentinel*, No. 1, Jan. 1997, Published by the IIA and the IIA Control Self-Assessment Center.
15. Hill, Gordon 'Embedding Turnbull, achieving a managed risk culture.' *Internal Auditing and Risk Management*, p. 30.
16. Institute of Internal Auditors, UK&Ireland, Position Statement 2004, The Role of Internal Audit in Enterprise-wide Risk Management.
17. Speech by James Lam at the IQPC Enterprise Risk Management Conference, 25 March 1999.

Chapter 4

INTERNAL CONTROLS

Introduction

We have referred to corporate governance and risk management; and internal control forms the third component of this stool. Good governance is dependent on a management that understands the risks it faces and is able to keep control of the business. *Brink's Modern Internal Auditing* suggests that internal control is the most important and fundamental concept that an internal auditor must understand.[1] This chapter covers the following areas:

4.1 Why Controls?

The Committee of Sponsoring Organizations (COSO) of the Treadway Commission have suggested that (www.coso.org):

> Senior executives have long sought ways to better control the enterprises they run. Internal controls are put in place to keep the company on course toward profitability goals and achievement of its mission, and to minimize surprises along the way. They enable management to deal with rapidly changing economic and competitive environments, shifting customer demands and priorities, and restructuring for future growth. Internal controls promote efficiency, reduce risk of asset loss, and help ensure the reliability of financial statements and compliance with laws and regulations. Because internal control serves many important purposes, there are increasing calls for better internal control systems and report cards on them. Internal control is looked upon more and more as a solution to a variety of potential problems.

Where there are risks to the achievement of objectives, which mean failure is a strong possibility, controls have to be put in place to address these risks. If not failure becomes likely. At the same time, controls cost money and they have to be worthwhile. A lot depends on the risk appetite and what is considered acceptable as opposed to unacceptable to the organization and its stakeholders.

Poor controls lead to losses, scandals, failures and damage the reputation of organizations in whatever sector they are from. Where risks are allowed to run wild and new ventures are undertaken without a means of controlling risk, there are likely to be problems.

The control banner is being waved by many authorities and regulators. For example, the Securities and Exchange Commission (SEC) regulations require organizations to devise and maintain a system of internal accounting control. While the Turnbull report (see Chapter 2) suggests that:

> A company's system of internal control has a key role in the management of risks that are signifi-cant to the fulfilment of its business objectives. A sound system of internal control contributes to safeguarding the shareholders' investment and the company's assets. (para.10) Internal control. . . facilitates the effectiveness and efficiency of operations, helps ensure the reliability of internal and external reporting and assists compliance with laws and regulations. (para.11)

One writer has highlighted the dynamic of controls by saying that the purpose of any control system is to attain or maintain a desired state or condition.[2] We can build on the view that control is about achieving objectives, dealing with risk and keeping things in balance by introducing our basic first model of control in Figure 4.1.

FIGURE 4.1   Internal control (1).

An organization will set clear objectives and then assess the inherent risks to achieving these objectives. Before it can reach the black achievements box, there needs to be a control strategy put in place to provide a reasonable expectation of getting there. The control strategy will be derived from a wider risk management strategy, but will have as a key component focused and effective systems of internal control. Effective controls are measures that work and give a reasonable probability of ensuring that operations are successful and resources protected. Viewing internal control as a dynamic concept that runs across an organization as opposed to a series of basic procedures takes the topic to a higher level. Turnbull provides some background as to what makes up a sound system of internal control:

> An internal control system encompasses the policies, processes, tasks, behaviours and other aspects of a company that, taken together:
>
> • facilitate its effective and efficient operation by enabling it to respond appropriately to significant business, operational, financial, compliance and other risks to achieving the company's objectives. This includes the safeguarding of assets from inappropriate use or from loss and fraud, and ensuring that liabilities are identified and managed;
> • help ensure the quality of internal and external reporting. This requires the maintenance of proper records and processes that generate a flow of timely, relevant and reliable information from within and outside the organisation;
> • help ensure compliance with applicable laws and regulations, and also with internal policies with respect to the conduct of business. (para. 20)

Management's Responsibilities

Turnbull has made clear where control responsibility lies in an organization:

> The board of directors is responsible for the company's system of internal control. It should set appropriate policies on internal control and seek regular assurance that will enable it to satisfy itself that the system is functioning effectively. The board must further ensure that the system of internal control is effective in managing risks in the manner which it has approved. (para. 16)

While the board sets overall direction, it is management who must implement good controls by considering the following:

Determine the need for controls Managers must be able to isolate a situation where there is a need for specific internal controls and respond appropriately.

Design suitable controls Once the need for controls has been defined, management must then establish suitable means to install them.

Implement these controls Managers are then duty-bound to ensure that the control processes are carefully implemented.

Check that they are being applied correctly Management and not internal audit is responsible for ensuring that control mechanisms are not being by-passed but are fully applied as they were originally intended.

Maintain and update the controls This feature is also important in that securing control is a continuous task that should be at the forefront of management concerns.

Inclusion of the above noted matters within any appraisal scheme that seeks to judge management's performance We would expect management to consider the application of controls as part of management skills and training.

Internal Audit's Role

The internal auditor has to be concerned about the state of control in the organization. The pace has been set by the IIA whose Performance Standard 2120 goes straight to the point: 'The internal audit activity should assist the organisation in maintaining effective controls by evaluating their effectiveness and efficiency and by promoting continuous improvement.' The auditors' role regarding systems of internal control is distinguished from management's in that it covers:

- Assessing those areas that are most at risk in terms of the key control objectives that we have already mentioned (i.e. MIS, compliance, safeguarding assets and VFM).
- Defining and undertaking a programme for reviewing these high profile systems that attract the most risk.
- Reviewing each of these systems by examining and evaluating their associated systems of internal control to determine the extent to which the five key control objectives are being met.
- Advising management whether or not controls are operating adequately and effectively so as to promote the achievement of the system's/control objectives.

- Recommending any necessary improvements to strengthen controls where appropriate, while making clear the risks involved for failing to effect these recommended changes.
- Following up audit work so as to discover whether management has actioned agreed audit recommendations.

The IIA's Implementation Standard 2120.A1 provides four key aspects of the scope of controls:

Based on the results of the risk assessment, the internal audit activity should evaluate the adequacy and effectiveness of controls encompassing the organisation's governance, operations, and information systems. This should include:

- Reliability and integrity of financial and operational information.
- Effectiveness and efficiency of operations.
- Safeguarding of assets.
- Compliance with laws, regulations, and contracts.

The IIA go on to make quite clear that the nature of internal audit's work incorporates this assessment of risk and suitable control models (Performance Standard 2100): 'The internal audit activity should evaluate and contribute to the improvement of risk management, control and governance processes using a systematic and disciplined approach.'

Even when internal audit is working on consulting engagements, as opposed to assurance-based work, there is still the need to consider whether controls are sound, as established by IIA Implementation Standard 2120.C1 which says: 'During consulting engagement's, internal auditors should address controls consistent with the engagements objectives and should be alert to the existence of any significant control weaknesses.'

Building the Control Model

One important feature of control relates to the need to contain activity within set limits or boundaries. We can amend our model to incorporate these limits in Figure 4.2.

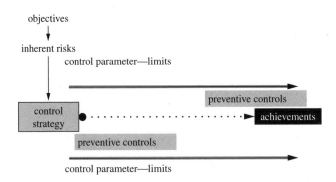

FIGURE 4.2   Internal control (2).

So activity moves an organization towards achieving its objectives, by keeping the activities within prescribed standards. The dotted black line moves dead straight to the achievement box and preventive controls are set which ensure everything is contained within the upper and lower control parameters. Constraining, containing and restricting controls are applied at the boundaries to ensure that only the right people get in the organization, they only do the right things and they cannot access anything that falls outside their remit. Note that Section 4.6 provides more detail about different types of controls. The trend towards devolved organizations where each business unit is pretty well autonomous depends on a series of boundaries set at local levels throughout the organization, each local unit having their own perception of how these boundaries should be set, and how much leeway is given on either side of the limits. There is some move towards recentralizing some of the support services and so making corporate alignment much easier.

Making Controls Work

Control may be seen as one of the single most important topics that the auditor needs to master. The main justification for the internal auditing function revolves around the need to review systems of internal control with all other audit activities being to an extent subsidiary to this task. A good understanding of the concept of control and how controls may be applied in practice is an important skill that takes many years to fully acquire. There are a number of issues that underlie the concept of controls:

- Controls are all means devised to promote the achievement of agreed objectives.
- All controls have a corresponding cost and the idea is that the ensuing benefits should be worth the required outlay.
- Controls belong to those who operate them and should not be viewed in isolation.
- Internal control is all about people since controls work well only if they are geared to the users' needs in terms of practicality and usefulness.
- Overcontrol is as bad as undercontrol in that it results in the impression that someone, somewhere is monitoring activity whereas this may not be the case in reality.
- Entropy is the tendency to decay and all control systems will underachieve where they are not reviewed and updated regularly.
- The organizational culture affects the type of control features that are in place, which may be bureaucratic or flexible in nature.

4.2 Control Framework – COSO

The wide view of controls means that internal controls cover all aspects of an organization and there is a clear need for a way of pulling together control concepts to form an integrated whole, that is a control framework. The Committee of Sponsoring Organizations (COSO) of the Treadway Commission devised one such model that has an international recognition as a useful standard. All larger organizations need a formal control framework as a basis for their systems of internal control and IIA Implementation Standard 2120.A4 notes the importance of a set of organizational criteria that the auditor can use to review control systems (www.coso.org):

> Adequate criteria are needed to evaluate controls. Internal auditors should ascertain the extent to which management has established adequate criteria to determine whether objectives and goals have been accomplished. If adequate, internal auditors should use such criteria in their evaluation. If inadequate, internal auditors should work with management to develop appropriate evaluation criteria.

In the past the silo approach has been to consider whatever individual system we were auditing at the time. Systems were defined and audited, while the resultant report detailed the weak areas and how they could be improved. There is no possible way the aggregation of separate internal audit reports over a period could be used to comment on the overall state of controls in an organization. It is only by considering the adopted control model that the internal auditor is able to make board level declarations concerning internal control. In fact we can develop our control model to reflect the valuable platform provided by the control framework in Figure 4.3.

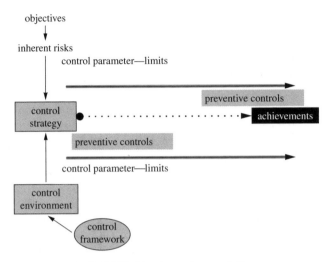

FIGURE 4.3   Internal control (3).

The control framework needs to be in place to promote the right control environment. Some might argue that the control environment in turn inspires an organization to build a suitable framework, although we will see that our first framework, COSO, incorporates the control environment as a separate component. The framework drives the environment, which in turn enables an organization to develop its control strategy in response to the assessment of various risks to achieving objectives. Risk assessment and control design is fragmented when not attaching to a clear control framework and any audit effort not directed at the big picture will itself be less valuable. The next areas to cover are based around the COSO components and the entire model is shown in Figure 4.4 before we describe each part.

FIGURE 4.4   The COSO model.

The COSO website (www.coso.org) gives the official background to their work:

In 1985 the National Commission of Fraudulent Financial Reporting, known as the Treadway Commission, was created through the joint sponsorship of the AIPCA, American Accounting Association, FEI, IIA and Institute of Management Accountants. Based on its recommendations a task force under the auspices of the Committee of Sponsoring Organisations conducted a review of internal control literature. The eventual outcome was the document Internal Control—Integrated Framework. COSO emphasised the responsibility of management for internal control.

Each component of the COSO model is dealt with next.

Control Environment

Turning once again to the COSO website (www.coso.org), their summary of the control environment follows:

The control environment sets the tone of an organization, influencing the control consciousness of its people. It is the foundation for all other components of internal control, providing discipline and structure. Control environment factors include the integrity, ethical values and competence of the entity's people; management's philosophy and operating style; the way management assigns authority and responsibility, and organizes and develops its people; and the attention and direction provided by the board of directors.

Risk Assessment

The COSO website (www.coso.org) provides a summary of where risk assessment fits into the control equation:

Every entity faces a variety of risks from external and internal sources that must be assessed. A precondition to risk assessment is establishment of objectives, linked at different levels and internally consistent. Risk assessment is the identification and analysis of relevant risks to achievement of the objectives, forming a basis for determining how the risks should be managed. Because economic, industry, regulatory and operating conditions will continue to change, mechanisms are needed to identify and deal with the special risks associated with change.

Control Activities

The COSO website (www.coso.org) provides a summary of where this aspect fits into their model:

Control activities are the policies and procedures that help ensure management directives are carried out. They help ensure that necessary actions are taken to address risks to achievement of the entity's objectives. Control activities occur throughout the organization, at all levels and in all functions. They include a range of activities as diverse as approvals, authorizations, verifications, reconciliations, reviews of operating performance, security of assets and segregation of duties.

Information and Communication

The COSO website (www.coso.org) provides a summary of where this aspect fits into their model:

Pertinent information must be identified, captured and communicated in a form and timeframe that enable people to carry out their responsibilities. Information systems produce reports, containing operational, financial and compliance-related information, that make it possible to run and control the business. They deal not only with internally generated data, but also information about external events, activities and conditions necessary to informed business decision-making and external reporting. Effective communication also must occur in a broader sense, flowing down, across and up the organization. All personnel must receive a clear message from top management that control responsibilities must be taken seriously. They must understand their own role in the internal control system, as well as how individual activities relate to the work of others. They must have a means of communicating significant information upstream. There also needs to be effective communication with external parties, such as customers, suppliers, regulators and shareholders.

Monitoring

The COSO website (www.coso.org) provides a summary of where this aspect fits into their model:

Internal control systems need to be monitored—a process that assesses the quality of the system's performance over time. This is accomplished through ongoing monitoring activities, separate evaluations or a combination of the two. Ongoing monitoring occurs in the course of operations. It includes regular management and supervisory activities, and other actions personnel take in performing their duties. The scope and frequency of separate evaluations will depend primarily on an assessment of risks and the effectiveness of ongoing monitoring procedures. Internal control deficiencies should be reported upstream, with serious matters reported to top management and the board. There is synergy and linkage among these components, forming an integrated system that reacts dynamically to changing conditions. The internal control system is intertwined with the entity's operating activities and exists for fundamental business reasons. Internal control is most effective when controls are built into the entity's infrastructure and are a part of the essence of the enterprise. 'Built in' controls support quality and empowerment initiatives, avoid unnecessary costs and enable quick response to changing conditions. There is a direct relationship between the three categories of objectives, which are what an entity strives to achieve, and components, which represent what is needed to achieve the objectives. All components are relevant to each objective's category. When looking at any one category—the effectiveness and efficiency of operations, for instance—all five components must be present and functioning effectively to conclude that internal control over operations is effective.

The COSO model is quite dynamic in that it covers most aspects of structures and processes that need to be in place to provide control. It is difficult to know how a board can state that it has reviewed its systems of internal control without reference to a comprehensive model or criteria for evaluating these controls at a corporate level. COSO simply asks five key questions:

1. Do we have the right foundations to control our business? (control environment)
2. Do we understand all those risks that stop us from being in control of the business? (risk assessment)
3. Have we implemented suitable control activities to address the risks to our business? (control activities)
4. Are we able to monitor the way the business is being controlled? (monitoring)
5. Is the control message driven down through the organization and associated problems and ideas communicated upwards and across the business? (communication and information)

If we can assess the quality of the responses to these five questions, we are on the way to achieving control and being able to demonstrate to all parties that their business concerns are in safe hands, even though no absolute guarantees are possible.

4.3 Control Framework – CoCo

The COSO framework is a powerful tool in that it allows an organization to focus on key structures, values and processes that together form this concept of internal control, far outside the narrow financial focus that used to be the case. The individual is part of the process but it can be hard to get a corporate solution down to grassroots. The criteria of control (CoCo) is a further control framework that can mean more to teams and individuals and includes an interesting learning dynamic. CoCo was developed by the Canadian Institute of Chartered Accountants (CICA) and is now an international standard. The CICA website (www.cica.ca) gives an account of their understanding of control as a platform for the criteria that was developed:

> Control needs to be understood in a broad context. Control comprises those elements of an organization (including its resources, systems, processes, culture, structure and tasks) that, taken together, support people in the achievement of the organization's objectives. The effectiveness of control cannot be judged solely on the degree to which each criterion, taken separately, is met. The criteria are interrelated, as are the control elements in an organization. Control elements cannot be designed or evaluated in isolation from each other. Control is as much a function of people's ethical values and beliefs as it is of standards and compliance mechanisms. Control should cover the identification and mitigation of risks. These risks include not only known risks related to the achievement of a specific objective but also two more fundamental risks to the viability and success of the organization:
>
> 1. failure to maintain the organization's capacity to identify and exploit opportunities;
> 2. failure to maintain the organization's capacity to respond and adapt to unexpected risks and opportunities, and make decisions on the basis of the telltale indications in the absence of definitive information.

The principles may be organized according to the four groupings of the CICA criteria of control framework as illustrated in Figure 4.5.

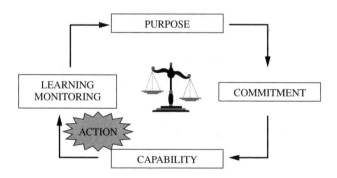

FIGURE 4.5   The CoCo model.

The main components are explained below:

Purpose   The model starts with the need for a clear direction and sense of purpose. This includes objectives, mission, vision and strategy; risks and opportunities; policies; planning; and performance targets and indicators. It is essential to have a clear driver for the control criteria and since controls are about achieving objectives, it is right that people work to the corporate purpose. Much work can be done here in setting objectives and getting people to have a stake in the future direction of the organization. The crucial link between controls and performance targets is established here as controls must fit in with the way an organization measures and manages performance to make any sense at all.

Commitment   The people within the organization must understand and align themselves with the organization's identity and values. This includes ethical values, integrity, human resource policies, authority, responsibility and accountability, and mutual trust. Many control systems fail to recognize the need to get people committed to the control ethos as a natural part of the way an organization works. Where people spend their time trying to 'beat the system', there is normally a lack of commitment to the control criteria. The hardest part in getting good control is getting people to feel part of the arrangements.

Capability   People must be equipped with the resources and competence to understand and discharge the requirements of the control model. This includes knowledge; skills and tools; communication processes; information; co-ordination; and control activities. Where there is a clear objective, and everyone is ready to participate in designing and installing good controls, there is still a need to develop some expertise in this aspect of organizational life. Capability is about resourcing the control effort by ensuring staff have the right skills, experience and attitudes not only to perform well but also to be able to assess risks and ensure controls make it easier to deal with these risks. Capability can be assisted by training and awareness seminars, either at induction or as part of continuing improvement programmes.

Action   This stage entails performing the activity that is being controlled. Before employees act, they will have a clear purpose, a commitment to meet their targets and the ability to deal with problems and opportunities. Any action that comes after these prerequisites has more chance of leading to a successful outcome.

Monitoring and learning   People must buy into and be part of the organization's evolution. This includes monitoring internal and external environments, monitoring performance, challenging assumptions, reassessing information needs and information systems, follow-up procedures, and assessing the effectiveness of control. Monitoring is a hard control in that it fits in with inspection, checking, supervising and examining. Challenging assumptions is an important soft control in that it means people can develop and excel. Each activity is seen as part of a learning process that lifts an organization to a higher dimension. Some organizations employ people who have tried and failed to start their own high risk venture, on the basis that they have had invaluable experiences that, if they have learnt lessons from, will make them stronger and much more resilient in growing a new business. Organizations that are based around blame cultures will not encourage positive learning experiences, and will interpret controls as mechanisms for punishing people whose performance slips. The CoCo criteria encourages a positive response to feedback on activities.

4.4 Other Control Models

COSO and CoCo are well-known control frameworks and they provide most of what is needed for an organization to consider when developing its own framework. There are, however, other sources of information to assist this task of getting control understood, addressed and reported.

Control Objectives for Information and Related Technology

This control standard, known as CobiT, 3rd edition, covers security and control for information technology (IT) systems in support of business processes and is designed for management, users and auditors. Several definitions are applied to this standard including:

- **Control:**   The policies, procedures, practices and organizational structures designed to provide reasonable assurance that business objectives will be achieved and that undesirable events will be prevented or detected and corrected.
- **IT control objective:**   Statement of the desired results of purpose to be achieved by implementing control procedures in a particular IT activity.
- **IT governance:**   A structure of relationships and processes to direct and control the enterprise in order to achieve the enterprise's goals by adding value while balancing risk versus returns over IT and its processes.

CobiT has four main components (domains) and for these domains there are a further 34 high level control processes:

- planning and organization;
- acquisition and implementation;
- delivery and support;
- monitoring.

Basle Committee on Banking Supervision

This committee reflects the work on internal controls for banking organizations developed by the Basle committee on Banking Supervision which is a committee of banking supervisory authorities established by the central bank governors of the group of ten countries in 1975. It consists of senior representatives of bank supervisory authorities and central banks from Belgium, Canada, France, Germany, Italy, Japan, Luxembourg, the Netherlands, Sweden, Switzerland, the United Kingdom and the United States. It usually meets at the Bank for International Settlements in Basle, where its permanent secretariat is located. The committee has spent some time developing principles of internal control that relate to the banking environment and they developed a Framework for Internal Control Systems in Banking Organisations in September 1998. The work on internal control provided a good platform for their guidance on operational risk management in February 2003, based on ten key principles:

- **Principle 1:**   The board of directors should be aware of the major aspects of the bank's operational risks as a distinct risk category that should be managed, and it should approve and periodically review the bank's operational risk management framework. The framework should provide a firm-wide definition of operational risk and lay down the principles of how operational risk is to be identified, assessed, monitored, and controlled/mitigated.
- **Principle 2:**   The board of directors should ensure that the bank's operational risk management framework is subject to effective and comprehensive internal audit by operationally independent, appropriately trained and competent staff. The internal audit function should not be directly responsible for operational risk management.
- **Principle 3:**   Senior management should have responsibility for implementing the operational risk management framework approved by the board of directors. The framework should be

consistently implemented throughout the whole banking organisation, and all levels of staff should understand their responsibilities with respect to operational risk management. Senior management should also have responsibility for developing policies, processes and procedures for managing operational risk in all of the bank's material products, activities, processes and systems.

- **Principle 4:**　Banks should identify and assess the operational risk inherent in all material products, activities, processes and systems. Banks should also ensure that before new products, activities, processes and systems are introduced or undertaken, the operational risk inherent in them is subject to adequate assessment procedures.
- **Principle 5:**　Banks should implement a process to regularly monitor operational risk profiles and material exposures to losses. There should be regular reporting of pertinent information to senior management and the board of directors that supports the proactive management of operational risk.
- **Principle 6:**　Banks should have policies, processes and procedures to control and/or mitigate material operational risks. Banks should periodically review their risk limitation and control strategies and should adjust their operational risk profile accordingly using appropriate strategies, in light of their overall risk appetite and profile.
- **Principle 7:**　Banks should have in place contingency and business continuity plans to ensure their ability to operate on an ongoing basis and limit losses in the event of severe business disruption.
- **Principle 8:**　Banking supervisors should require that all banks, regardless of size, have an effective framework in place to identify, assess, monitor and control/mitigate material operational risks as part of an overall approach to risk management.
- **Principle 9:**　Supervisors should conduct, directly or indirectly, regular independent evaluation of a bank's policies, procedures and practices related to operational risks. Supervisors should ensure that there are appropriate mechanisms in place which allow them to remain apprised of developments at banks.
- **Principle 10:**　Banks should make sufficient public disclosure to allow market participants to assess their approach to operational risk management.[2]

In terms of all organizations across all public and private sectors, it is important that each decides what to do about its system of internal control. There are several options:

1. Do nothing. On the basis that individual controls are in place and working and that this is good enough to satisfy stakeholders.
2. Document the existing control arrangements and develop them further to reflect an agreed corporate internal control framework.
3. Invent a model. Each organization may develop a unique perception of its controls and have this as its corporate internal control framework.
4. Adopt an existing published framework. Here the organization will simply state that it has adopted COSO, or CoCo or some version that the regulators promote.
5. Adapt an existing framework to suit the context and nuances of the organization in question. An international control framework may then be used as a benchmark to develop a tailored framework that fits the organization in question.
6. Selectively use all the available published material as criteria to develop a control framework that suits. Similar to 5 above but draws from all available sources of published guidance.

Whatever the chosen solution, each organization should publish a policy on internal control and in developing the policy, it will become clear that decisions have to be made along the lines suggested by options 1 to 6.

4.5 Links to Risk Management

We may expand our control model to include two more features. The first is CRSA where inherent risks are considered and assessed in a workshop setting to ensure any controls that need updating are firmly related to the risks that have been debated. The second addition is the corporate governance arrangements involving the role and responsibilities of the main board and audit committee. Control models that fail to link their mission to the governance structures will flounder. In fact, it is the governance arrangements that drive the risk assessments, which in turn drives the adopted processes and controls put in place. In this way the model assumes some depth and links the control effort back to the main board in Figure 4.6.

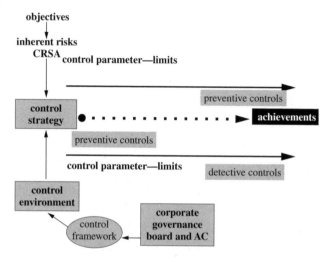

FIGURE 4.6 Internal control (4).

Changing risks call for changing controls and, for example, a shift towards e-procurement may allow local managers to place orders direct with suppliers and so appear to override central buying controls. But strict criteria over suppliers, goods, prices and so on forced through the adopted information system (and associated database) can themselves act as a central buying control and so shift the control focus to automated processes with head office intervention where appropriate. The equation is quite simple. Controls are needed if they guard against an unacceptable risk to the business or if they are part of a legal or regulatory compliance regime. In fact these later controls guard against the risk of failing to comply with the regime. Controls that do not pass these two tests may well be discarded, since they in turn cause a risk to the business by increasing costs and/or slowing down the organization.

4.6 Control Mechanisms

Control mechanisms are all those arrangements and procedures in place to ensure the business objectives may be met. They consist of individual mechanisms used by people and processes throughout the organization and they should exhibit certain defined attributes:

1. They should be clearly defined and understood by all users. Where a procedure is not fully appreciated by staff there will definitely be problems associated with compliance. They should be simple to operate and make sense.

2. Mechanisms should be established to monitor the extent to which control is being applied in practice. Control is a process that starts with setting standards and ends with reviewing the extent to which this has been successful.
3. Their use should be agreed by management and the staff who operate them. This factor should be used by the auditors to ensure they get managers to 'own' recommendations that impact on the systems of internal control.

Types of Controls

Principal controls may be categorized in a number of different ways. One way is to view them as being classified as follows:

1. **Directive**—to ensure that there is a clear direction and drive towards achieving the stated objectives.
2. **Preventive**—to ensure that systems work in the first place.
3. **Detective**—to pick up transaction errors that have not been prevented.
4. **Corrective**—to ensure that where problems are identified they are properly dealt with.

A combination of the above types of controls is essential to address the four key questions:

1. How do we get the right culture and drive to ensure these risks are appreciated and anticipated?
2. How do we install specific measures to prevent the risks that we now understand?
3. How can we find out if, despite our best efforts, things are still going wrong?
4. How can we plan in advance to address problems that we detect, particularly when they represent a significant risk to our business?

Many feel that a heavy dependence on detective and corrective controls may suggest an imbalance where upfront direction and prevention have not been adequately resourced.

Controls in Practice

Controls need to work well. There is one view that they should be 'SMART' in that they should be:

- Specific.
- Measurable.
- Achievable.
- Results oriented.
- Timely.

Some of the more traditional control mechanisms that may be applied in practice include:

1. Authorization   The act of authorizing something brings with it the process of granting permission on behalf of the organization.

2. Physical access restrictions   Physical access measures should be applied to information through, say, passwords, access restrictions to desktop computers and an overall policy covering buildings security.

3. Supervision   This control tends to have a dual nature whereby staff are observed first hand by their line managers, while at the same time these supervisors are available to help and assist their subordinates.

4. Compliance checks We have already discussed compliance as a fundamental component of the control systems and the way it is part of the process of doing things properly.

5. Procedures manuals As a high level control, the organization should set corporate standards that cover at least the following areas:

- Financial regulations covering income, expenditure, cash, banking, general accounting, contracts and related matters.
- Staff handbook covering recruitment, training and development, performance, discipline and so on.
- Purchasing code of practice on goods and services acquired by the organization.
- Code of personal conduct with guidance on gifts and hospitality.
- Computer standards on the use of computer systems and security procedures.

6. Recruitment and staff development practices We have indicated that most controls are based around what people do and the people factor cannot be ignored.

7. Segregation of duties This control brings into play more than one individual during any one transaction, which can lead to an actual gain or benefit.

8. Organization The way an organization is structured can promote or impair good control. Clear reporting lines that establish links between accountability, responsibility and authorization is a good starting place.

9. Sequential numbering of documents and controlled stationery Valuable documents such as orders, cheque requisitions and cheques themselves have an in-built control in terms of the sequential numbers.

10. Reconciliations The act of balancing one system to another does in itself engender control.

11. Project and procurement management Most organizations have established ongoing change programmes to push ahead or simply keep up with the competition and heightened expectations from stakeholders.

12. Financial systems controls Most of the well-known specific controls over basic payments, income, sales, purchasing, inventory and other financial-based systems should be firmly in place.

13. IT security All organizations use information systems and these will tend to be automated with internal networks and links to the Internet.

14. Performance management Another key control that should be firmly in place is related to a process whereby outputs and overall performance are examined by line management. The performance system should be:

- Simple.
- Reliable.
- Accepted by all.
- Driven by the board.
- Flexible.
- Reflect accountabilities.
- Forward-looking based on the corporate vision.

- Based on a clear and fair policy.
- Linked into the organization's value system.
- Linked to objectives and their achievement.
- Based on a good reporting system that provides information that is timely, regular, reliable, comparable, clear (e.g. graphs) and not bogged down with excessive detail and which links clearly into personal accountabilities.
- Based on a learning dynamic.
- Tailored to the operation.
- In line with the culture or be part of a culture change initiative.
- Responsive to changing risk management strategies.
- More than anything, challenging.

The Suitability of Controls

In terms of assessing the suitability of systems of internal control, there are some danger signs that should be looked for that might lower the efficiency of the control environment as follows:

- Ability of senior management to override accepted control.
- Lack of staff and vacant posts.
- Poor control culture.
- Staff collusion.
- Reliance on a single performance indicator.
- Reliance on memory.
- Retrospective transaction recording.
- Uncontrolled delegation of tasks.

4.7 Importance of Procedures

The previous section on control mechanisms outlined the different types of controls that are available when designing a suitable system of controls. As such, we can now refine our control model in Figure 4.7 to incorporate the additional features that have been described.

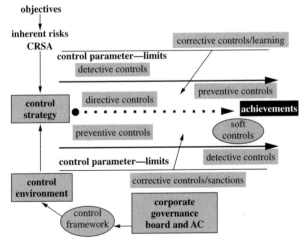

FIGURE 4.7 Internal control (5).

The preventive controls were already on our model and they revolve around the upper and lower control parameters, above and below the achievements line. We then set additional levels outside the two parameters and locate detective controls outside the control parameters. These detective controls will pick up transactions and activity that fall outside the acceptable limits (parameters) or appear likely to go outside these limits. The detective controls will tend to be information-based and will ring alarms when management intervention is needed to deal with activity that either has gone or appears to be going haywire. Corrective controls as we have discussed are measures designed to put right any deviations that have been detected and hence the arrowed lines start at the corrective control and then go back inside the control parameters. The final addition is soft controls that focus on the hearts and minds of people to encourage them to take responsibility for their controls and to take action where appropriate. There is a complicated view of control and a more simple version. The complicated view is based around our control model and recognizes the wide variety and range of controls that can be applied to getting the job done. The simple view is that most risks to operations can be mitigated through better procedures, that is ways of doing the job. Hence the importance of good procedures as a major arm of the risk management strategy. We can base our discussion of procedures around an amended version of a model (in Figure 4.8) first used in the book *Internal Control: A Manager's Journey.*[3]

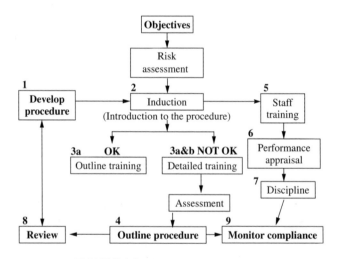

FIGURE 4.8   Implementing procedures.

Once the operational risk assessment has identified the need for tighter procedures, the task is then set to make and issue an improved version for staff. By going through the nine-stage model, there is a better chance to get procedures both correct, understood and accepted in the operation in question. Taking each stage of the model in turn:

1. **Development**—this involves reviewing the underlying processes, simplifying them and working with users—then drafting an agreed document that reflects the required activities.
2. **Induction**—it is important to introduce the procedure to new starters and show existing staff a new or improved procedure.
3. **The training manual**—may be broken down into two levels. Where staff are assessed as able to apply procedures, an outline manual ('a') can be provided. Where this is not the case, a more comprehensive package ('a&b') with exercises can be given to them to work through.

4. **Outline**—after the training or induction period, it is possible to turn to a short-cut outline document with key tasks and processes summarized for use thereafter.
5. **Training**—the skills of staff affect the degree to which procedures are successful. The training on procedures is mainly about knowledge and to supplement this, we should also seek to develop the underlying skills and the appropriate attitudes as a parallel training initiative.
6. **Appraisal**—Link the way staff are using procedures in their performance appraisal framework. In this way, it is seen to have some meaning for the work people do and their individual development programmes.
7. **Discipline**—this is a fall-back position, where if all else fails staff may need to be disciplined for breach of procedure.
8. **The review process**—which should be straightforward in that it entails keeping the procedure relevant, vibrant and up to date.
9. **Compliance**—this stage deals with compliance and it is the line manager's responsibility to ensure staff comply with procedure. This is best done by getting staff to understand how they can monitor themselves, and supporting them in this task.

There is a lot to the simple view of better control, which is based on better procedures. Because procedures are so important to the business it is worthwhile resourcing efforts to get them focused on known risks and integrated into the way people work.

4.8 Integrating Controls

The control model comes back into the frame with a few additional features covering: performance, communications, and policy, competence and training as in Figure 4.9.

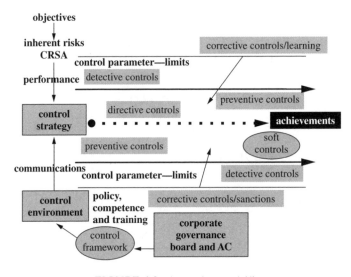

FIGURE 4.9   Internal control (6).

Each of these is now explained:

1. Performance   The process of assessing risk must fit and be integrated with the performance management system.

2. Communications   The control model is improved by the addition of good communications in the organization.

3. Policy, competence and training   The crucial pivot for the control model is the Policy on Internal Control.

One further point is to reconsider the corrective controls that have appeared in the control model. The upper version has an add-on (learning) which suggests that people need to learn from their experiences where controls have failed, or they do not respond to changes in risk profiles or there have been near-misses that suggest a problem. This ongoing learning and improvement is based on the assumption that most problems experienced by an organization can be traced to a failing in control of sorts. The lower version of corrective controls in the model has a different add-on (sanctions) which suggests that corrective controls that address a failing of directive or preventive controls may be the result of breach of procedure and/or negligence by one or more employees. Here an organization must be firm and determine whether control failure is a learning opportunity or the result of outright staff misconduct. This factor must be built into the control model to deal with those rare circumstances where people have failed to live up to the standards expected from them with no reasonable excuse. Sanctions may include warning, demotion and transfers, as well as ultimately dismissal. If sanctions are used as a first resort and are the norm in dealing with avoidable control failure, there is likely to be a blame culture in place and the control model will be seen by most employees as an enforced constraint that creates stress, tension and unfair practices. Which is the opposite to what the model is seeking to achieve. If, on the other hand, the control model acts as a corporate interpretation of the means to manage risk and ensure the business is successful, it reverts to the positive footing for control that it is intended to be.

4.9 The Fallacy of Perfection

The greater the uncertainty of achieving objectives, the more measures are needed to reduce this uncertainty. But the measures will normally cost money and time and will tend to involve doing more work, to get to the end result and may be suggested that:

- Controls tend to cost money and slow an organization down.
- Controls are needed to help manage risks to an organization's business.
- Controls cannot guarantee success.
- Control is effected through people and dependent on the way they behave and relate to each other.
- Even the best-managed organization can fail.
- The fallacy is that controls will ensure success and it is just a question of how many measures are needed and how they should be best implemented.

Thus, while internal control can help an entity achieve its objectives, it is not a panacea.

4.10 Internal Control Awareness Training

If everyone had a clear understanding of internal controls and they were motivated to establish good controls in line with risk-assessed operations and functions within an organization, then controls are more likely to work. Staff awareness training is one way of getting the message across the organization, and is often missed out of the CRSA exercises that are now becoming popular.

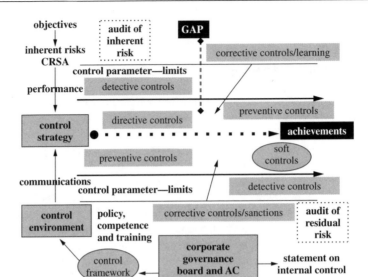

FIGURE 4.10   Internal control (7).

We can refer to the final version of our control model and use this as the basis for awareness seminars. The final version appears in Figure 4.10.

The additional items to complete the model are described:

Audit of inherent risk   Superimposed on the control model is the role of internal audit and external audit.

Audit of residual risk   Internal audit will also be concerned that the risks that remain after controls have been applied are fully understood and acceptable.

Statement of internal control   One important constituent of the control model is the feed into the published statement on internal control.

Gap   The final part of the control model consists of a single 'gap' that breaks through the upper and lower control parameters. This gap may be defined as 'an extra capacity to allow for growth and the potential to reach outside the norm, challenge existing assumptions and search for new corporate inspiration'.

Staff control awareness seminars should be designed to suit the organization and needs of the employees. The training may be multimedia-based where the learning points are achieved through interactive sessions via the corporate intranet. Or it may be possible for people to work in small teams of twos or threes, taking turns to use the computer interface. The best impact method is through actual seminars/workshops wherever possible. Also two presenters (or facilitators) will provide better results if the resources are available. The starting place for this type of activity involves several main drivers:

- A corporate policy on risk and internal control.
- The board's involvement.
- Staff competencies that include a good understanding of internal control concepts, design and review.

- A resource (trainer) that is able to lead the training event.
- A commitment to sound controls that means time is found for training programmes.

If these forces are in place, then there is a good chance that an organization may empower its people to take responsibility for ensuring there are good systems of internal control both protecting and promoting the business.

Summary and Conclusions

The internal control concept is crucial to business success. There are models and guidance and hundreds of specific measures that can be used to develop and maintain a good system of internal control. There are reporting standards that ask the board to report on internal control and ensure that this is linked to a suitable system for assessing risk and formulating a wider risk management strategy. Controls tend to form a major component of the risk management, and there are some controls that are standard requirements implicitly or explicitly. If there is a sound system of corporate governance in place and if this underpins a robust control environment then an organization may develop a control policy, perhaps as part of the risk policy. Where these considerations have been addressed then control awareness training may be carried out to turn ideas into practice. Where none of the control infrastructure that has been mentioned is in place, then board awareness seminars on internal control may be used to start the ball rolling. The internal auditor needs to be able to assess the organization in terms of these types of issues before any useful internal audit work can begin. The consulting role of internal audit argues that the auditor may help set up the necessary infrastructure (control framework) while the assurance role suggests that internal audit can go on to make sure the framework is owned by managers and that it makes sense and works well. It is difficult to talk about risk management without talking about internal control, as they are both necessary aspects of ensuring the business succeeds.

Chapter 4: Multi-Choice Questions

Having worked through the chapter the following multi-choice questions may be attempted. (See Appendix A for suggested answer guide and Appendix B where you may record your score.)

1. **Which is the most appropriate sentence?**
   Turnbull has made clear where control responsibility lies in an organization:
   a. The board of directors is responsible for the company's system of internal control. It should set appropriate policies on internal control and seek regular assurance that will enable it to satisfy itself that the system is functioning effectively.
   b. The audit committee is responsible for the company's system of internal control. It should set appropriate policies on internal control and seek regular assurance that will enable it to satisfy itself that the system is functioning effectively.
   c. The senior management is responsible for the company's system of internal control. It should set appropriate policies on internal control and seek regular assurance that will enable it to satisfy itself that the system is functioning effectively.
   d. The board of directors is responsible for the company's system of internal control. It should design appropriate procedures on internal control and seek regular assurance that will enable it to satisfy itself that the system is functioning effectively.

2. Insert the missing words:

The internal auditor has to be concerned about the state of control in the organization. The pace has been set by the IIA whose Performance Standard 2120 goes straight to the point: 'The internal audit activity should assist the organisation in maintaining effective controls by evaluating their effectiveness and efficiency and by promoting . . . .'

a. the audit role.

b. good performing staff.

c. perfection and performance.

d. continuous improvement.

3. Which is the least appropriate sentence?

The IIA's Implementation Standard 2120.A1 provides four key aspects of the scope of controls:

a. Reliability and integrity of financial and operational information.

b. Effectiveness and efficiency of management decisions

c. Safeguarding of assets.

d. Compliance with laws, regulations, and contracts.

4. Insert the missing words:

The . . . . sets the tone of an organization, influencing the control consciousness of its people. It is the foundation for all other components of internal control, providing discipline and structure.

a. control environment.

b. personnel section.

c. code of ethics.

d. internal audit team.

5. Which item is wrong?

The main components of CoCo are explained below:

a. Purpose and commitment.

b. Capability and consistency.

c. Action.

d. Monitoring and learning.

6. Which item is wrong?

CobiT has four main components (domains) and for these domains there are a further 34 high level control processes:

a. planning and organization.

b. acquisition and implementation.

c. delivery and support.

d. monitoring and discipline.

7. Which is the most appropriate sentence?

a. Controls are needed if they guard against an unacceptable risk to the business or if they are part of a legal or regulatory compliance regime. In fact these later controls guard against the risk of failing to comply with the regime. Controls that do not pass these two tests may not be discarded, since they in turn cause a risk to the business by increasing costs and/or slowing down the organization.

b. Controls are needed if they guard against an unacceptable risk to the business or if they are part of a legal or regulatory compliance regime. In fact these later controls guard against the risk of failing to comply with the regime. Controls that pass these two tests may well be discarded, since they in turn cause a risk to the business by increasing costs and/or slowing down the organization.

c. Controls are needed if they guard against an acceptable risk to the business or if they are part of a legal or regulatory compliance regime. In fact these later controls guard against the risk of failing to comply with the regime. Controls that do not pass these two tests may well be discarded, since they in turn cause a risk to the business by increasing costs and/or slowing down the organization.

d. Controls are needed if they guard against an unacceptable risk to the business or if they are part of a legal or regulatory compliance regime. In fact these later controls guard against the risk of failing to comply with the regime. Controls that do not pass these two tests may well be discarded, since they in turn cause a risk to the business by increasing costs and/or slowing down the organization.

8. Which is the least appropriate item?

Principal controls may be categorized in a number of different ways. One way is to view them as being classified as follows:

a. Directive—to ensure that there is a clear direction and drive towards achieving the stated objectives.

b. Preventive—to ensure that systems work in the first place.

c. Detective—to pick up transaction errors before they happen.

d. Corrective—to ensure that where problems are identified they are properly dealt with.

9. Which is the least appropriate item?

Controls need to work well. There is one view that they should be 'SMART', in that they should be:

a. Special.

b. Measurable.

c. Achievable.

d. Results oriented and timely.

10. Which is the least appropriate item?

The greater the uncertainty of achieving objectives, the more measures are needed to reduce this uncertainty. But the measures will normally cost money and time and will tend to involve doing more work to get to the end result, and it may be suggested that:

a. Controls tend to cost money and speed up an organization.

b. Controls are needed to help manage risks to an organization's business.

c. Controls cannot guarantee success.

d. Control is effected through people and dependent on the way they behave and relate to each other and even the best-managed organization can fail.

References

1. Moeller, Robert and Witt, Herbert (1999) *Brink's Modern Internal Auditing*, 5th edition, New York: John Wiley and Sons Inc.

2. BASEL Committee on Banking Supervision, Sound Practice for the Management and Supervision of Operational Risk, February 2003, Bank for International Settlements

3. Pickett, K. H. S and Pickett, Jennifer M (2001) *Internal Control: A Manager's Journey*, New York, John Wiley and Sons Inc.

Chapter 5

THE INTERNAL AUDIT ROLE

Introduction

This chapter covers the role of internal auditing and describes what it takes to become a good auditor. The areas covered are:

5.1 Why Auditing?

Before we delve into the standard features of the internal audit role, we issue a challenge to the reader. The challenges for the internal audit profession are found in the early chapters of the book, that is corporate governance, risk management and control. These developments set the context for the audit role. Now we need to explore how such challenges may be met.

5.2 Defining Internal Audit

The starting place for internal audit theory is the definition of internal audit. A standard definition is made up of important issues that form the basic framework of internal audit principles. The Institute of Internal Auditors' (IIA) definition appears once again:

> Internal auditing is an independent, objective assurance and consulting activity designed to add value and improve an organisation's operations. It helps an organisation accomplish its objectives by bringing a systematic, disciplined approach to evaluate and improve the effectiveness of risk management, control and governance processes.

We can analyse the IIA's formal definition in detail by examining each of the material concepts:

'Internal auditing'   The service is provided within the organization and is distinct from the external audit role (but see 'activity' below). Years ago the IIA considered changing the name of internal auditing to reflect the modern and increasingly professional approach. No alternative was forthcoming and the idea was dropped.

'Independent'   The concept of independence is fundamental. Internal auditing cannot survive if it is not objective. All definitions of internal audit feature an element of independence, although its extent, and how it is achieved, is a topic in its own right. The audit function must have sufficient status and be able to stand back from the operation under review for it to be of use. If this is not achieved, then this forms a fundamental flaw in the audit service and some internal audit functions may not be able to subscribe to the standards.

'Assurance and consulting'   This part of the definition refers to the fundamental shift in the role of internal audit. The shift makes clear that the past tinkering with the advice and consulting aspect of auditing is now a full-blown additional consultancy arm of the function. Internal audit may provide advice and assistance to management in a way that best suits each manager's needs. Even consulting work should take on board the impact of risks and IIA Implementation Standard 2110.C1 says that: 'during consulting engagements, internal auditors should address risk consistent with the engagement's objectives and should be alert to the existence of other significant risks'. Meanwhile the primary role of internal audit is to provide independent assurances that the organization is, or is not, managing risk well. Internal audit can provide assurance on the extent to which controls are able to address risks but cannot give any absolute guarantees. There is help at hand and Implementation Standard 1220.A3 clarifies this point by saying that: 'The internal auditors should be alert to the significant risks that might affect objectives, operations, or resources. However assurance procedures alone, even when performed with due professional care, do not guarantee that all significant risks will be identified.'

'Activity'   The fact that the internal audit function is an activity is important. This means it is a defined service, although not necessarily located within the organization (e.g. it may be outsourced).

'Designed to add value'   As a service, auditing has to form a client base and understand the needs of the organization. Here the service role should lead to a defined benefit to the organization rather than internal audit working for its own mysterious goals. Adding value should be uppermost in the minds of chief audit executives (CAE) and this feature should drive the entire audit process.

'And improve an organization's operations'   This brings into play the notion of continuous improvement. The auditors are really there to make things better and not inspect and catch people out. In one sense, if the CAE cannot demonstrate how the auditors improve the business, there is less reason to resource the service.

'It helps an organization accomplish its objectives'   The task of internal audit is set firmly around the organization's corporate objectives. Making an organization successful is the key driver for corporate governance (a badly governed organization will not be successful), for risk management (where risks to achieving objectives are the main focus) and internal controls (that seek to ensure objectives are realized). Moreover, it is the search for long-term corporate success that must steer the internal audit shop, or there is little point setting up the team.

'Systematic, disciplined approach'   Internal audit is now a full-blown profession. This means it has a clear set of professional standards and is able to work to best practice guidelines in delivering a quality service. One measure of this professionalism is that the organization can expect its auditors to apply a systematic and disciplined approach to its work. Be it consulting or assurance work, IIA Performance Standard 2040 requires that: 'The CAE should establish policies and procedures to guide the internal audit activity.'

'Evaluate and improve'   We have mentioned the need to focus on making improvements in the organization and part of this search for improvement entails making evaluations. Internal audit set what is found during an audit against what should be present to ensure good control. This necessarily entails the use of evaluation techniques that are applied in a professional and impartial manner to give reliable results. Many review teams leave out the evaluation aspect of review work and simply ask a few questions or check a few records and their results are not robust. Internal audit, on the other hand, has built into its definition the formal use of evaluation procedures to support steps to improve operations.

'Effectiveness'   Effectiveness is a bottom-line concept based on the notion that management is able to set objectives and control resources in such a way as to ensure that these goals are in fact achieved. The link between controls and objectives becomes clear, and audit must be able to understand the fundamental needs of management as it works to its goals. The complexities behind the concept of effectiveness are great, and by building this into the audit definition, the audit scope becomes potentially very wide.

'Risk management, control and governance processes'   These three related concepts have been covered in early chapters of the book and set the parameters for the internal audit role. Organizations that have not developed vigorous systems for these matters will fail in the long run and fall foul of regulators in the short term. The internal auditors are the only professionals who have these dimensions of corporate life as a living and breathing component of their role. They should therefore be the first port of call for anyone who needs to get to grips with corporate governance and IIA Performance Standard 2130 makes it clear that the internal audit activity should assess and make appropriate recommendations for improving the governance process in its accomplishment of the following objectives:

- Promoting appropriate ethics and values within the organization.
- Ensuring effective organizational performance management and accountability.
- Effectively communicating risk and control information to appropriate areas of the organization.
- Effectively coordinating the activities of and communicating information among the board, external and internal auditors and management.

The assurance role of internal auditing needs to be understood. Assurance implies a form of guarantee that what appears to be the case is in fact the case, based on a reliable source of confirmation that all is well. The more impartial and professional the source of these assurances, the more reliable they become.

The Four Main Elements

The scope of internal auditing is found in the Institute of Internal Auditors' Implementation Standard 2110.A2 which states that:

> The internal audit activity should evaluate risk exposures relating to the organization's governance, operations and information systems regarding the:
>
> - Reliability and integrity of financial and operational information.

- Effectiveness and efficiency of operations.
- Safeguarding of assets.
- Compliance with laws, regulations, and contracts.

Reliability and integrity of financial and operational information   Internal auditors review the reliability and integrity of financial and operating information and the means used to identify, measure, classify and report such information.

Effectiveness and efficiency of operations   Internal auditors should appraise the economy and efficiency with which resources are employed. They should also review operations or programmes to ascertain whether results are consistent with established objectives and goals and whether the operations are being carried out as planned.

Safeguarding of assets   Internal auditors should review the means of safeguarding and, as appropriate, verifying the existence of such assets.

Compliance with laws, regulations and contracts   Internal auditors should review the systems established to ensure compliance with those policies, plans, procedures, laws, regulations and important contracts that could have a significant impact on operations and reports, and should determine whether the organization is in compliance.

Internal audit reviews the extent to which management has established sound systems of internal control so that objectives are set and resources applied to these objectives in an efficient manner. This includes being protected from loss and abuse. Adequate information systems should be established to enable management to assess the extent to which objectives are being achieved via a series of suitable reports. Controls are required to combat risks to the achievement of value for money and it is these areas that internal audit is concerned with. Compliance, information systems and safeguarding assets are all prerequisites to good value for money.

Implications of the Wide Scope

The scope of internal auditing defined above is necessarily wide and this has several implications:

1. Expertise   Great expertise is required from auditors to enable them to provide advice on the wide range of key control objectives.

2. Safeguarding assets   It is necessary to establish who is responsible for investigating frauds since this is resource-intensive.

3. The compliance role   Controls over compliance may include an inspection routine and audit's role in this should be clearly defined.

4. Information systems   The audit of management information systems (MIS) is crucial since this may involve reviewing MIS as part of operational audits, or these systems can be audited separately.

5. Value for money   The concept of economy, efficiency and effectiveness (or VFM) is another sensitive issue. Auditors can assist management's task in securing good arrangements for promoting VFM or alternatively undertake a continual search for waste and other poor VFM.

6. *Management needs*   A wide scope requires a good understanding of the operations being reviewed and it is necessary to include management's needs in the terms of reference by adopting a more participative style.

7. *Specialists*   The four elements of the key control objectives may require specialists in each of the defined areas and the level of expectation may place great demands on the audit service.

5.3 The Audit Charter

The audit charter may be used in a positive fashion to underpin the marketing task that is discharged by audit management. It can also be used to defend audit services in the event of a dispute or an awkward audit. The charter formally documents the *raison d'être* of the audit function. It is important that all audit departments both develop and maintain a suitable charter. The Institute of Internal Auditors has issued a statement of responsibilities that covers the role of internal auditing and this document may be used to form the basis of such a charter. The audit charter constitutes a formal document that should be developed by the CAE and agreed by the highest level of the organization. If an audit committee exists then it should be agreed in this forum although the final document should be signed and dated by the chief executive officer. The audit charter establishes audit's position within the organization and will address several issues:

1. The nature of internal auditing
3. The scope of audit work
5. Audit's authority

2. The audit objectives
4. Audit's responsibilities
6. Outline of independence

Structure of the Charter

It is possible to outline a suitable structure for the charter bearing in mind the different models that will be applied by different types of organizations per Figure 5.1.

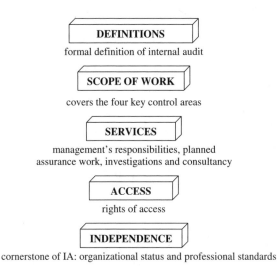

DEFINITIONS
formal definition of internal audit

SCOPE OF WORK
covers the four key control areas

SERVICES
management's responsibilities, planned assurance work, investigations and consultancy

ACCESS
rights of access

INDEPENDENCE
cornerstone of IA: organizational status and professional standards

FIGURE 5.1   Structure of the audit charter.

The Audit Charter—an Example

Each individual charter will vary depending on the needs of the organization, views of the CIA and type of services offered. We have produced a charter for a fictional company, Keystone Ltd.

KEYSTONE AUDIT SERVICES—AUDIT CHARTER

This audit charter sets out the role, authority and responsibilities of the internal audit function and has been formally adopted by Keystone Ltd. on 1 January 20xx.

1. Role

Internal auditing is an independent, objective assurance and consulting activity designed to add value and improve an organization's operations. It helps organizations accomplish their objectives by bringing a systematic, disciplined approach to evaluate and improve the effectiveness of risk management, control and governance processes. Internal audit is concerned with controls that ensure:

- reliability and integrity of financial and operating information
- effectiveness and efficiency of operations
- safeguarding of assets
- compliance with laws, regulations and contracts.

2. Responsibilities

Management is responsible for maintaining an adequate system of internal control to manage risks to the organization. Internal audit will provide assurance services to management, the board and the audit committee in terms of reviewing the adequacy of these systems of internal control. Internal audit will also provide a consulting role in helping promote and facilitate the development of effective systems of risk management and internal control. In addition, and subject to the availability of resources, audit will seek to respond to management's requests for investigations into matters of fraud, probity and compliance. Internal audit will provide advice on addressing these problems, which remain the responsibility of management. Furthermore, internal audit shall have no responsibilities over the operations that it audits over and above the furnishing of recommendations to management. The results of consulting and ad hoc projects requested by management will be used to inform internal audit's position on assurances where appropriate.

3. Plans

Internal audit is required to publish an annual audit plan to the board and audit committee and perform the audits that are contained within this plan, to the standards set out in the audit manual. Annual audit plans will be based on the risk assessments carried out by management and the board and take into account issues derived from the current audit strategy that is approved by the audit committee.

4. Reports

All audit reports will be cleared with the relevant management and once agreed will be copied to the appropriate director, the audit committee and external audit. Management is expected to implement all agreed audit recommendations within a reasonable time frame and each audit will be followed up to assess the extent to which this has happened. The audit committee will be given a summary of audits where agreed recommendations have not been implemented by management without reasonable explanation. The audit committee will also receive a summary of all audits where management have decided not to implement an audit recommendation without reasonable explanation. The overall results of audit work will be reported quarterly to the audit committee (who in turn report to the board of directors). Internal audit is also required to furnish an annual assurance on the state of internal control in the organization.

5. Access

Internal audit has access to all officers, buildings, information, explanations and documentation required to discharge the audit role. Any interference with this right of access will be investigated and, if found to be unreasonable, will be deemed a breach of organizational procedure and dealt with accordingly.

6. Independence

Internal audit is required to provide an objective audit service in line with professional auditing standards (as embodied within the audit manual) and the auditor's code of ethics. To this end it is essential that sufficient independence attaches to this work for it to have any impact on Keystone Ltd. This is dependent on sufficient organizational status and the ability to work to professional standards and the audit committee will undertake an ongoing review of the impact of these two factors.

CHIEF EXECUTIVE   **CHAIR OF AUDIT COMMITTEE**
DATE   **DATE**

5.4 Audit Services

The role of internal auditing is wide. Within the context of improving risk management, control and governance processes, the type of work undertaken to add value to an organization will vary greatly. It all depends on the context and best use of resources. Internal audit shops that focus on the corporate governance arrangements, rather than take on any work that comes its way, will tend to have a better direction. The remit is the audit charter, the parameters are the professional standards while the context is the success criteria that is set by the organization. Within these factors will fall the range of audit products that are on offer. These may include one or more of the following possible interpretations of the audit role. Note the following are listed internal audit services selected at random from various websites that feature internal audit shops from both private and public sector organizations:

- Cyclical audit (stock petty cash payroll).
- Investigations into specific problems.
- Responding to requests by management.
- Operational efficiency and effectiveness reviews.
- Internal control reviews.
- Fraud investigations.
- Compliance reviews.

- Reviewing controls over revenue, contracts administration and operational expenses.
- Acting as a contact point for allegations of fraud, waste and abuse.
- Information system reviews.
- Financial and compliance audits.
- Performance audits.
- Internal control reviews and testing poor areas.
- Investigative audits into reported irregularities.
- Verify assets and review safeguards.
- Evaluation of reporting systems and procedures.
- Cost saving reviews.
- Review of administration and accounting controls.
- Financial and performance audits.
- Revenue audits.
- Management studies into cost savings, problems in technical support and performance.
- Special reviews of projects.
- Control self-assessment facilitation.
- Environmental audits.
- Auditing the change management process.
- Operational audits.
- Computer audits.
- Control self-assessment questionnaire design and analysis.
- Issuing guidance to staff on internal control.
- Value driven internal consultancy, acting as change agents.
- Business process analysis.
- Business risk assessments.
- Quality advocates and reviews.
- Providing measures to strengthen mechanisms to achieving objectives.
- Evaluation of corporate governance processes.
- Working with management on their risk management practices.
- Advising clients on risk exposures and measures to remedy.
- Review risk management arrangements.
- Provide practical solutions and supporting management in implementing them.
- Participating in major information systems projects.
- Reviews to improve quality of management processes.
- Communicate risk information to clients.
- Operational auditing (or management audits).
- Financial systems audits, accounting and financial reporting.
- Compliance auditing on adherence to laws, regulations, policies and procedures—concentrating on improved controls to help compliance.
- Computer auditing during development stage.
- Audit approach determined by discussion with management but final result remains an internal audit prerogative.
- Advice to managers when making changes to procedure.
- Training in risk and control awareness.
- Provision of independent assurance on internal controls.
- General advice and guidance on control related issues.
- Operate follow-up system for outstanding audit recommendations.
- Evaluate action plans made in response to audit recommendations.

- Liaison and joint projects with external audit.
- Special projects as requested by management.
- Management reviews of new or existing programmes, systems, procedures.
- Control consciousness seminars.
- Recommendations for enhancing cost-effective control systems.
- Monitoring financial information and reporting results.
- Reviews of fixed assets, cash receipts, budgets, purchasing and accounting routines.
- Surprise audits over cash funds, accounting records, employee records, observation of operations, and inventory records.
- Accountability and fraud awareness training.
- Projects to improve quality of information or its context for decision making.
- Reviews of e-commerce arrangements and security.
- Audits of internal control structures, efficiency and effectiveness and best practice.
- Safeguarding assets (and information) using verification of asset registers, inventories and the adopted security policy.

5.5 Independence

There are several key IIA Attribute Standards that make clear the significance of auditors' independence:

- 1100: the internal audit activity should be independent, and internal auditors should be objective in performing their work.
- 1110: the internal audit activity should report to a level within the organization that allows the internal audit activity to fulfil its responsibilities.
- 1110.A1: the internal audit activity should be free from interference in determining the scope of internal auditing, performing work, and communicating results.
- 1120: internal auditors should have an impartial, unbiased attitude and avoid conflicts of interest.
- 1130: if independence or objectivity is impaired in fact or appearance, the details of the impairment should be disclosed to appropriate parties. The nature of the disclosure will depend upon the impairment.
- 1130.A1: internal auditors should refrain from assessing specific operations for which they were previously responsible. Objectivity is presumed to be impaired if an auditor provides assurance services for an activity for which the auditor had responsibility within the previous year.
- 1130.A2: assurance engagements for functions over which the CAE has responsibility should be overseen by a party outside the internal audit activity.
- 1130.C1: internal auditors may provide consulting services relating to operations for which they had previous responsibilities.
- 1130.C2: if internal auditors have potential impairments to independence or objectivity relating to proposed consulting services, disclosure should be made to the engagement client prior to accepting the engagement.

The Meaning of Independence

Independence means that management can place full reliance on audit findings and recommendations. There are many positive images that are conjured up by this concept of independence:

1. Objectivity   Behind this word is a whole multitude of issues that together form a complex maze. The main problem is that the whole basis of objectivity stems from a human condition of correctness and fair play. Any models that involve a consideration of the human condition have to deal with many psychological matters, and at times irrational behaviour. Although objectivity is located in the mind, it is heavily influenced by the procedures and practices adopted.

2. Impartiality   Objectivity may be seen as not being influenced by improper motives while impartiality is not taking sides. The question of impartiality is important because there is a view that internal audit, like all other units, will work in a politically advantageous way. This may result in audit taking the side of the most powerful party in any work that impacts on the political balances within an organization. If this is allowed to occur unchecked then the audit evidence that supports any audit report may be secured with a view to assisting one side only.

3. Unbiased views   When an audit report states that 'the audit view is ...' this should provide a comment on the state of internal controls. Where used to provide an advantage for the audit function, credibility is risked. The other aspect of audit bias is where certain officers/sections have been earmarked as 'poor, uncooperative or suspect ...' We go into an audit looking for any material that supports our original contentions. If taken to the extreme, the audit function will become a hit squad, conjuring up cases against people it does not like. It is difficult to build professional audit standards using this model.

4. Valid opinion   Readers of audit reports require the auditors to complete work to professional standards with the audit opinion properly derived from this work. This opinion must make sense having reference to all relevant factors. The audit role is not to please nominated parties or simply maintain the status quo; it is to present audit work in a professional and objective manner.

5. No spying for management   Professional objectivity means that audit does not fall into the trap of acting as spies for management, particularly where managers feel that their staff are not performing.

6. No 'no-go' areas   There are senior managers who adopt a particularly aggressive stance to managing their areas of responsibility. All outsiders are treated with great suspicion. In fact there is a correlation between professional incompetence and this threatening posture, i.e. the less able the manager the more aggressive he/she becomes. If this results in certain areas being deemed out of bounds to internal audit then this means that audit's independence is impaired and they will have a lesser role. If audit can be kept away from certain areas then this restricts the audit field, and if this trend is allowed to continue it could set a damaging precedent. The net result may be that the audit field becomes relegated to defined parts of the organization only. This is playing at auditing far removed from the demands of any professionally based audit practice.

7. Sensitive areas audited   To achieve its full status internal audit must be able to audit sensitive areas. Unlike the no-go areas, this potential barrier arises where the necessary skills and techniques are not available to the audit unit thus making it impossible to cover high-level areas. Where the audit scope is set within basic accounting systems for low-level checking, little important work can be undertaken and audit independence will not have been secured.

8. Senior management audited   There is a view that system controls are primarily located within the management processes that underpin the operations. Where audit fails to incorporate this factor into the scope of audit work, a great deal will be missed. The problem is that managers may not wish to be audited, particularly where this exposes gaps in their responsibility to establish sound controls. The CAE will have a quiet life where he/she works only at a detailed operational level and ignores the whole management process. Again this restricts the audit role and so adversely impacts on the auditor's independence.

9. No backing-off   We do not expect auditors to back down without a valid reason when confronted by an assertive manager. This is not to say that auditors march unchecked across the organization, unaware of any disruption they might be causing to front line operations. It does, however, mean that they will pursue audit objectives to the full in a diplomatic and professional manner. If this is not the case then audit will be vulnerable to criticism from all sides. Audit reports would then reflect what managers allowed the auditor to do rather than the work required to discharge the terms of reference for the audit. In this instance audit can claim very little real independence.

The above provides a foundation for the audit practice at the heart of the audit role. This distinguishes it from management consultancy and other review agencies who provide professional review services but only to the terms of reference set by management. These factors must be in place for the audit function to have any real impact on the organization.

Reconciling the Consultancy Branch

The internal auditing arena is now facing a real threat to independence where it is being asked to reconcile two forces that are at times in conflict. The client might wish to have internal audit perform a series of consultancy projects generated by ad hoc problems that they as managers may experience. The professional auditing standards seek to promote audits that involve reviews of control systems as a service to the entire organization as a wider concept. The conflict arises where the problems referred to audit by management result from inadequacies in controls. The act of propping up management reinforces the view that management need not concern itself about controls and that, if there are control faults, audit will solve the ensuing problems. Here independence falls by the wayside and a response-based audit service is resourced to the detriment of organizational controls.

5.6 Audit Ethics

The Institute's Code of Ethics extends beyond the definition of internal auditing to include two essential components:

1. Principles that are relevant to the profession and practice of internal auditing;
2. Rules of conduct that describe behaviour norms expected of internal auditors. These rules are an aid to interpreting the Principles into practical applications and are intended to guide the ethical conduct of internal auditors.

Principles
Internal auditors are expected to apply and uphold the following principles:

Integrity
The integrity of internal auditors establishes trust and thus provides the basis for reliance on their judgement.

Objectivity

Internal auditors exhibit the highest level of professional objectivity in gathering, evaluating, and communicating information about the activity or process being examined. Internal auditors make a balanced assessment of all relevant circumstances and are not unduly influenced by their own interests or by others in forming judgements.

Confidentiality

Internal auditors respect the value and ownership of information they receive and do not disclose information without appropriate authority unless there is a legal or professional obligation to do so.

Competency

Internal auditors apply the knowledge, skills and experience needed in the performance of internal auditing services.

Rules of Conduct

1. Integrity

Internal auditors:

1.1 Shall perform their work with honesty, diligence, and responsibility.
1.2 Shall observe the law and make disclosures expected by the law and the profession.
1.3 Shall not knowingly be a party to any illegal activity, or engage in acts that are discreditable to the profession of internal auditing or to the organization.
1.4 Shall respect and contribute to the legitimate and ethical objectives of the organization.

2. Objectivity

Internal auditors:

2.1 Shall not participate in any activity or relationship that may impair or be presumed to impair their unbiased assessment. This participation includes those activities or relationships that may be in conflict with the interests of the organization.
2.2 Shall not accept anything that may impair or be presumed to impair their professional judgement.
2.3 Shall disclose all material facts known to them that if not disclosed, may distort the reporting of activities under review.

3. Confidentiality

Internal auditors:

3.1 Shall be prudent in the use and protection of information acquired in the course of their duties.
3.2 Shall not use information for any personal gain or in any manner that would be contrary to the law or detrimental to the legitimate and ethical objectives of the organization.

4. Competency

Internal auditors:

4.1 Shall engage only in those services for which they have the necessary knowledge, skills and experience.
4.2 Shall perform internal auditing services in accordance with the Standards for the Professional Practice of Internal Auditing.
4.3 Shall continually improve their proficiency and the effectiveness and quality of their services.

The code of ethics is in fact a series of codes, each of which depends on the individual auditor, the audit unit and the entire organization. If there are gaps in any of these three parts, then a suboptimal position arises. The code of ethics creates a special bond between the auditor and the employer. The internal auditor's position is easily abused and there are not many officers who will question the auditor's behaviour particularly where it appears that audit reports to some unseen higher authority. The code counters this problem and should be applied in an educational mode where auditors are encouraged to adopt the code as part of the training and development process.

5.7 Police Officer versus Consultant

Most audit textbooks make reference to the impact that internal audit has not only on systems but also on people, and stress the importance of understanding human behaviour. This is sometimes extended by the view that auditors face various complicated issues because of their special position in the organization. The alternatives to the word 'Audit' from a standard thesaurus include the following terms:

examination   review
investigation   inspection
scrutiny

These terms do not conjure up the concept of a helpful, value-add service and here we tackle the fallout of negativity and the need to manage this problem by adopting the stance that merely being genuine is not enough. One has to seriously consider one's position and the impact of the applied audit policies on the behavioural aspects of this role, to uncover any actual or potential barriers to good performance. Alan Marshall outlines his approach when asked by someone, 'So what do you do for a living?': 'The word "audit" has negative connotations, fostering the image of tick and turn ... When announcing that I work as internal auditor ... perhaps the most frustrating reaction is "Ah! You're an accountant. You check people's books, don't you?" '[1]

Human Behavioural Aspects

This covers a wide area and touches on topics such as industrial psychology, communication skills and group theory. Auditors should be skilled in dealing with people and as such this aspect is seen as a valid audit skill. Unfortunately this skill does not always form part of the auditors' professional training and development programme. In fact a poor recruitment policy may result in bringing in auditors who see little value in developing good interpersonal skills. The old-fashioned detailed checker had little time to discuss the real-life issues that fall outside the scope of the audit programme. Nowadays auditors are required to do more than operate on a detailed technical level; they are expected to be able to converse openly with senior management.

Dealing with People

There are certain obstacles that the internal auditor may come across when carrying out audit work, many of which relate to the behavioural aspects of work:

1. Traditional tick and check   Many auditors are seen as checkers who spend their time ticking thousands of documents and records.

2. The audit snoop   Line management and the various operatives may resent the audit as being mainly based on management's wishes to spy on them using audit staff for this unsavoury task.

3. Role of audit   There are audits that are undertaken and completed with a final report issued some time after the event that have little meaning to the operatives affected by the work.

4. Interviewing   An audit interview may be a highly pressurized event for a more junior member of staff and, if the auditor fails to recognize this, many barriers to communications may arise.

5. Audit committee   The relationship with the audit committee is a factor in the success of the audit function.

6. Poor cousin of external audit   Where the internal auditors merely support the external audit function, the relationship may leave little scope for professional development.

7. Fear and hostility   Auditors who feel that hostile management has something to hide will perpetuate a cycle where they probe, management resists, they probe harder and so on.

8. Advisor/inspector conflict   Problems will ensue where auditors are convinced that they are advisors whereas they are seen by management as only checkers.

9. Image problems   Internal audit departments can have a poor reputation. This will affect the type of contact that is had with other members of the organization since one has to earn rather than demand respect.

Understanding and Participating with Management

Where an auditor understands management and the management process it is easier to work in a partnership mode. The participative approach brings audit closer to a consultancy role where management needs are foremost. Many audit departments have moved along this route and the explanatory models suggest that a continuum may be designed where one may move further along the direction of participation. It must, however, be noted that the more participation that is promoted, the greater the strain in maintaining a satisfactory level of independence. As such there will be limits on how far one might go. It is possible to use an established model of audit styles ranging from a traditional through to a participative style. There is a continuum for each of the components of this established model as shown in Table 5.1.

TABLE 5.1   Traditional versus participative styles.

Factor	Traditional style	Participative style
Role	Policeman	Advisor
Authority	Formal	Informal
Source of authority	Office	Personal attributes
Sanction	Coercion	Suggestion

These are two extremes which might on the one hand mean that an audit function is imposed on management to police the organization. Alternatively, the audit service may be more like a partnership with audit providing professional advice in line with management's needs. Clearly modern internal auditing is moving towards the partnership role with management as it does not report to itself, or work towards its own mysterious goals. The auditor should recognize the culture that exists in the area being audited and ensure that audit recommendations are framed in a way that fits into management's needs. Participative auditing means working with management rather than auditing them. This is in line with the view that controls belong to management and they should be encouraged to maintain and improve them.

The Expectation Gap

Client expectations of traditional internal audit services typically consist of:

- A check on remote establishments to ensure that they are complying with procedures.
- The investigation of frauds where they have been detected within the organization.
- Investigations into employees who cause concern to management in terms of breaching procedure.
- A continuous programme of checks over the output from various financial systems to assess whether these are correct.
- On-the-spot advice as to whether proposed management decisions are acceptable in terms of compliance with procedure and best practice.
- Ad hoc investigations requested by members of the corporate management team.
- Additional resources for computer system development projects.

The rules to be applied to managing this situation may be set out as:

1. Isolate two ranges of clients. The audit committee who will be the client for audit work (risk-based systems auditing), and managers who can receive additional consultancy services.
2. Make sure the audit committee understands the concept of planned systems audits and that a basic block of resources must be reserved for this task.
3. Provide consultancy as additional services that are clearly distinguished from audit work. Ensure that management understands that they are responsible for compliance, information systems, fraud investigations and achieving value for money.
4. Publicize the audit role through suitable brochures, website presentations and correspondence.
5. Encourage managers to take a long-term view in promoting sound controls and so avoid the many problems that are derived from poor arrangements. This is a long process but is assisted by oral presentations in control that audit may provide to management.

In terms of dealing with management, there are several important considerations to be borne in mind:

1. Time: Busy managers find it difficult to assign time (and their staff's time) to deal with the auditor. Arrangements will have to be agreed to suit all sides and it is here that negotiation skills will come to the fore.

2. Terms of reference: The opening terms of reference for the audit are always a difficult matter as each side feels the other out. There is always an element of suspicion from the client which itself is located in the whole issue of change management. The auditor must recognize the two main worries of the client:

- That the auditor may wish to recommend changes that will adversely affect the manager's position.
- That the auditor may in fact be investigating him, the operating manager.

3. Audit approach: The audit approach and general attitude will have an impact on the resulting negotiations. It is generally accepted that negotiation is about compromise and securing benefits for all sides in contrast to a win/lose stance.

4. Bottom line: Sawyer's view of internal audit sees it as a function that seeks to leave the operation in a better position than it was before the audit. This does not mean that every detailed recommendation must be immediately implemented by management. It is based more on the view that management should be consulted and, where essential, they will take on board recommendations, although open to negotiation. It requires the auditor to negotiate recommendations and differentiate between those that are essential, important and merely useful. Using this approach, a little may be given up for the sake of progress in other areas.

5.8 Managing Expectations through Web Design

This section gives a brief review of some of the material that is being set up on internal audit websites. A consideration of a sample of the websites of various internal audit shops makes for interesting reading. Some of the material that is being posted on these websites includes the following frequently asked questions (the reader may wish to choose some of these for their own website):

1. Why this guide?
2. What is internal audit?
3. Overall mission statement?
4. Vision?
5. What is the audit objective?
6. Why do we have internal audit?
7. Who are the internal auditors?
8. How are we organized?
9. Difference between the audit and management role?
10. Difference between external and internal audit?
11. Why do we need internal audit?
12. How is internal audit independent?
13. How does the audit committee come in?
14. Where does internal audit authority come from?
15. Scope of audit work?
16. What does internal audit do?
17. How are areas selected for audit?
18. How does this fit in with risk management?
19. What is CRSA and do we not do our own audit using this tool?
20. Does management have any involvement in setting audit terms of reference?
21. What if you feel you do not need to be audited?

22. How can you facilitate the progress of the audit?
23. Do we have any set values?
24. Professional standards?
25. What takes place during an audit?
26. How long do audits last?
27. What is audit testing?
28. What occurs after the audit?
29. Where do the reports go?
30. Follow-up procedures?
31. Do we accept requests from management?
32. What do managers need to know about risk and controls?
33. Do we conduct surprise audits?
34. What do we do about fraud?
35. What does internal audit not do?
36. Who audits the auditors?
37. Complaints procedure?

5.9 Audit Competencies

The first thing that needs to be in place to ensure competent internal auditors is effective human resource policies and practices. Here we are concerned with the attributes of successful internal auditors. The IIA Practice Advisory 1210-1 deals with proficiency and requires that each internal auditor should possess certain knowledge, skills, and other competencies:

- proficiencies in applying internal auditing standards and procedures . . .
- proficiency in accounting principles and techniques . . .
- an understanding of management principles . . .
- appreciation of accounting, economics, commercial law, taxation, finance, quantitative methods and IT.
- skilled at dealing with people and communicating . . .
- skilled in oral and written communications . . .

CAE should establish suitable criteria for education and experience for filling internal auditing positions . . . the IA staff should collectively possess the knowledge and skills essential to the practice of the profession within the organization.

The organization of the future will be a conveyor of ideas with the sourcing of products and services a secondary issue. The customer says what they want, and the organization delivers. Meanwhile the organization also helps the customer raise their sights in envisioning what is available. In this way, the organization of the future is a collection of visions and intellects brought together by a dynamic information and communications network. The importance of getting the right competencies in staff has never been more crucial to business success, and internal auditing is no exception. Some of the attributes that the competent internal auditor needs to demonstrate include the following (in no particular order):

- Ability to apply innovative and creative thinking.
- Ability to work to agreed timescales and account for time.
- Able to add value to the organization.
- Able to appreciate concerns of stakeholders and focus on needs of the customer.
- Able to appreciate new ideas and embrace and encourage change.

- Able to establish credibility with senior management and at grassroots.
- Able to function within flexible working arrangements.
- Able to plan work and have a sense of urgency in performing the audits.
- Able to quickly build relationships but retain professional stance.
- Able to work under pressure and set priorities.
- Ambitious and confident without being overbearing.
- Appreciation of business environment and new ventures.
- Appreciative enquiry—looking for the positive in human undertakings based on the great energies that come from success and accomplishments.
- Balance and common sense with an overall sense of fairness and diplomacy.
- Basic technical skill—financial, legal, economics, accounting, auditing, computing, statistics, other analytical techniques, database and spreadsheet use, data interrogations and so on.
- Can cope with travel requirements and overnight stays.
- Commercial awareness.
- Committed to continuous learning and open to training and development.
- Committed to working within set corporate policies and section procedures.
- Communications skills, oral, public speaking, writing, report writing, effective listening, written and interpersonal skills at all levels.
- Diplomatic but persistent where required.
- Emotional intelligence and good balance of emotions such as anger, sadness, fear, enjoyment, love, surprise, disgust, shame—and humility. The ability to apply social skills such as trustworthiness, empathy, adaptability.
- Enthusiastic, task-oriented person, able to focus on the job in hand.
- Facilitation skills with an emphasis on challenge and co-ordination.
- Formal report writing.
- General management skills and able to provide direction, delegate and monitor results through performance review.
- Global perspective and interest in international developments.
- Good balance of consulting and assurance approaches and able to reconcile possible conflicts between helping people and reviewing systems.
- Good decision making and judgement with no special bias to self-interests.
- Good interviewing technique and able to empathize with the client.
- Good problem solver and able to weigh up pros and cons of different options and to see around the problem through to solutions.
- Intellectual capacity and able to see things for what they are and ascertain causal relationships between problem, cause and effect.
- Interpersonal skills recognizing group dynamics and people behaviour.
- Leadership and drive with a clear sense of direction.
- Mature and professional enough to deal with different types of people and operate across different cultures.
- Negotiation skills and some tenacity in sticking to crucial points.
- Objectivity and independence with an ability to remain impartial.
- Practical edge in applying policy and an understanding of any limitations.
- Presentation skills.
- Project management skills.
- Self-motivated with good initiative, and enthusiastic even when performing mundane tasks.
- Some commitment to developing a career in internal audit.
- Task-focused and good at applying energies to delivering results.

- Team player—able to buy into team working and team tasks with an understanding of the importance of being friendly, participative and helpful, and having fun where possible.
- Track record of achievement and completion of tasks.
- Understanding of internal audit procedures and quality requirements.
- Understanding of modern audit techniques including corporate governance, risk management and control.
- Understands big picture but can respond to detail when required, notwithstanding apparent ambiguity.

The new look creates a very demanding role. It includes all those aspects that make a good traditional auditor with a hard nose and deep concern with getting to the truth, and the new approach of being a top-flight consultant on risk and control issues.

5.10 Training and Development

Training is an important aspect of developing internal auditors, and has to be carefully planned in line with a career developmental programme. The year 2002 saw the introduction of a new syllabus for the IIA.UK&Ireland that sought a wider coverage of the audit world and related areas. This now provides two levels of qualification, the practitioner level (PIIA) and the more advanced professional level (MIIA). The professional level builds on and extends the subjects that are covered at practitioner stage. As well as internal auditing topics, there is coverage of financial and general management, information systems and a new module dedicated to the topic of corporate governance and risk management. The advanced internal auditing paper is based around a case study that is available before the examination date, so reflecting the growing trend towards more practical work. The PIIA topics are: organization and management, accounting and financial systems, internal auditing, business information systems auditing, and corporate governance and risk management. The MIIA topics are: advanced management, financial management, advanced information systems auditing, and advanced internal auditing. There are also two skills modules that the students are required to complete on communication and client/auditor relations and effective delivery of an audit. More recently, the IIA.UK&Ireland have developed a certificate in Corporate Governance and Risk Management. As well as formal qualifications, there is an entire spectrum of developing people at work that includes:

- Training—programmes for getting people to learn to do things differently.
- Development—untaught activity to increase/improve performance.
- Education—formal courses to develop knowledge and qualifications.
- Learning—acquiring better skills, knowledge and attitudes.

There are various ways that audit staff may be trained and developed:

1. Specialist skills training via internal or external skills workshops   These can be extremely efficient in terms of auditor development.

2. Professional training   This may be based on passing examinations of a defined professional body such as the Institute of Internal Auditors, which is a completely different form of training from skills-based courses.

3. The training co-ordinator   Appointing a training co-ordinator is a positive way of promoting various training programmes, particularly where the co-ordinator can undertake some of the actual training.

4. Directed reading   This is one way of encouraging auditors to research aspects of internal audit. The department should subscribe to all relevant journals and publications.

5. Training through work   Programmed audits enable audit management to ensure auditors are rotated and exposed to a variety of audits and experiences. It is possible to designate smaller audits as 'training audits' where they form part of the auditors' personal development programme.

6. The audit review   The audit review process enables audit managers and team leaders to direct the work of junior staff and also provides experience in staff management.

7. Professional affiliations   These can be part of continuing professional development (CPD) and stimulate group discussions.

8. The audit manual   This sets out the defined methods and procedures required to discharge the audit mission.

Training is part of the managerial process and as such forms only one constituent of the overall system of human resource management. It cannot be seen in isolation from the other techniques for developing audit staff. Not all auditors remain in the audit shop for long periods of time. This 'short-stay syndrome' results because organizations view internal audit as an ideal place to train managers. There are many who do not view internal audit as a career in its own right and, for example, trainee accountants may wish to return to main line accountancy after a spell in audit. This poses a problem in that extensive training is lost on audit staff who will not remain with the department for long. All staff should be developed and those who may wish eventually to leave auditing will simply be replaced by other auditors. Vacancies create scope for internal promotions for auditors who excel via their development programmes. The only concern is that short-stay staff should not be placed on professional qualification programmes as these last several years and require a major commitment to a career in internal auditing.

Summary and Conclusions

The challenge has been set by the corporate governance, risk management and control dimensions that now drive both the business world and public services. The definition of internal auditing has been changed to reflect this factor, and audit charters are being torn up and rewritten to secure this important focus. Everything else that happens in internal audit flows from the changes, charter and heightened expectations.

Chapter 5: Multi-Choice Questions

Having worked through the chapter the following multi-choice questions may be attempted. (See Appendix A for suggested answer guide and Appendix B where you may record your score.)

   I. **Which is the least appropriate item?**
       Performance Standard 2130 makes it clear that the internal audit activity should assess and make appropriate recommendations for improving the governance process in its accomplishment of the following objectives:
       a. Promoting appropriate ethics and values within the organization.
       b. Ensuring effective organizational performance management and accountability.

c. Effectively communicating risk and control information to appropriate areas of the organization.

d. Effectively co-ordinating the activities of and communicating information among the board, external auditors, other companies and regulators.

2. Which is the most appropriate item?
a. Internal auditors should review the systems established to ensure compliance with those policies, plans, procedures, laws, regulations and important contracts that could have a significant impact on operations and reports, and should determine whether the organization is in compliance.

b. Internal auditors should review the systems established to ensure compliance with those policies, plans, procedures, laws, regulations and important contracts that could have a significant impact on operations and reports, and should determine whether the organization is competent.

c. Internal auditors should ensure compliance with those policies, plans, procedures, laws, regulations and important contracts that could have a significant impact on operations and reports, and should determine whether the organization is in compliance.

d. Internal auditors should design the systems established to ensure compliance with those policies, plans, procedures, laws, regulations and important contracts that could have a significant impact on operations and reports, and should determine whether the organization is in compliance.

3. Insert the missing words:
The . . . . constitutes a formal document that should be developed by the CAE and agreed by the highest level of the organization. If an audit committee exists then it should be agreed in this forum although the final document should be signed and dated by the chief executive officer.
a. audit plan.
b. audit charter.
c. audit manual.
d. audit report.

4. Which is the least appropriate item?
There are several key IIA Attribute Standards that make clear the significance of auditors' independence:
a. 1100: the internal audit activity should be independent, and internal auditors should try to be objective in performing their work.

b. 1110: the internal audit activity should report to a level within the organization that allows the internal audit activity to fulfil its responsibilities.

c. 1110.A1: the internal audit activity should be free from interference in determining the scope of internal auditing, performing work, and communicating results.

d. 1120: internal auditors should have an impartial, unbiased attitude and avoid conflicts of interest.

5. Insert the missing word:
Independence means that management can place full reliance on . . . .
a. the audit manual.
b. management assurances.
c. draft audit reports.
d. audit findings and recommendations.

6. Which item is wrong?

The IIA's rules of conduct that apply to internal auditors cover four areas:

a. Integrity.

b. Objectivity.

c. Confidentiality.

d. Consistency.

7. Which is the most appropriate sentence?

a. The old-fashioned detailed checker had little time to discuss the real-life issues that fall outside the scope of the audit programme. Nowadays auditors are required to do more than operate on a detailed technical level; they are expected to be able to converse openly with other auditors.

b. The old-fashioned detailed checker had little time to discuss the real-life issues that fall outside the scope of the audit programme. Nowadays auditors are only required to operate on a detailed technical level; they are not expected to be able to converse openly with senior management.

c. The old-fashioned detailed checker had little time to discuss the real-life issues that fall outside the scope of the audit programme. Nowadays auditors are required to do more than operate on a detailed technical level; they are expected to be able to converse openly with senior management.

d. The old-fashioned detailed checker had a lot of time to discuss the real-life issues that fall outside the scope of the audit programme. Nowadays auditors are required to do more than operate on a detailed technical level; they are expected to be able to converse openly with senior management.

8. Which is the least appropriate sentence?

As well as formal qualifications, there is an entire spectrum of developing people at work that includes:

a. Training—programmes for getting people to learn to do things differently.

b. Development—untaught activity to increase/improve performance.

c. Education—formal courses to develop knowledge and qualifications.

d. Learning—acquiring better qualifications

9. Insert the missing word:

The '. . . . .' results because organizations view internal audit as an ideal place to train managers.

a. short-stay syndrome.

b. professional auditor.

c. untrained auditor.

d. career auditor.

10. Which is the most appropriate sentence?

a. The challenge has been set by the corporate governance, risk management and control dimensions that now drive both the business world and public services. The definition of internal auditing has been changed to reflect this factor, and audit charters are being torn up and rewritten to secure this important focus.

b. The challenge has been set by the corporate governance, risk management and control dimensions that now drive the private sector. The definition of internal auditing has been changed to reflect this factor, and audit charters are being torn up and rewritten to secure this important focus.

c. The challenge has been set by the corporate governance, risk management and control dimensions that now drive the public sector. The definition of internal auditing has been changed to reflect this factor, and audit charters are being torn up and rewritten to secure this important focus.

d. The challenge has been set by the corporate governance, risk management and control dimensions that now drive both the business world and public services. The definition of internal auditing has been changed to reflect this factor, and audit reports are being torn up and rewritten to secure this important focus.

Reference

1. Marshall, Alan 'So what do you do for a living?' *Internal Auditing*, May 1994, p. 17.

Chapter 6

PROFESSIONALISM

Introduction

Internal audit is now a complete profession and features in most larger organizations in all sectors. This entails the use of competent staff, a respected role in the organization and robust quality assurance arrangements that underpin the defined services that are provided. This chapter covers the following areas:

6.1   Audit Professionalism
6.2   Internal Auditing Standards
6.3   Due Professional Care
6.4   Professional Consulting Services
6.5   The Quality Concept
6.6   Defining the Client
6.7   Internal Review and External Review
6.8   Marketing the Audit Role
6.9   Audit Feedback Questionnaire
6.10 Continuous Improvement
        Summary and Conclusions
        Chapter 6: Multi-Choice Questions

6.1 Audit Professionalism

Internal auditing needs defined standards and this contributes to the development of professional audit services. Notwithstanding the problem of securing a truly international dimension to internal auditing, the Global Institute of Internal Auditors seeks to represent a worldwide position. This exciting development may have a profound impact on the profession and is mentioned again in the final chapter of *The Essential Handbook*. Before studying the various standards attached to internal auditing we list the main features of a professional discipline:

1. Training programme	2. Common body of knowledge
3. Code of ethics	4. Sanctions
5. Control over services	6. Qualified practitioners
7. Morality	8. Technical difficulty
9. Examinations	10. Journals
11. Professional body	12. Compliance with rules
13. Service to society	

Internal auditing is able to meet all of the above measures and is now firmly established as a professional discipline. This has been a huge achievement as, ten to twenty years ago, it certainly was not the case. Having a firm professional base allows the internal audit community to plan for the future and track the way it needs to progress as its newly acquired high profile places it firmly on the boardroom agenda.

6.2 Internal Auditing Standards

The IIA have described their original objectives in 1941 when they were first established (www.theiiaorg.com):

> To cultivate, promote, and disseminate knowledge and information concerning internal auditing and subjects related thereto; to establish and maintain high standards of integrity, honor, and character among internal auditors; to furnish information regarding internal auditing and the practice and methods thereof to its members etc.

Since then the IIA has moved on to develop their Professional Practices Framework (PPF) which contains the basic elements of the profession. It provides a consistent, organized method of looking at the fundamental principles and procedures that make internal auditing a unique, disciplined and systematic activity. The purpose of the standards is to:

1. Delineate basic principles that represent the practice of internal auditing as it should be.
2. Provide a framework for performing a broad range of value-added internal audit activities.
3. Establish the basis for the measurement of internal audit performance.
4. Foster improved organizational processes and operations.

The PPF consists of:

- Standards for the Professional Practice of Internal Auditing and the Code of Ethics which have to be followed by all practising (IIA) internal auditors.
- Practice Advisories are pronouncements that are strongly recommended and endorsed by the IIA.
- Development and Practice Aids—research, books, seminars, conferences, etc.—developed or endorsed by the IIA.

A main part of the PPF is attribute and performance standards. Attribute standards describe the defining character of organizations and individuals performing internal audit services, while performance standards describe the nature of internal audit services and provide quality criteria against which to measure performance, and the individual implementation standards are used to augment the attribute and performance standards by helping employ them in particular types of engagements. The standards cover both assurance services and client-based consulting. Over 2004 the IIA clarified the status of their standards and made it clear that the use of the word 'should' means that the related standard is a mandatory obligation. This tightening up of the standards adds to the professionalism of internal auditing.

ATTRIBUTE STANDARDS

1000—Purpose, Authority, and Responsibility

The purpose, authority, and responsibility of the internal audit activity should be formally defined in a charter, consistent with the *Standards*, and approved by the board.

1000.A1—The nature of assurance services provided to the organization should be defined in the audit charter. If assurances are to be provided to parties outside the organization, the nature of these assurances should also be defined in the charter.

1000.C1—The nature of consulting services should be defined in the audit charter.

1100—Independence and Objectivity

The internal audit activity should be independent, and internal auditors should be objective in performing their work.

1110—Organizational Independence

The chief audit executive should report to a level within the organization that allows the internal audit activity to fulfil its responsibilities.

1110.A1—The internal audit activity should be free from interference in determining the scope of internal auditing, performing work, and communicating results.

1120—Individual Objectivity

Internal auditors should have an impartial, unbiased attitude and avoid conflicts of interest.

1130—Impairments to Independence or Objectivity

If independence or objectivity is impaired in fact or appearance, the details of the impairment should be disclosed to appropriate parties. The nature of the disclosure will depend upon the impairment.

1130.A1—Internal auditors should refrain from assessing specific operations for which they were previously responsible. Objectivity is presumed to be impaired if an **internal** auditor provides assurance services for an activity for which the **internal** auditor had responsibility within the previous year.

1130.A2—Assurance engagements for functions over which the chief audit executive has responsibility should be overseen by a party outside the internal audit activity.

1130.C1—Internal auditors may provide consulting services relating to operations for which they had previous responsibilities.

1130.C2—If internal auditors have potential impairments to independence or objectivity relating to proposed consulting services, disclosure should be made to the engagement client prior to accepting the engagement.

1200—Proficiency and Due Professional Care

Engagements should be performed with proficiency and due professional care.

1210—Proficiency

Internal auditors should possess the knowledge, skills, and other competencies needed to perform their individual responsibilities. The internal audit activity collectively should possess or obtain the knowledge, skills, and other competencies needed to perform its responsibilities.

1210.A1—The chief audit executive should obtain competent advice and assistance if the internal audit staff lacks the knowledge, skills, or other competencies needed to perform all or part of the engagement.

1210.A2—The internal auditor should have sufficient knowledge to identify the indicators of fraud but is not expected to have the expertise of a person whose primary responsibility is detecting and investigating fraud.

1210.A3—Internal auditors should have knowledge of key information technology risks and controls and available technology-based audit techniques to perform their assigned work.

However, not all internal auditors are expected to have the expertise of an internal auditor whose primary responsibility is information technology auditing.

1210.C1—The chief audit executive should decline the consulting engagement or obtain competent advice and assistance if the internal audit staff lacks the knowledge, skills, or other competencies needed to perform all or part of the engagement.

1220—Due Professional Care

Internal auditors should apply the care and skill expected of a reasonably prudent and competent internal auditor. Due professional care does not imply infallibility.

1220.A1—The internal auditor should exercise due professional care by considering the:

- Extent of work needed to achieve the engagement's objectives.
- Relative complexity, materiality, or significance of matters to which assurance procedures are applied.
- Adequacy and effectiveness of risk management, control, and governance processes.
- Probability of significant errors, irregularities, or noncompliance.
- Cost of assurance in relation to potential benefits.

1220.A2—In exercising due professional care the internal auditor should consider the use of computer-assisted audit tools and other data analysis techniques.

1220.A3—The internal auditor should be alert to the significant risks that might affect objectives, operations, or resources. However, assurance procedures alone, even when performed with due professional care, do not guarantee that all significant risks will be identified.

1220.C1—The internal auditor should exercise due professional care during a consulting engagement by considering the:

- Needs and expectations of clients, including the nature, timing, and communication of engagement results.
- Relative complexity and extent of work needed to achieve the engagement's objectives.
- Cost of the consulting engagement in relation to potential benefits.

1230—Continuing Professional Development

Internal auditors should enhance their knowledge, skills, and other competencies through continuing professional development.

1300—Quality Assurance and Improvement Program

The chief audit executive should develop and maintain a quality assurance and improvement program that covers all aspects of the internal audit activity and continuously monitors its effectiveness. This program includes periodic internal and external quality assessments and ongoing internal monitoring. Each part of the program should be designed to help the internal auditing activity add value and improve the organization's operations and to provide assurance that the internal audit activity is in conformity with the *Standards* and the *Code of Ethics*.

1310—Quality Program Assessments

The internal audit activity should adopt a process to monitor and assess the overall effectiveness of the quality program. The process should include both internal and external assessments.

1311—Internal Assessments

Internal assessments should include:

- Ongoing reviews of the performance of the internal audit activity; and
- Periodic reviews performed through self-assessment or by other persons within the organization, with knowledge of internal audit practices and the *Standards*.

1312—External Assessments

External assessments, such as quality assurance reviews, should be conducted at least once every five years by a qualified, independent reviewer or review team from outside the organization.

1320—Reporting on the Quality Program

The chief audit executive should communicate the results of external assessments to the board.

1330—Use of "Conducted in Accordance with the Standards"

Internal auditors are encouraged to report that their activities are "conducted in accordance with the *International Standards for the Professional Practice of Internal Auditing*." However, internal auditors may use the statement only if assessments of the quality improvement program demonstrate that the internal audit activity is in compliance with the *Standards*.

1340—Disclosure of Noncompliance

Although the internal audit activity should achieve full compliance with the *Standards* and internal auditors with the *Code of Ethics*, there may be instances in which full compliance is not achieved. When noncompliance impacts the overall scope or operation of the internal audit activity, disclosure should be made to senior management and the board.

PERFORMANCE STANDARDS

2000—Managing the Internal Audit Activity

The chief audit executive should effectively manage the internal audit activity to ensure it adds value to the organization.

2010—Planning

The chief audit executive should establish risk-based plans to determine the priorities of the internal audit activity, consistent with the organization's goals.

2010.A1—The internal audit activity's plan of engagements should be based on a risk assessment, undertaken at least annually. The input of senior management and the board should be considered in this process.

2010.C1—The chief audit executive should consider accepting proposed consulting engagements based on the engagement's potential to improve management of risks, add value, and improve the organization's operations. Those engagements that have been accepted should be included in the plan.

2020—Communication and Approval

The chief audit executive should communicate the internal audit activity's plans and resource requirements, including significant interim changes, to senior management and to the board for review and approval. The chief audit executive should also communicate the impact of resource limitations.

2030—Resource Management

The chief audit executive should ensure that internal audit resources are appropriate, sufficient, and effectively deployed to achieve the approved plan.

2040—Policies and Procedures

The chief audit executive should establish policies and procedures to guide the internal audit activity.

2050—Coordination

The chief audit executive should share information and coordinate activities with other internal and external providers of relevant assurance and consulting services to ensure proper coverage and minimize duplication of efforts.

2060—Reporting to the Board and Senior Management

The chief audit executive should report periodically to the board and senior management on the internal audit activity's purpose, authority, responsibility, and performance relative to its plan. Reporting should also include significant risk exposures and control issues, corporate governance issues, and other matters needed or requested by the board and senior management.

2100—Nature of Work

The internal audit activity should evaluate and contribute to the improvement of risk management, control, and governance processes using a systematic and disciplined approach.

2110—Risk Management

The internal audit activity should assist the organization by identifying and evaluating significant exposures to risk and contributing to the improvement of risk management and control systems.

2110.A1—The internal audit activity should monitor and evaluate the effectiveness of the organization's risk management system.

2110.A2—The internal audit activity should evaluate risk exposures relating to the organization's governance, operations, and information systems regarding the

- Reliability and integrity of financial and operational information.
- Effectiveness and efficiency of operations.
- Safeguarding of assets.
- Compliance with laws, regulations, and contracts.

2110.C1—During consulting engagements, internal auditors should address risk consistent with the engagement's objectives and be alert to the existence of other significant risks.

2110.C2—Internal auditors should incorporate knowledge of risks gained from consulting engagements into the process of identifying and evaluating significant risk exposures of the organization.

2120—Control

The internal audit activity should assist the organization in maintaining effective controls by evaluating their effectiveness and efficiency and by promoting continuous improvement.

2120.A1—Based on the results of the risk assessment, the internal audit activity should evaluate the adequacy and effectiveness of controls encompassing the organization's governance, operations, and information systems. This should include:

- Reliability and integrity of financial and operational information.
- Effectiveness and efficiency of operations.
- Safeguarding of assets.
- Compliance with laws, regulations, and contracts.

2120.A2—Internal auditors should ascertain the extent to which operating and program goals and objectives have been established and conform to those of the organization.

2120.A3—Internal auditors should review operations and programs to ascertain the extent to which results are consistent with established goals and objectives to determine whether operations and programs are being implemented or performed as intended.

2120.A4—Adequate criteria are needed to evaluate controls. Internal auditors should ascertain the extent to which management has established adequate criteria to determine whether objectives and goals have been accomplished. If adequate, internal auditors should use such criteria in their evaluation. If inadequate, internal auditors should work with management to develop appropriate evaluation criteria.

2120.C1—During consulting engagements, internal auditors should address controls consistent with the engagement's objectives and be alert to the existence of any significant control weaknesses.

2120.C2—Internal auditors should incorporate knowledge of controls gained from consulting engagements into the process of identifying and evaluating significant risk exposures of the organization.

2130—Governance

The internal audit activity should assess and make appropriate recommendations for improving the governance process in its accomplishment of the following objectives:

- Promoting appropriate ethics and values within the organization.
- Ensuring effective organizational performance management and accountability.
- Effectively communicating risk and control information to appropriate areas of the organization.
- Effectively coordinating the activities of and communicating information among the board, external and internal auditors and management.

2130.A1—The internal audit activity should evaluate the design, implementation, and effectiveness of the organization's ethics-related objectives, programs and activities.

2130.C1—Consulting engagement objectives should be consistent with the overall values and goals of the organization.

2200—Engagement Planning

Internal auditors should develop and record a plan for each engagement, including the scope, objectives, timing and resource allocations.

2201—Planning Considerations

In planning the engagement, internal auditors should consider:

- The objectives of the activity being reviewed and the means by which the activity controls its performance.

- The significant risks to the activity, its objectives, resources, and operations and the means by which the potential impact of risk is kept to an acceptable level.
- The adequacy and effectiveness of the activity's risk management and control systems compared to a relevant control framework or model.
- The opportunities for making significant improvements to the activity's risk management and control systems.

2201.A1—When planning an engagement for parties outside the organization, internal auditors should establish a written understanding with them about objectives, scope, respective responsibilities and other expectations, including restrictions on distribution of the results of the engagement and access to engagement records.

2201.C1—Internal auditors should establish an understanding with consulting engagement clients about objectives, scope, respective responsibilities, and other client expectations. For significant engagements, this understanding should be documented.

2210—Engagement Objectives

Objectives should be established for each engagement.

2210.A1—Internal auditors should conduct a preliminary assessment of the risks relevant to the activity under review. Engagement objectives should reflect the results of this assessment.

2210.A2—The internal auditor should consider the probability of significant errors, irregularities, noncompliance, and other exposures when developing the engagement objectives.

2210.C1—Consulting engagement objectives should address risks, controls, and governance processes to the extent agreed upon with the client.

2220—Engagement Scope

The established scope should be sufficient to satisfy the objectives of the engagement.

2220.A1—The scope of the engagement should include consideration of relevant systems, records, personnel, and physical properties, including those under the control of third parties.

2220.A2—If significant consulting opportunities arise during an assurance engagement, a specific written understanding as to the objectives, scope, respective responsibilities and other expectations should be reached and the results of the consulting engagement communicated in accordance with consulting standards.

2220.C1—In performing consulting engagements, internal auditors should ensure that the scope of the engagement is sufficient to address the agreed-upon objectives. If internal auditors develop reservations about the scope during the engagement, these reservations should be discussed with the client to determine whether to continue with the engagement.

2230—Engagement Resource Allocation

Internal auditors should determine appropriate resources to achieve engagement objectives. Staffing should be based on an evaluation of the nature and complexity of each engagement, time constraints, and available resources.

2240—Engagement Work Program

Internal auditors should develop work programs that achieve the engagement objectives. These work programs should be recorded.

2240.AI—Work programs should establish the procedures for identifying, analyzing, evaluating, and recording information during the engagement. The work program should be approved prior to its implementation, and any adjustments approved promptly.

2240.CI—Work programs for consulting engagements may vary in form and content depending upon the nature of the engagement

2300—Performing the Engagement

Internal auditors should identify, analyze, evaluate, and record sufficient information to achieve the engagement's objectives.

2310—Identifying Information

Internal auditors should identify sufficient, reliable, relevant, and useful information to achieve the engagement's objectives.

2320—Analysis and Evaluation

Internal auditors should base conclusions and engagement results on appropriate analyses and evaluations.

2330—Recording Information

Internal auditors should record relevant information to support the conclusions and engagement results.

2330.AI—The chief audit executive should control access to engagement records. The chief audit executive should obtain the approval of senior management and/or legal counsel prior to releasing such records to external parties, as appropriate.

2330.A2—The chief audit executive should develop retention requirements for engagement records. These retention requirements should be consistent with the organization's guidelines and any pertinent regulatory or other requirements.

2330.CI—The chief audit executive should develop policies governing the custody and retention of engagement records, as well as their release to internal and external parties. These policies should be consistent with the organization's guidelines and any pertinent regulatory or other requirements.

2340—Engagement Supervision

Engagements should be properly supervised to ensure objectives are achieved, quality is assured, and staff is developed.

2400—Communicating Results

Internal auditors should communicate the engagement results.

2410—Criteria for Communicating

Communications should include the engagement's objectives and scope as well as applicable conclusions, recommendations, and action plans.

2410.AI—Final communication of engagement results should, where appropriate, contain the internal auditor's overall opinion and or conclusions.

2410.A2—Internal auditors are encouraged to acknowledge satisfactory performance in engagement communications.

2410.A3—When releasing engagement results to parties outside the organization, the communication should include limitations on distribution and use of the results.

2410.C1—Communication of the progress and results of consulting engagements will vary in form and content depending upon the nature of the engagement and the needs of the client.

2420—Quality of Communications

Communications should be accurate, objective, clear, concise, constructive, complete, and timely.

2421—Errors and Omissions

If a final communication contains a significant error or omission, the chief audit executive should communicate corrected information to all parties who received the original communication.

2430—Engagement Disclosure of Noncompliance with the *Standards*

When noncompliance with the *Standards* impacts a specific engagement, communication of the results should disclose the:

- *Standard(s)* with which full compliance was not achieved,
- Reason(s) for noncompliance, and
- Impact of noncompliance on the engagement.

2440—Disseminating Results

The chief audit executive should communicate results to the appropriate parties.

2440.A1—The chief audit executive is responsible for communicating the final results to parties who can ensure that the results are given due consideration.

2440.A2—If not otherwise mandated by legal, statutory or regulatory requirements, prior to releasing results to parties outside the organization, the chief audit executive should:

- Assess the potential risk to the organization.
- Consult with senior management and/or legal counsel as appropriate
- Control dissemination by restricting the use of the results.

2440.C1—The chief audit executive is responsible for communicating the final results of consulting engagements to clients.

2440.C2—During consulting engagements, risk management, control, and governance issues may be identified. Whenever these issues are significant to the organization, they should be communicated to senior management and the board.

2500—Monitoring Progress

The chief audit executive should establish and maintain a system to monitor the disposition of results communicated to management.

2500.A1—The chief audit executive should establish a follow-up process to monitor and ensure that management actions have been effectively implemented or that senior management has accepted the risk of not taking action.

2500.C1—The internal audit activity should monitor the disposition of results of consulting engagements to the extent agreed upon with the client.

2600—Resolution of Management's Acceptance of Risks

When the chief audit executive believes that senior management has accepted a level of residual risk that *may be* unacceptable to the organization, the chief audit executive should discuss the matter with senior management. If the decision regarding residual risk is not resolved, the chief audit executive and senior management should report the matter to the board for resolution.

The IIA Code of Ethics

The purpose of the Institute's Code of Ethics is to promote an ethical culture in the profession of internal auditing. A code of ethics is necessary and appropriate for the profession of internal auditing, founded as it is on the trust placed in its objective assurance about risk management, control and governance. The Institute's Code of Ethics extends beyond the definition of internal auditing and has been described in Chapter 5.

6.3 Due Professional Care

Taking care during the audit process is becoming an increasingly onerous requirement for the internal auditor. The dismissal of two internal auditors by Allied Irish Bank's US subsidiary (Allfirst) in the wake of the activities of rogue trader John Rusnak provides a powerful illustration of the concept of due professional care. The need to take care is reinforced by Attribute Standard 1220 (Due Professional Care) which states that internal auditors should apply the care and skill expected of a reasonably prudent and competent internal auditor. Due professional care does not imply infallibility. As a short-cut to isolating the principles upon which the elements of an audit are based, we may seek to devise a model in Figure 6.1.

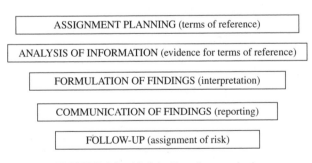

FIGURE 6.1   Model of baseline standards.

Each individual audit has to meet a set of baseline standards if it is to be of acceptable quality, and as such the components outlined above will have to be firmly in place. If this is not the case then there is a strong argument to conclude that the audit has not been performed properly.

6.4 Professional Consulting Services

The definition of internal auditing makes it clear that it is an assurance and consulting activity. The IIA has defined an assurance service as: 'An objective examination of evidence for the purpose of providing an independent assessment of risk management, control, or governance processes for the organisation. Examples may include financial, compliance, systems security, and due diligence engagements.' While consulting services are defined as: 'Advisory and related client service activities, the nature and scope of which are agreed upon with the client and which are intended to add value and improve an organisation's operations. Examples include counsel, advice, facilitation, process design, and training.' The primary players in assurance work are the auditor, the client and the third party to whom assurance is being provided, while for consulting work it is simply the auditor and the client. Assurance work is well understood by the internal audit community and over the years there has been 'creeping consulting' normally in the form of advice and information on request from the line managers. What has not happened before is the offer of a formal consulting service based around the corporate governance, risk management and control dimensions. Many auditors simply suggest that they will do more consulting work, but may not appreciate that this is an entire industry, with set standards and methods, many of which are similar to internal audit techniques.

What is Management Consulting?

IIA Implementation Standard 1000.C1 states that the nature of consulting services should be defined in the charter. But just what is the nature of this work? After considering several different definitions Milan Kubr came up with the following: 'Management consulting is an independent professional advisory service assisting managers and organisations to achieve organisational purposes and objectives by solving management and business problems, identifying and seizing new opportunities, enhancing learning and implementing changes.'[1]

The Institute of Management Consultants (IMC) has prepared a code of conduct that is binding on its members and which is based on three key principles of:

1. Meeting the client's requirements.
2. Integrity, independence, objectivity.
3. Responsibility to the profession and to the IMC.

Moreover members have to ensure that in publicizing work or making representations to a client, the information given:

- Is factual and relevant.
- Is neither misleading nor unfair to others.
- Is not otherwise discreditable to the profession.

In terms of adding value, we can return to Milan Kubr for a consideration of the two main aspects of consulting work being:

- The technical dimension, which concerns the nature of the management or business processes and problems faced by the client and the way in which these problems can be analysed and resolved.
- The human dimension, i.e. interpersonal relationships in the client organisation, people's feelings about the problem at hand and their interest in improving the current situation, and the interpersonal relationship between the consultant and the client.[2]

The IIA see a crossover between consulting work and the assurance role, which is unique to the audit position where strict confidentiality may not be an absolute. Implementation Standard 2110.C2 makes it clear that: 'Internal auditors should incorporate knowledge of risks gained from consulting engagements into the process of identifying and evaluating significant risk exposures of the organisation.'

6.5 The Quality Concept

The IIA's Attribute Standard 1300 (Quality Assurance and Improvement Program) states that:

> The CAE should develop and maintain a quality assurance and improvement program that covers all aspects of the internal audit activity and continuously monitors its effectiveness. The program included periodic internal and external quality assessments and ongoing monitoring. Each part of the program should be designed to help the internal auditing activity add value and improve the organization's operations and to provide assurance that the internal audit activity is in conformity with the Standards and the Code of Ethics.

There is a lot being said about quality assurance, as this appears to be one of the standard management buzzwords. Quality is about:

- Knowing your business.
- Knowing your customers and understanding how they see your business.
- Looking for and dealing with problems.
- Having a way of finding out what stakeholders think of the service.
- Relating all problems to systems that need to be improved. In other words risks to success should be identified, assessed and managed.
- Being very concerned about the section's reputation and overall standing in the organization.
- A clear focus on value for money.
- Resourcing the drive for quality.
- Having efficient and effective procedures.
- Having the quality role built into all staff and ensuring audit managers review and supervise work with this in mind.
- Developing assessment models that can be used to judge whether quality standards are being met.
- Adopting a culture of getting things right and continually improving.

Several Attribute Standards address the quality concept:

> **1310**—The internal audit activity should adopt a process to monitor and assess the overall effectiveness of the quality program. The process should include both internal and external assessments.

> **1311**—Internal assessments should include:
> - Ongoing reviews of the performance of the internal audit activity; and
> - Periodic reviews performed through self-assessment or by other persons within the organisation, with knowledge of internal auditing practices and the Standards.

> **1312**—External assessments, such as quality assurance reviews, should be conducted at least once every five years by a qualified, independent reviewer or review team from outside the organisation.

> **1320**—The CAE should communicate the results of external assessments to the board.

6.6 Defining the Client

Professionalism and quality is about giving the client what they both want and need. This simple concept becomes more involved for internal auditors because we have several different stakeholders and because we deliver both assurance and consulting services. In the past, people who received audit services were simply known as auditees. However, we have moved on from here and there are various views on exactly how we deliver the audit service. The first point is that internal audit has moved away from a 'them and us' battleground as made crystal clear by many commentators:

> Abbey National's new chief internal auditor tells Neil Hodge what he thinks makes an invaluable audit function. . . 'Internal audit needs to make sure that it works as a kind of "controls consultant". It is definitely not tenable for internal audit just to sit back and pull management plans apart, however justified their criticism might be. Auditors need to work with management—not against it—and this needs to be made explicit in internal audit's dealings with the board. . .'

> Once we understood and accepted the fact that internal auditing's customers included virtually everyone in the organization, we were prepared to initiate a survey process that would help us learn how well we were serving these customers. We determined that our audit process could be reduced to five basic categories that would be relevant to our customers:
> * audit planning
> * performance of audits
> * the reporting of results
> * our response to ad hoc requests for assistance
> * auditor professionalism[3]

6.7 Internal Review and External Review

Quality can be promoted by clear standards and effective supervision to ensure these standards are understood and employed throughout the audit shop. The CAE should also install a system of internal assessment to review whether everything is as it should be. The IIA's Attribute Standard 1311 requires the CAE to provide an internal assessment which should include:

* Ongoing reviews of the performance of the internal audit activity; and
* Periodic reviews performed through self-assessment or by other persons within the organization, with knowledge of internal auditing practices and the Standards.

The internal review will consider various aspects of an audit that has been recently completed including the way it was performed and the standards that were applied.

External Review

The IIA's Attribute Standard 1312 requires that: 'external assessments, such as quality assurance reviews, should be conducted at least once every five years by a qualified, independent reviewer or review team from outside the organisation'. There are various options for commissioning this wide ranging review:

External audit—Here an overemphasis on financial systems and support for the external audit role may bias the work.

Internal audit departments in groups of companies—An informal policy of not criticizing each other may invalidate the work. Or fierce competition may make the review less than objective.

Reciprocal arrangements—Here companies may review each other, although confidentiality may be a real problem.

> Other external auditors—Using other companies' external auditors helps reduce bias but they would still tend to have a financial orientation.
>
> Consultant—A consultant who specializes in internal audit reviews will probably be the best choice in terms of skills, independence and final result.

The CAE should use the results of the external review to help form a strategy for improving the audit function and producing an effective quality programme. The review will look at whatever is set in the agreed terms of reference, which as suggested could come from a risk workshop. However, it may well include some of the following areas:

1. Audit charter—mission and vision and buy-in from staff and stakeholders.
2. Organizational status.
3. Independence.
4. Codes of conduct and internal disciplinary mechanisms.
5. Mix between assurance and consulting activity.
6. Audit strategy and whether it fits with corporate strategy of organization.
7. Relations with the board, senior manager and general reputation.
8. Interface with audit committee and whether best practice measures used to keep the audit committee informed.
9. Links with external audit and internal review teams.
10. Performance measurement system and whether this makes sense—also links with performance reporting systems.
11. Communications and participation between auditors and also with external parties—whether use is made of web-based material.
12. Mix of specialist such as fraud, IT, projects, contract and other areas.
13. Complaints procedure and whether this picks up all significant problems.
14. Structure and flexibility—in response to changes and strategies.
15. Staff competence, qualification and CPD.
16. Morale levels among auditors, and remuneration and retention rates—why do people leave internal audit?, policies on secondment, career auditors and short-term placements.
17. Formal training programmes.
18. Research into developing best practice and links with professional bodies, local universities, conferences, and international developments. Do the audit staff keep themselves up to date?
19. Planning systems and the annual audit plan.
20. Budgets and budgetary control also cost per audit day.
21. Extent to which audit is accomplishing its objectives.
22. Planning and control of audit assignments and supervision arrangements.
23. Working papers, standards and compliance (also extent of automation, protection, security, retention, back-up and confidentiality).
24. Level of equipment such as laptops, communication links, etc.
25. Balance work–life issues and use of flexible approaches such as working from home.
26. Measures to encourage diversity among staff.
27. Quality assurance systems and whether internal reviews are adequate—the review will start with considering outcomes of recent internal reviews.
28. Due professional care and measures taken to ensure professionalism and consistency—including the use of the audit manual.

29. Compliance mechanisms to ensure laws and regulations are adhered to.
30. The adopted value add proposition and whether this is being achieved.

The list is, in one sense, open ended—it really depends on the risks that form the basis of the terms of reference for the review. Where the three-pronged approach of supervision, internal and/or external review uncovers a problem to do with non-compliance, this problem needs to be addressed. Senior management and the board need to be informed where this impacts the overall scope or operation of internal audit, including a lack of external assessment (Practice Advisory 1330-1: Use of 'Conducted in Accordance with the Standards'). The results of any review of quality and compliance within internal audit should be reported back to the party who requested the assessment in the first place (Practice Advisory 1320-1: Reporting on the Quality Program) and an appropriate action prepared from the findings and recommendations. The CAE is responsible for following up this action plan.

6.8 Marketing the Audit Role

The IIA distance learning manuals have made clear the need for internal audit to prove its position in an organization:

> In this day and age no function has the right to exist. Each must be able to demonstrate how it adds value to the organisation, and can expect to be continually questioned about its role and contribution. Although internal audit is primarily a review function it is increasingly coming under the same scrutiny as every other part of an organisation and must be able to justify its existence.[4]

There are those who argue that the unique feature of the internal audit function, that relates to its independence, in some way means that there is no need to adopt a market-based orientation in the way services are delivered. They may go on to suggest that if we let managers define the way internal audit works then we become little more than consultants. This view is misconceived as it fails to recognize that internal audit is a service to the organization and not to itself, although there are some considerations that impact on a purist view of marketing. One useful way of assessing whether our marketing efforts have interfered with the levels of independence that we should have achieved is to apply the basic acid test:

> If internal audit were instantly removed from the organization, would certain operations collapse?

A purist's view would insist that this question receives a negative answer to reinforce the concept of the audit services being free from operational involvement. The dilemma, from a marketing angle, is that this exposes the audit role and makes it akin to a dispensable commodity. This problem warrants further exploration since there is an inherent conflict between the marketing concept and the independence test that must be recognized and managed by the CAE when the marketing mix is being considered:

- **The product** Here we consider whether the audit work that is being provided fits with the requirements of the organization.

- **The price** The costs of the audit work should be subject to ongoing review so as to work to an optimum profile.
- **Promotion** This may be seen more as being built into the public relations function as a way of selling the audit image and underlying services.

The Audit Budget

Clients pay for audit services through for example, a quarterly fee charging system, and it is essential that the charges are linked into the audit budget. We need to recover whatever it costs to provide the audit service and the main annual cost components are shown in Table 6.1.

TABLE 6.1   Audit cost profile.

Item	£
Salaries	
Staff expenses	
Office accommodation	
General admin. overheads	
Equipment	
Other expenses	
Total cost	

By dividing the total annual costs over the projected number of chargeable audit hours for the year (normally 214), we can arrive at a recovery hourly rate. By increasing this hourly rate we may achieve a trading surplus as a contribution to non-recoverable time and purchases such as expenditure on computer equipment. The hourly charge-out rate will vary by grade of auditor and this factor will be entered into the time monitoring system. Alternatively, a rough indicator of the hourly rate may be calculated by using the following formula:

$$\frac{\text{Annual salary } (\times 1.5)}{\text{Chargeable hours for the year}} = \text{Hourly rate}$$

The time charging system will allow audit management to monitor the extent to which the budgeted income is being achieved and this will be reported quarterly to audit management. The audit committee, as well as having a general overseeing role, may also request certain reviews and will be charged accordingly. The CAE will probably advise the audit committee on any necessary corporate reviews. Note that management should not generally be able to refuse a planned audit review, but may negotiate the timing or ask to negotiate additional work where there are sufficient audit resources available. Managers may in addition request details of audit's planning, risk analysis and time charging mechanisms.

Creating the Audit Image

Audit needs to formulate and maintain an appropriate image and one auditor who breaches professional behaviour may tarnish the reputation of the whole department. The audit image is based around the standards set out in the audit manual and the auditor code of conduct. In addition it requires the following features of the internal auditor:

- Politeness, having regard to the need to respect fellow officers at whatever grade.
- Being positive by building constructive working relations with management.

- Sensitivity to management's needs.
- Respect for confidentiality with an understanding of the damage that idle gossip can do.
- A team-based audit approach working with and alongside management.
- A hard-working attitude with a constant mission to encourage management to promote good controls.
- A desire to explain the role of audit and promote the audit service wherever possible.

It may be an idea to organize a series of seminars (or a slot at the corporate annual conference) and deliver the new-look internal audit approach.

6.9 Audit Feedback Questionnaire

One way of achieving a degree of feedback from the client is to obtain a response to a formal questionnaire that makes enquiries about the audit service. The purpose of the survey should be explained in a covering memo from the CAE, the main objectives being:

- To obtain the client's view on the benefits secured from the audit.
- To isolate any communication problems that may have been experienced by the client.
- To assess whether the client's perceived needs have been met.
- To identify any adjustments to marketing strategy and audit methodologies that may be required.

The client survey operates at two levels: one as an assignment follow-up while the other looks for more general comments that are not linked to any particular audit. An Audit Effectiveness Questionnaire, along with a covering memorandum from the CAE, may be given to the client by the lead field auditor and once the audit has been completed it will be returned direct to the CAE. It is felt that allowing the field auditors to distribute and explain the survey dispels the view that the CAE does not trust them. The arrangement whereby the form is filled in by the client and returned direct to the CAE ensures that the client may be quite open in their views. Audit working papers will note any disagreement that the auditors may have had with the client and this point should be taken on board when reviewing the survey results. A wider survey may also be carried out from time to time, which can be used to provide feedback on audit's overall impact on management, for use in formulating audit marketing plans.

6.10 Continuous Improvement

To make a start on noting a few comments on the quality drive we can mention the points made by the founding father of the quality movement, Dr Edwards Deming:

1. An organization must have a consistent message about quality.
2. There must be a commitment to change and continual improvement.
3. Defect prevention rather than detection.
4. Build partnerships with suppliers.
5. Constantly improve.
6. Train in a way which makes everyone responsible for their own quality.
7. Supervision must encourage and support, not chase.
8. Drive out 'fear' of improvement.
9. Break down department barriers to foresee problems and improve quality.
10. Don't set unrealistic targets.

11. Enable employees to have pride in their work.
12. Train and educate.
13. Create an organizational structure which supports all of the above.

Meanwhile the three key drivers for the marketing campaign have been noted as just as crucial to the survival of an in-house audit team:

Many internal auditors have failed to appreciate what marketing can offer them and even worse, have become complacent about themselves and the role that they play within their organisation. Marketing can achieve many benefits not least:

- the opportunity to truly demonstrate to the organisation the value added by internal audit.
- the ability to raise internal audit's profile so that it is invited to the 'top table' and involved in key projects within the organisation.
- the opportunity to ensure that the organisation does not consider outsourcing internal audit as a serious option.[5]

Having the following three mechanisms in place promotes continuous learning and success:

1. A clear role definition and service base that responds to changing needs of stakeholders.
2. Procedures that are efficient, flexible and focused on achieving service delivery standards.
3. A staff development system that ensures continuous revitalization of skills, attitudes and approaches.

Summary and Conclusions

The quality movement has been established for many years and there are various standards, guidelines and tools that can be used to incorporate quality into the internal audit shop. Moreover, there are benchmarks, measures and full-blown accreditation schemes that can be used so as to avoid reinventing the wheel. In one sense, we could argue that an independent review activity must have its own house in order before it can embark on this review activity with any real credibility. The IIA standards make it clear that there must be a system of quality assurance in place and that any non-compliance should be formally reported. There is really no excuse for failing to reach the exacting levels of performance and profiles that many internal audit shops are achieving. Professional standards abound, and the IIA with their professional practices framework have been knocking on the boardroom door for many years now. Professional standards create the targets that need to be aimed at, even where the audit shop is small. It is essential that each internal audit team tracks developments in the professional standards and incorporates new aspects into their own policies and interpretations of the audit role.

Chapter 6: Multi-Choice Questions

Having worked through the chapter the following multi-choice questions may be attempted. (See Appendix A for suggested answer guide and Appendix B where you may record your score.)

1. Which is the least appropriate sentence?
   The purpose of the IIA standards is to:
   a. Delineate demanding principles that represent the practice of internal auditing as it should be.

b. Provide a framework for performing a broad range of value-added internal audit activities.

c. Establish the basis for the measurement of internal audit performance.

d. Foster improved organizational processes and operations.

2. Which item is wrong?

The IIA's Professional Practices Framework consists of:

a. Standards for the Professional Practice of Internal Auditing and the Code of Ethics which have to be followed by all practising (IIA) internal auditors.

b. Practice Advisories are pronouncements that are strongly recommended and endorsed by the IIA.

c. Development and Practice Aids—research, books, seminars, conferences, etc.— developed or endorsed by the IIA.

d. Best practice guides prepared by leading audit functions.

3. Insert the missing words:

IIA Attribute Standard 1000:

The purpose, authority, and responsibility of the internal audit activity should be formally defined in a charter, consistent with the *Standards*, and approved by . . . .

a. the management.

b. chief audit executive.

c. external auditor.

d. the board.

4. Which is the most appropriate sentence?

IIA Attribute Standard 1210:

a. Internal auditors should possess the personality, skills and other competencies needed to perform their individual responsibilities. The internal audit activity collectively should possess or obtain the knowledge, skills and other competencies needed to perform its responsibilities.

b. Internal auditors should possess the knowledge, skills and other competencies needed to perform their individual responsibilities. The internal audit activity collectively should possess or obtain the knowledge, skills and other competencies needed to perform its responsibilities.

c. Internal auditors should possess the knowledge, skills and other competencies needed to perform their individual responsibilities. Each auditor should possess the knowledge, skills and other competencies needed to perform internal audit's responsibilities.

d. Internal auditors should possess the knowledge and skills needed to perform their individual responsibilities. The internal audit activity collectively should possess or obtain the knowledge and skills needed to perform its responsibilities.

5. Insert the missing words

IIA Attribute Standard 1300:

The chief audit executive should develop and maintain a quality assurance and improvement program that covers all aspects of the internal audit activity and . . . .

a. continuously monitors its effectiveness.

b. monitors its effectiveness.

c. continuously monitors its staff.

d. continuously report its effectiveness.

6. Insert the missing word

IIA Attribute Standard 1312:

External assessments, such as quality assurance reviews, should be conducted at least once every . . . . years by a qualified, independent reviewer or review team from outside the organization.

a. two.
b. four.
c. five.
d. seven.

7. Which is the most appropriate sentence?

IIA Performance Standard 2010:

a. The chief audit executive should establish plans to determine the priorities of the internal audit activity, consistent with the organization's goals.
b. The chief audit executive should establish risk-based plans to determine the priorities of the internal audit activity, consistent with the organization's goals.
c. The chief audit executive should establish risk-free plans to determine the priorities of the internal audit activity, consistent with the organization's goals.
d. The chief audit executive should establish risk-based plans to determine the risks of the internal audit activity, consistent with the organization's goals.

8. Insert the missing words:

IIA Performance Standard 2060:

The chief audit executive should report periodically to the board and senior management on the internal audit activity's purpose, authority, responsibility, and performance relative to its plan. Reporting should also include . . . . and control issues, corporate governance issues, and other matters needed or requested by the board and senior management.

a. significant risk exposures.
b. all risk exposures.
c. significant risk opportunities.
d. significant risk probabilities.

9. Which is the most appropriate sentence?

IIA Implementation Standard 2110.C1:

a. During assurance engagements, internal auditors should address risk consistent with the engagement's objectives and be aware of the existence of other significant risks.
b. During consulting engagements, internal auditors should address risk consistent with the audit committee's objectives and be alert to the existence of other significant risks.
c. During consulting engagements, internal auditors should address risk consistent with the engagement's objectives and be alert to the existence of other assurance risks.
d. During consulting engagements, internal auditors should address risk consistent with the engagement's objectives and be alert to the existence of other significant risks.

10. Insert the missing words:

IIA Performance Standard 2600:

When the chief audit executive believes that senior management has accepted a level of residual risk that . . . . unacceptable to the organization, the chief audit executive should discuss the matter with senior management. If the decision regarding residual risk is not resolved, the chief audit executive and senior management should report the matter to the board for resolution.

a. is certainly.
b. may be.
c. is not.
d. should be.

References

1 Kubr, Milan (ed.) (2002) *Management Consulting, A Guide to the Profession*, 4th edition, International Labour Organisation, p. 10.
2 Kubr, Milan (ed.) (2002) *Management Consulting, A Guide to the Profession*, 4th edition, International Labour Organisation p. 5.
3 'Abbey Road'. *Internal Auditing and Business Risk*, Aug. 2002, p. 29.
4 *Internal Auditing, Distance Learning Module* (2002) Institute of Internal Auditors, UK&Ireland.
5 'Lex service: marketing internal audit effectively'. *Internal Auditing and Business Risk*, Nov. 2000, p. 30.

Chapter 7

THE AUDIT APPROACH

Introduction

Internal auditing may be performed in many different ways and there are a variety of models that may be applied to discharging the audit role. The organization will define its audit needs and this will help to establish which types of audit services are provided. The CAE is then charged with providing this service to professional auditing standards. This chapter explores some of these different approaches and the way that they relate to the role of internal auditing. Moreover, an audit department will contain different types of auditors who collectively discharge the audit function. Internal auditing is about evaluating risk management and internal controls and this should be a central theme in most audit work. The sections addressed here are as follows:

7.1 The Systems Approach

There are many different ways that internal auditing may be approached: some are investigatory/ transactions-based while others move towards a systems approach. There is an argument that the most efficient use of audit resources occurs where one concentrates on reviewing systems as opposed to examining individual systems' transactions. It is possible to use force-field analysis to weigh up the factors that together define the actual audit approach that is applied in any organization. These forces may be set out in Figure 7.1. Each of these factors will apply pressure in defining the way that the audit role is discharged and some of the influences may appear as shown in Table 7.1.

In terms of professional standards, there are aspects of an organization that clearly fall within the scope of audit work. Performance Standard 2100 means that the internal audit activity should assist the organization by identifying and evaluating significant exposures to risk and contributing to the improvement of risk management and control systems. In terms of systems work Implementation Standard 2110.A1 asks that the internal audit activity evaluates and contributes to the improvement of risk management control and governance systems. While Implementation

FIGURE 7.1   Factors impacting on the audit approach.

TABLE 7.1   Factors: main requirements.

Body	Requirements
The CAE	Review of systems of risk management and satisfying audit committee, the board and other audit clients.
Audit committee	Systems of corporate governance, risk management and control validated, and accounting and accountability issues resolved.
Line management	Management problems solved and help with establishing good risk management.
Professional practice	Assurance and consulting role of internal audit.

Standard 2110.A2 makes it clear that the internal audit activity should evaluate risk exposures relating to the organization's governance, operations and information systems regarding the:

- Reliability and integrity of financial and operational information.
- Effectiveness and efficiency of operations.
- Safeguarding of assets.
- Compliance with laws, regulations, and contracts.

These systems need to be assessed by internal audit as part of the assurance role. There is a choice in the way internal auditing is carried out and although professional standards do set conceptual guidelines, they do not promote a particular methodology. The final approach will result from a combination of factors that affect the audit role and resultant work carried out. The premise upon which *The Essential Handbook* is founded considers risk-based systems auditing as a valid interpretation of the assurance role of internal audit, with all other matters falling under the generic term investigations—most of which is part of the consulting service along with direct assistance and advice in establishing business risk management. Systems thinking is based on viewing operations and events as processes with the flows as shown in Figure 7.2.

Defining a system:

A set of objects together with relationships between these objects and their attributes connected or related to each other in such a manner as to form an entirety or whole.

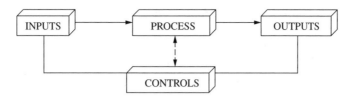

FIGURE 7.2   A basic system.

There is a number of concepts that underpin systems theory:

- **Connected components**
- **Affected by being in a system**
- **Assembly of components does something**
- **Assembly identified as being of special interest**

Entropy

This may be seen as a disorder, disorganization, lack of patterning or randomness of organization of systems. A closed system tends to increase in entropy over time in that it will move towards greater disorder and randomness. Entropy provides a justification for the audit role as systems break down and controls deteriorate over time unless they are reviewed and made to keep pace with changing risks. The trend to removing tiers of management to achieve budget reductions may have a major impact on systems controlled through supervisory reviews by line and middle management. The balance of controls should change with restructuring. If not, the imbalance becomes part of the overall entropy where a deterioration in controls impairs the successful functioning of the system. Systems are designed to ensure an objective is achieved in the best way possible and it has been said that: 'Systems thinking is the way we can discern some rules, some sense of pattern and events, so we can prepare for the future and gain some influence over it.'[1]

We are concerned with reviewing and then advising management on their systems of internal controls that discharge the four objectives mentioned earlier. So an activity should be undertaken with due regard for compliance with laws and procedures and this feature should be built into the system. Systems in control will subscribe to these key control features, in contrast to those that are at risk. IIA Performance Standard 2060 includes the following line: 'Reporting should also include significant risk exposures and control issues, corporate governance issues, and other matters needed or requested by the board and senior management.'

Stages of Risk-based Systems Auditing (RBSA)

Systems thinking is used twice in RBSA. First, we break down operations as systems, components of a system, subsystems, parallel systems and parent systems. An overview may be adopted and links between operations may be identified and understood. Second, RBSA is in fact a systematic audit approach in itself, with defined stages and clear links between each step, and there are a number of matters to be considered at each stage:

Define clear objectives for the stage   What we are aiming to achieve should be clearly stated at each stage so that the actual output can be measured against this.

Plan the work and approach to be adopted   Planning is a continuous process that occurs before the audit and throughout the various above-mentioned stages. It is possible to set a separate time budget for the stage and then seek to monitor hours charged before finalizing the audit. It is also possible to carry out a review of work as the stage is completed to provide an ongoing supervision of the project by audit management.

Obtain a good understanding of the risks to the operation   This may be achieved through analysis, discussion with client staff or through a structured workshop where the client team members consider their risks and how they impact on their business and team goals.

Define any testing strategy   Testing is applied at ascertainment (walkthrough), compliance (after evaluation) and substantive testing (after evaluation and compliance tests). The detailed work programme may be drafted and agreed as the appropriate stage is arrived at.

Define the techniques that will be used   Audit techniques such as interviewing, flowcharting, database interrogation, control self-assessment, negotiating and statistical sampling should be agreed again at the relevant stage of the audit. This will assist timing the work and enable additional skill needs to be identified.

Brief staff working on the project   With a team approach it is useful to break down each stage so that a briefing can be held to discuss problem areas, progress and other matters. Not only will this act as a feedback device but it will also promote team working where ideas are exchanged.

Ensure that the work is formally documented   Standardized documentation ensures all key points are covered and that the work is fully recorded. The stage end is a convenient time to consider whether the documentation meets quality standards (according to the audit manual) and contains all the necessary detail. The opportunity to obtain missing material is more readily available during and not after the audit. There is an obvious link between this and the audit manager review procedure.

Look for high levels of unmitigated risk   It is good practice to report as the audit progresses to save time and ensure that the report is fresh and dynamic. The auditor has the opportunity to assess the impact on the work done so far on the report and the testing strategy that will have to be developed at some stage. Details of excessive risk can enter the report so long as the repercussions have been tested. Since evaluation of risk occurs throughout the audit, the whole package of views on the ability of key controls to mitigate risk is developed as work progresses. This is a major part of the auditor's work.

Agree the direction of work for the next stage   The link between stages comes naturally from the systems approach to auditing as one moves smoothly from one to another. The direction of the next stage must be considered by the auditor not only from a planning point of view, but also from the wider perspective of whether work should be expanded, curtailed or adjusted. This is the point to discuss matters with the audit manager and also advise that the stage in question is complete.

7.2 Control Risk Self-Assessment (CRSA)

Control risk self-assessment is a tool that is used by businesses to promote risk management in teams, projects, through processes and generally throughout the organization. This tool can be used by the executive board, partners, middle management, work teams and of course internal audit. In other words, CRSA is both a management tool and audit technique depending on what the CAE wishes to apply to the audit process and the views of the corporate body. The IIA's Practice Advisory 2120.A1-2 (Using Control Self-Assessment for Assessing the Adequacy of Control Processes) suggests that CRSA is: 'A methodology encompassing self-assessment surveys and facilitated workshops called CSA is a useful and efficient approach for managers and internal auditors to collaborate in assessing and evaluating control procedures. In its purest form, CSA integrates business objectives and risks and control processes.' Returning to our model of business systems, we can illustrate where CRSA fits into the process of managing risks in Figure 7.3.

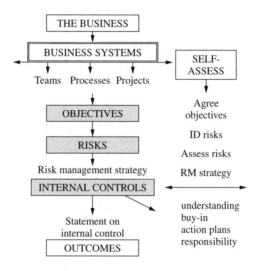

FIGURE 7.3   Risk-based auditing.

All business systems have objectives, risks and ways of managing these risks. CRSA is a process for agreeing the set objectives, identifying the inherent risks that stop one from achieving the objectives and then working out which risks are most significant. Chapter 3 on risk management provides information on the risk management cycle and the way risks may be categorized and assessed. This section simply describes the CRSA technique where it is used in workshop mode. Having isolated the key risks, the team members will go on to refine their strategy for managing the risks, which will tend to focus on internal controls as a main component of the strategy. Note that Chapter 4 deals with internal control in some detail. Allowing the work team (or project team, or representatives from a cross-organization process) to assess their risk management strategy leads to a better understanding of the specific risks and controls in question, more buy-in as people agree their approach and ensure action plans are realistic. And the CRSA approach reinforces the view that the responsibility for controls lies with those that operate them and those that manage the operations.

CSRA and Internal Controls

Some see CRSA workshops as ways of developing contingency plans to protect the business interests and for new ventures that are being developed. In fact, many see internal control as mainly relating to disaster recovery and contingency planning, particularly in response to the threat of terrorist attacks. Many risk workshops focus on retaining key staff, and providing back-up arrangements for senior figures or top specialists in the event of an accident or other reasons for their non-availability. Other workshops concentrate on specific projects and ways of managing the risks to larger and more important projects. The traditional view of internal control relates them to measures such as authorization and segregation of duties used for examples of basic accounting systems. One way of analysing this variation of views is to suggest that there are four main types of environments that tend to be subject to risk assessment consisting of process, project, people and preparedness as in Figure 7.4.

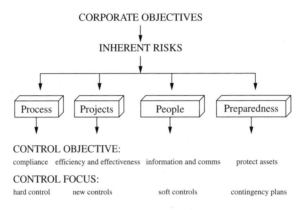

FIGURE 7.4   Types of CRSA.

While in practice there are numerous types of CRSA events, we can suggest four basic approaches:

1. Process   Here CRSA is used to review typical controls found in a business process with a view to checking whether the controls are robust and complied with. An example may be a CRSA workshop for the finance team who prepare the group final accounts. The basic controls over information, adjustments, feeder systems, closing accounts, reconciliations and so on will be considered in the light of changing risks (e.g. the risk of financial misstatement) and controls fine-tuned where required. Compliance with these controls also becomes a main consideration. The systems of internal control will tend to revolve around set procedures and information systems, that is 'hard controls to ensure things are done properly'.

2. Projects   These CRSA events will be part of the standard risk assessment and preparation of risk registers that most project management methodologies recommend. Project risk will consist of a combination of the project going wrong and the outcome being poor, late or over budget. Controls will revolve around the way the project is managed and if this involves a large new venture an entire set of new controls may be designed and adopted. The focus is on innovation and flexibility and the production of brand new controls that fit the bill. Moreover, risks may also be seen as upside risk that means we take out excessive controls to ensure new opportunities can be exploited.

3. People   Some CRSA workshops try to address people issues as the main driver. Here the issues and problems that affect the way the team operates and relates to each other, in the pursuit of business objectives are considered. The idea being to isolate the problems (risks) and solutions (controls) to encourage better performance. A focus on soft controls in terms of people issues is the key factor that drives these types of behavioural workshops. Experienced CRSA proponents like Paul Makosz have promoted the importance of soft controls and have described them as the Sleeping Giant. Moreover James Roth has suggested that... 'you actually have less audit risk when you devote time to evaluating soft controls, because they are more important to controlling an organisation than the hard control activities'.[2] In one CRSA-based workshop the background was to identify why the operation was suffering from dysfunction and to:

- Identify the current inhibitors that prevent the team performing to the best of class standard.
- Envision how the service could improve in the short, medium and long term.
- Drill down on each of the inhibitors to identify the processes and systems failure or weakness that would prevent or hinder service improvements.
- Develop a detailed action plan necessary for the service to improve.
- Share best practice wherever possible to aid systems/process improvement.

The workshop sought to assess the risks that could either prevent or accelerate the achievement of the business objectives and considered:

1. How the team sees itself.
2. How the team would like to see itself.
3. What changes are needed to get there.

The findings from the event included that:

- Significant risks and threats face the operation.
- These risks are not being well managed.
- Control focus is reactive not proactive.
- The operation is not performing well as a team.
- There are no clearly understood service objectives.
- Many silos are in place based on where staff stand in the hierarchy.
- This has given rise to a blame culture—no collective ownership of problems.
- All staff want to see improvements.
- There are different perceptions of problems from staff, supervisors and managers.

A series of focus groups was set up to tackle problems and help improve the service based on an action plan and a newly agreed vision for the service.

4. Preparedness This type of workshop is growing in popularity and consists of considering the types of risks that could impact the integrity of the corporate resource, that is the buildings, the staff, the knowledge, information systems and products or services. The context is the heightened awareness of accidents, sabotage, terrorism and natural disasters that could wipe out a corporate asset overnight. These workshops concentrate on scenario planning and result in risk mitigation strategies, insurance cover and fully resourced contingency plans. Many people now see risk as mainly associated with wide-scale disasters that can stop an organization in its tracks. The emphasis is on protection of assets and containing any potential damage to the continued operation of the business.

The Internal Audit Role

The IIA have accepted the consulting aspect of helping to establish CRSA in organizations against the background of the internal auditors' expertise in this area. Professional Practices Pamphlet

98–2 makes it clear that: 'The IIA recommends using the synergy created by the interaction of the auditor–facilitator and CSA participants to add increased value to the organisation through the internal auditing function.'[3]

Some internal auditors feel they need to stand back from the CRSA drive and allow management to assume full responsibility for managing operational risk. Others have thrown themselves into the development and lead from the front under the 'value add' banner. Still others kick-start CRSA in their organizations then stand back and validate the system when it has settled down to some extent. There is no finite solution and much depends on the approach that is adopted. Whatever the final format, the internal auditor must be equipped with the right skills to perform the role as required by Implementation Standard 1210.C1 which states that: 'The CAE should decline the consulting engagement or obtain competent advice and assistance if the internal audit staff lacks the knowledge, skills or other competencies needed to perform all or part of the engagement.'

7.3 Facilitation Skills

The CRSA process depends on a good control environment and open communications that engender trust and confidence. People will participate and add to a CRSA workshop if they:

- Are committed to the workshop objective.
- Have something of value to add.
- Believe that their opinion will be appreciated.
- Understand the CRSA process and where it fits into the business.
- Have confidence in the way the workshop is applied.

Where each of the above aspirations are achieved, there is a good chance that the entire CRSA process will be successful. A few poorly administered workshop events will soon spread the word across the organization that these should be avoided at all costs. Conversely, several positive events will engender a view that they are worthwhile and even enjoyable. A facilitator gets people to do things for themselves. Ideally the CRSA facilitator should have a good understanding of:

- What makes for a good facilitator.
- Groups and how they behave.
- Learning styles and how people make progress.
- Risk and control concepts.
- Different styles of facilitation ranging from passive through to aggressive.
- What could go wrong in a workshop.
- How to make the event successful.

7.4 Integrating Self-Assessment and Audit

The internal auditor may review the CRSA process and the way it is developed and applied in an organization, or the internal auditor may provide a consulting service to help facilitate the CRSA process in a hands-on manner. Since no one can be a judge in their own case, these two approaches can create a potential problem. As mentioned earlier, some audit teams start off the CRSA process then withdraw to a position of safety and resume the review roles thereafter. Other teams split their staff into audit and consulting services and make sure that the CRSA facilitation aspect of audit is kept separate from the main risk-based assurance work. Meanwhile, the IIA Performance Standard 2201 on planning considerations states quite clearly that:

In planning the engagement, internal auditors should consider:

- The objectives of the activity being reviewed and the means by which the activity controls its performance.
- The significant risks to the activity, its objectives, resources and operations and the means by which the potential impact of risk is kept to an acceptable level.
- The adequacy and effectiveness of the activities risk management and control systems compared to the relevant control framework or model.
- The opportunity for making significant improvements to the activity's risk management and control systems.

In other words, the internal auditor should recognize the risk management activity in the area that is being audited and take on board all the effort the client is making to manage risks and establish good controls. This is endorsed by Implementation Standard 2210.A1 which makes it clear that: 'Internal auditors should conduct a preliminary assessment of the risks relevant to the activity under review. Engagement objectives should reflect the results of this assessment.'

If we produce a complete model of the CRSA/audit process it may look something like Figure 7.5.

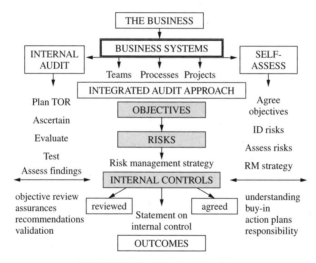

FIGURE 7.5   Risk-based auditing.

A mixture of audit objectivity and testing alongside the inside knowledge and commitment from the self-assessment process may create a useful solution. This integrated approach mixes audit with the close involvement of client staff in workshop format to identify risks and help define suitable solutions. Two new boxes are added to the model: reviewed and agreed, that is the risk management process will have been objectively reviewed by internal audit and also agreed by the people who actually operate the system, creating many benefits.

7.5 Fraud Investigations

Fraud is big business and the real scale may be unknown. Frauds arise when 'things go wrong' and this has implications for the system of internal control. An analysis of theft and fraud in government departments for 2001 reported that while some 51% of government bodies who had completed the return reported no frauds, the other 49% reported 539 cases to a value of £1.6 million. The types of fraud reported included:

Types of fraud:	Number	Value
fraudulent encashment of payable instruments	1%	1%
misappropriation of cash	14%	4%
theft of assets	33%	25%
works services projects	2%	3%
travel and subsistence	12%	8%
instruments of payment received on false documents	6%	49%
false claims for hours worked	11%	3%
other	21%	7%

Some of the main risk areas for employee fraud include:

Debtors	Cash
Payroll	Large capital contracts
Revenue contracts	Major computer acquisitions
Computer access	Portable attractive items (e.g. laptops)
Public sector benefits	Government grants
Expenses	Stock
Cheques drawn	Creditors and payments
Mortgages	Pensions
Petty cash	Recruitment references
Overtime and employee claims	Confidential information
Subsidy claims	Credit cards
Computer memory chips	Corporate knowledge
Employee bonus schemes	Procurement

Defining Fraud

The IIA define fraud as: 'Any illegal acts characterised by deceit, concealment or violation of trust. These acts are not dependent upon the application of threats of violence or physical force. Frauds are perpetrated by individuals, and organisations to obtain money, property or services; to avoid payment or loss of services; or to secure personal or business advantage.'

While the Association of Fraud Examiners (ACFE) define occupational fraud as: 'The use of one's occupation for personal enrichment through the deliberate misuse or misapplication of the employing organisation's resources or assets'.[4]

Fraud can develop where an innocent error has gone undetected so that the ability to breach a system's security becomes evident. Once a member of staff spots a system weakness, it can be used to perpetrate fraud. This weakness may consist of unclear procedures covering access privileges to a computerized system where there is little distinction between authorized and unauthorized work.

The Four Components

Fraud is an act of deceit to gain advantage or property of another with four main components:

1. **Motive.** There should be a motive for the fraud. This may be that the employee is dissatisfied or is in financial difficulties. In the case of non-employees there should be a reason why

the fraud is perpetrated. Good human resource management keeps employees satisfied and lowers non-financial motives for engaging in frauds.

2. **Attraction.** The gain or advantage secured must have an attraction for the perpetrator. This varies and may provide a gain for an associated person, e.g. a mortgage applicant.

3. **Opportunity.** There must be adequate opportunity. Someone may wish to defraud an organization and know exactly what is to be gained, but with no opportunity, it may never occur. Preventive control should be used to guard against the possibility of fraud by reducing opportunities. In fact a report by the University of Nottingham Business School (commissioned by Business Defence Europe) based on a study of 200 firms, claims that middle managers are particularly likely to defraud because they have an in-depth knowledge of how their firms work and know how to cover their tracks.[5]

4. **Concealment.** In contrast to theft, fraud has an element of concealment. It can be by false accounting which is a criminal offence. This makes it difficult to uncover and allows the fraud to be repeated.

The causes of fraud will vary but in terms of reported government fraud the causes of fraud have been listed as:

Causes:	Number	Value
Absence of proper control	24%	14%
Lack of separation of duties	1%	1%
Collusion with persons outside department	8%	31%
Failure to observe control procedures	50%	48%
Collusion within the department	3%	4%
Other	3%	2%[6]

Types of Fraud

There is no legal definition of fraud. The fraud may be carried out by insiders or outsiders and an organization may carry out fraud by, say, overstating its earnings. The Theft Act 1968 covers various offences and the offences associated with fraud are:

Theft   This includes obtaining property by deception and false accounting.

Bribery and corruption   The Prevention of Corruption Acts 1889 to 1916 apply to local government and provide that 'any money, gift or consideration paid or received shall be deemed to have been paid or received corruptly as an inducement or reward unless the contrary is proved'.

Forgery   A person is guilty of forgery if he makes a false instrument with the intention that he or another shall use it to induce someone to accept it as genuine and by reason of so accepting it, to do, or not to do some act to his own or some other person's prejudice.

Conspiracy   This involves the unlawful agreement by two or more persons to carry out an unlawful common purpose or a lawful common purpose by unlawful means. This would cover collusion to override internal controls.

There are other actions that fall under the generic category of fraud, including:

- Perjury.
- Concealment (of information).

- Fraudulent trading (e.g. unable to pay creditors).
- Conversion (e.g. fraudulently cashing a cheque).
- Financial misstatement.

Unauthorized removal and breach of internal procedures may also be investigated but these are seen as internal disciplinary matters with no criminal implications. Cybercrime is a growing problem and a survey by the Confederation of British Industry placed types of cybercrime in order of perceived threats:

viruses	hacking
illegal database access	adverse comments on the Internet
intellectual property infringement	legal liability issues
distorted versions of website	credit card fraud
securities and financial fraud	money laundering

The survey reported that the main perpetrators were hackers (45%), former employees (13%) and current employees (11%). [6]

The Regulation of Investigatory Powers Act 2000 created a new criminal offence and a tort of unlawful interception of communication being transmitted by certain means. Certain transmissions can be intercepted if authorized and the Secretary of State may issue interception warrants for certain purposes and to require the disclosure of an encryption key. Electronic signatures consist of a public encryption key linked to a private key so messages are secure as long as the authorized user transmits the message. The Electronic Communications Act 2000 allows this device to be submitted in court as evidence, as would a traditional signature. The Act contains arrangements for the Secretary of State to maintain a register of approved cryptography providers.

Money laundering is also a growing concern and it is an offence:

- For any person to provide assistance to a criminal to retain, conceal or invest funds if that person knows or suspects that the funds are the proceeds of crime. The definition of crime for money laundering purposes is now very wide and includes the proceeds of anything from theft to tax evasion.
- To prejudice a money laundering investigation by informing any third party that an investigation is underway.
- Not to report a suspicion of laundering relating to drugs or terrorism.

Indicators of Fraud

Frauds are normally found through luck or third-party information while some are discovered during audit reviews, or through controls or by line management. Indicators of fraud are:

- Strange trends where comparative figures move in an unexplained fashion.
- Rewritten and/or amended documents may be evidence of unauthorized alteration to cover up fraud.
- Missing documents may signal a fraud where items are sensitive such as unused cheques or order forms.
- Tipp-Ex (erasing fluid) applied to documents may indicate unauthorized alterations.
- Photocopies substituted for originals can be readily tampered with since the photocopy may make it impossible to uncover alterations to the original.
- Complaints from suppliers that do not tie in with the records should alert one to a potential problem.

- Social habits of staff are sometimes used as an example of a fraud indicator particularly where they appear to be living beyond their means.
- Other unusual situations or trends.

Many indicators go unnoticed and the problem arises when, after a fraud has been uncovered, there are criticisms that there was obviously something wrong that should have been spotted. There are employees who are alert to these signs and as long as the organization promotes alert behaviour this becomes an additional control. The only real remedy is effective controls.

Fraud Detection

The ACFE 2002 Report to the Nation suggests that the main sources of detection in the US (percentage shown in brackets) come from:

1. tip from employees (26%).	2. by accident (19%).
3. internal audit (18%).	4. internal control (15%).
5. external audit (11%)	6. tip from customer (9%).
7. anonymous tip (6%).	8. tip from vendor (5%).
9. notification by law enforcement (2%).[7]	

Defining Roles in an Organization

In terms of fraud detection Practice Advisory 1210.A2-2 makes clear the difference between management and internal audit's roles:

1. Management and the internal audit activity have differing roles with respect to fraud detection.
2. Management has responsibility to establish and maintain an effective control system at a reasonable cost.
3. A well-designed internal control system should not be conducive to fraud. Tests conducted by auditors, along with reasonable controls established by management, improve the likelihood that any existing fraud indicators will be detected and considered for further investigation.

The organization should negotiate the audit role in respect of frauds. Principles to be applied are:

1. The audit charter should establish the audit role in frauds.
2. The organization should define a clear policy on fraud and if this involves internal audit then it should say so. It may be that all frauds are reported in the first instance to internal audit.
3. Within the organizational policies, internal audit should establish a service level agreement that will describe the role in frauds. This should be agreed at audit committee.
4. Whatever is agreed, it is clear that management is wholly responsible for investigating and resolving their frauds and any internal audit involvement is, in reality, consultancy work.
5. The most effective model is where management resolves its own frauds while internal audit provides an advisory role.
6. Executive decisions should be made by management who should implement action required to solve the fraud.
7. Where audit investigates the fraud they should be careful not to become manipulated by management.
8. Once a fraud is resolved, audit must ensure that management recognizes its responsibilities to close internal control loopholes.

9. In terms of fraud detection, IIA Implementation Standard 1210.A2 makes it clear that: 'The internal auditor should have sufficient knowledge to identify the indicators of fraud but is not expected to have the expertise of a person whose primary responsibility is detecting and investigating fraud.'

The external auditor   The external auditor must ensure that management has taken reasonable steps to control fraud, and where this is insufficient it may be referred to in a management letter.

Internal compliance teams   Management may set up internal compliance teams to assist in promoting compliance with procedures. These teams do not relieve it of its responsibilities, since management must still be prepared to make executive decisions, even where based on recommendations made by internal auditors.

Personnel section   Personnel may be seen as an independent function that may be used to formally communicate between the alleged perpetrator/s and management and ensure that personnel polices are being adhered to.

Employees   All employees should understand the fraud policy and know how to report suspicions of fraud. The Public Interest Disclosure Act 1998 offers some protection for workers who disclose information to a manager or their employer if the whistleblower has a:

> reasonable suspicion that the malpractice has occurred, is occurring or is likely to occur and can make a protected disclosure (which includes reporting a criminal offence) in good faith where:

> - the whistleblower reasonably believed he would be victimised,
> - he raised the matter internally or with a prescribed regulator,
> - reasonable believed a cover-up was likely and there was no prescribed regulator; or he had already raised the matter internally or with the prescribed regulator.

Investigating Fraud

Although every fraud investigation will be unique, it is nonetheless possible to define certain key stages and devise standardized procedures that may be applied to each one. These may be summarized:

1. Allegation received   A clear policy should be established. The allegation can come from a variety of sources including:

- Detective controls—e.g. a bank reconciliation.
- Anonymous information—by phone or letter.
- Formal complaint—say from a supplier.
- Concerns expressed by a line manager about their staff.
- Whistleblowers' 'hotline'.
- Head office—on activities at a branch—say less cash accounted for.
- An audit—which has picked up an unexplained problem.
- Colleagues or friends who hear an employee boasting about underhand activities.
- The police who indicate that an employee is implicated in fraudulent activities.
- Pure accident.

2. Establish the basic facts before firm action is taken   Interview the person supplying information at their convenience. This gives the auditor a good idea as to the validity of the allegations as well as providing necessary background information. Contact names should be taken and a full write-up of the allegation made. A personal profile may be drawn up where there are defined suspects and information such as payroll, pension records, personnel, creditors, income, electoral register and Companies House may be used. It is possible to establish a defined list of details that relate to a suspect.

3. Carry out further background research   This includes securing all information available to the auditor without entering the area where the fraud is located. It involves reviewing previous audit files and documents that relate to the location. Special rules will apply to dealing with this designated area so that the investigation may proceed unimpaired. The following factors will assist this process:

- Identify the exact work area subject to the allegations.
- Isolate what goes on in this area including documentation and information received by the unit/branch/section.
- Establish the outputs in terms of documentation, returns, reports and services that come from the affected area.
- Establish the staff involved and isolate potential suspects.
- For each suspect compile a profile including name, age, role, job title, length of service, sex, description, car, address, National Insurance number and so on.
- Define reporting lines and structures in the section.
- Try to secure inventory lists and a record of assets (including computers held).

We may care to access all corporate information systems such as payroll, personnel, payments, ordering, stores, pensions and others in pursuit of the required information. It is as well to have several key contacts in personnel and other corporate sections where we may make discreet enquires about the people in question.

4. The preliminary report   This indicates whether the allegation may be true and should be investigated. An overall strategy should be defined. Management should be shown the report and a meeting held to discuss the implications.

5. Investigation plan   This plan should be derived from discussions with management and will indicate the approach, work required, resources and any contact with the police or other authorities. The preliminary report outlined above will be used to devise a plan of action and may set the tone for relevant meetings with senior managers. The plan should set in motion the agreed approach so that all parties to the matter have a clear role with timescales attached to each task.

6. Managerial support   The level of managerial support will depend on the fraud and the level at which it is alleged to have occurred. It is best to link with the level of management twice removed from the allegations.

7. Defining barriers   Throughout the investigation it is necessary to work out possible barriers to the investigation such as missing documents, sources of evidence, the culprit's presence, close associates of the culprit, the need for confidentiality and records being tampered with. Where any of the evidence is at risk, swift action must be taken.

8. _Initial strategy_   New information will come to light and the adopted strategy will alter as necessary. There are several options that may be considered, including:

- Suspend the employee in question immediately.
- Call in the local police (we may have already gone to them for initial advice).
- Undertake covert enquiries without alerting anyone not party to the exercise.
- Send out a general reminder to staff where a low level abuse of facilities is occurring.
- Carry out an audit of the area in question—this is particularly useful where spot checks are part of the normal audit approach.
- Carry out surveillance—we need to establish rules for this type of activity.

9. _Surveillance?_   Surveillance involves observing the activities of defined individuals without their knowledge. Watching, looking and gathering evidence does not generally breach privacy standards and is a useful way of securing information in a fraud investigation. But it is sensitive and must be handled with care. One approach is to formulate a formal policy based on the premise that it should only be used when absolutely necessary. Some argue surveillance should only be carried out by experts. Simple undercover operations can yield results particularly where this is the only way of obtaining proof of a fraud. To carry out surveillance:

- Plan the operation carefully.
- Do a trial run.
- Prepare by deciding resources and approach.
- Action should be anticipated and authorized activity distinguished from the unauthorized.
- If confronted during a surveillance initially try to deny it while avoiding a conflict situation.
- Always carry an ID card.
- Simple matters may be resolved through surveillance.
- Ensure that the individual's right to reasonable privacy is preserved.

10. _The full investigation_   Most of the investigation will involve obtaining confirmatory evidence in whatever form it is available. This may include reviewing documents, interviews, photographs, surveillance, analysis and/or tracing transactions. It is here that the real art of applying auditing techniques comes to the fore. We must seek to prove guilt by carefully compiling relevant evidence, although we should be careful not to be seen as acting as an _agent provocateur_. The resource issue must be resolved and this will alter as the investigation takes shape and changes direction. It will be linked to sensitivity and overall impact on the organization. Once we have agreed an appropriate course of action we need to consider the detailed plans. The format of the investigation will dictate the way it is structured and undertaken. In essence we take the view that a fraud cannot be said to have occurred unless we are able to present evidence that substantiates it. As such the plan will be aimed at securing the requisite evidence in the most convenient and reliable manner possible. This may consist of:

- Interviewing witnesses.
- Analysing documentation.
- Securing reports that tend to support the allegations.
- Computation of financial losses.
- Securing evidence of breach of procedure by comparing what happened with the approved procedure.
- Observing activities and recording the results.
- Reperforming calculations and reconciliation.

- Securing evidence from independent sources that corroborate or conflict with other available evidence. Perhaps to find out whether a cheque was received by a supplier listed on the payments database.
- Assessing whether a document is forged, altered or subject to a forged signature.

Much of the above is about interviewing witnesses and extracting relevant documentation. One point that should have been discussed at the outset is the objective of the investigation. Although this will be to prove that the fraud has occurred, it may also be used to bring a prosecution in a court of law. In addition, it may be used to present internal disciplinary charges to a specially convened panel.

11. Ongoing review and discussions with management As the investigation progresses its shape and form will alter as new information comes to light and all parties to the work become more familiar with the activities under review.

12. Interviews A key component of most fraud investigations is the interview process. Here most questions can be addressed by simply asking the right people. Interviews may be held with:

- Informants.
- Key witnesses.
- Line managers.
- Persons who may be useful to the enquiries.
- Suspects.

Each has a different purpose and will follow a different format. The most important interviews will be with witnesses, who should be asked to provide a formal witness statement, and the suspect(s) who may be asked to sign a formal interview record. Witnesses will write down in their own words what they saw and heard, as relating to the issues in hand, and be prepared to present this evidence in court and/or at an internal disciplinary. They may cross-reference their comments to various exhibits that will be attached to their statement and which were shown to them at the time the statement was taken. Suspects on the other hand will be asked to provide an explanation of evidence that points to them as perpetrators of the fraud in question. They should be cautioned in the appropriate format, which in the UK is:

> You do not have to say anything. But it may harm your defence if you do not mention something which you may later rely on in court. Anything you do say may be given in evidence.

This retains the right of silence but at the same time allows the prosecution to comment on any alibis that are produced at a later date. In addition the Police and Criminal Evidence Act lays down certain rules for interviewing suspects in terms of allowing the interview record to be submitted to a court of law. In summary these allow a right of silence and disallow practices that would constitute intimidation or duress. Most investigators now recognize that the suspect interview is not about extracting a confession. It is about presenting the evidence in front of the suspect to secure an explanation. If none is forthcoming then we would seek to progress the investigation to prosecution stage. We may encourage a full disclosure, but this is a decision for the suspect (having been given the opportunity to seek advice from their lawyer). Note that we would expect most formal interviews with suspects to be carried out by police officers.

13. Interim reports   Throughout the investigation interim reports should be issued setting out findings to date, implications and further work recommended.

14. The final report   This covers the necessary action that should be taken and may treat the activity as an internal matter or seek referral to the police.

15. Criminal prosecutions and internal disciplinaries   There tend to be two main results from fraud investigations. One is a referral to the police who will place a case before the Crown Prosecution Service with a view to bringing criminal proceedings against the parties in question. The other is that internal disciplinaries will be held against any employee where evidence points to their guilt in connection with the fraud.

16. Internal disciplinary action   Employee fraud should be dealt with under the internal disciplinary procedure as gross misconduct, which is a dismissible offence. Internal action is not dependent on any ongoing criminal prosecution and should be taken at the earliest possible opportunity. Even where a criminal case falls over the employer can still defend a dismissal resulting from the internal procedure which operates on the less demanding balance of probabilities (rather than beyond all reasonable doubt). The test here is whether the employer genuinely believed on reasonable grounds that the applicant was guilty of the offence in question.

17. Final completed report   We will complete the procedure by insisting that a final report is prepared on the fraud and action taken. This part is often missed as an employee is dismissed and the police take over the case. The confidential audit report may look like Figure 7.6.

EXECUTIVE SUMMARY

1. INTRODUCTION

allegation and initial response

2. INVESTIGATION

work carried out and detailed testing performed
a list of people interviewed will also be set out

3. DETAILED FINDINGS

detailed findings including suspects and evidence obtained

4. CONCLUSIONS AND RECOMMENDATIONS

action required in terms of police involvement and disciplinaries
a list of disciplinary charges should be set out if possible
a whole section would cover controls and required improvements
(as well as any urgent changes that should have already been implemented)

APPENDICES

schedule of losses—and details of recovery
results of police case and disciplinaries
any press releases and newspaper reports

FIGURE 7.6   Fraud investigation audit report—format.

Documentation

Each fraud investigation must be recorded in a formal file containing all the relevant documents that have been secured during the course of the investigation. When securing and storing documents from a fraud investigation:

- Handle all documents with care and protect them by placing them in suitable pockets. Preserve fingerprints by using forceps.
- Label all documents carefully (i.e. the pocket) and note date, time and location. Where a person admits using or having an association with a document, record this, e.g. a diary belongs to them.
- Do not write on the documents or attach any sticky labels.
- Do not attempt to reassemble documents by using adhesive.
- Make sure the original documents are retained.
- Try to obtain samples of handwriting from all suspects. The sample should match what it is being compared with.

Preventive Techniques

The investigative process is reactive in that it is initiated as a result of an alleged fraud. Steps may be taken to guard against fraud. The importance of establishing sound controls cannot be overemphasized as most frauds could have been avoided with proper controls. We must also question an organization which fully resources the investigation of fraud while ignoring the control implications.

Unfortunately those charged with performing these investigations may have little incentive to push the control angle if it will result in less work being available for them. Key controls include:

Good recruitment procedures	Independent checks over work
Supervision	Regular staff meetings
System of management accounts	An employee code of conduct
Up-to-date accounts	Good management information systems
Clear lines of authority	Publicized policy on fraud
Controlled profit margins	Good documentation
Good staff discipline procedures	Financial procedures
Management trails	Good communications
Good controls over cash income	Segregation of duties
Stores/equipment control	Anti-corruption measures
Fraud hotline	Good all-round systems of control
Well-trained and alert management	

Fraud risk management is now a major issue and, under its consulting arm, internal audit may need to spend some time helping managers ensure that the risk of fraud is properly understood and mitigated wherever possible. Note that any such activity should be carried out in conjunction with the corporate anti-fraud policy.

7.6 Information Systems Auditing

We return to IIA Implementation Standard 2110.A2 which states that the internal audit activity should evaluate risk exposures relating to the organization's governance, operations and information systems regarding the:

- Reliability and integrity of financial and operational information.
- Effectiveness and efficiency of operations.
- Safeguarding of assets.
- Compliance with laws, regulations, and contracts.

The information systems auditor has a particular interest in item one—the reliability and integrity of financial and operational information. Meanwhile Practice Advisory 2100-2 goes on to say that: 'Internal auditors should periodically assess the organisation's information security practices and recommend, as appropriate, enhancements to, or implementation of, new controls and safeguards.' Complicated information systems have major implications for the internal auditor. Auditing around the computer described the traditional approach to auditing computer-based systems. This meant adjusting the usual audit approach without applying additional expertise in computerized applications. Another term was the black box approach where the computer was seen as a foreign object to be ignored by the auditor. Nowadays the audit response must take on board strategic changes in automation otherwise audit is left behind. One response is to define an audit role that specializes in reviewing computerized information systems as 'information systems (IS) audit' and this is the subject of this section. There are differing views of IS audit with many believing that all audit sections should employ specialist auditors. Others feel there is no such animal as the IS auditor since tackling computerized applications is part of everyday audit life. Computer audit tends to be known as information systems auditing, as we move from the idea of auditing computers to the view that we are helping to turn raw data into a reliable and secure platform for decision making, as in Figure 7.7.

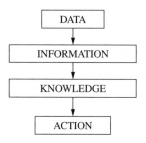

FIGURE 7.7   Control information.

Information Systems Risk

The risk of poor information systems and unreliable security and back-up arrangements leads to possible fraud, error, non-compliance with data protection rules, customer dissatisfaction and security breaches. Poor information systems can undermine an organization and its entire reputation may be at stake. The IIA.UK&Ireland's Information Technology Briefing Note Three covers Internet Security (A Guide for Internal Auditors) and suggests a number of IS risk areas:

Theft of proprietary information	Sabotage of data or networks
Eavesdropping	System penetration
Abuse of Internet access	Fraud
Denial of service	Spoofing
Viruses	

Meanwhile, a 2002 Computer Crime and Security Survey highlighted the growing problem of cybercrime:

Computer Crime continues to hit organizations hard, yet most don't report information security breaches to law enforcement, a recent U.S. survey reports. Ninety percent of the 503 U.S. organizations that responded have detected computer security breaches in the past

12 months and 80 percent acknowledged suffering financial losses, according to the seventh annual 'Computer Crime and Security Survey' conducted by the U.S. Federal Bureau of Investigation and the Computer Security Institute (CSI). The 44 percent of organizations that disclosed the amount of financial damage they suffered reported losses of $455.8 million. Last year, 85 percent of respondents detected computer crimes, and organizations lost $377.8 million, according to the 2001 survey.[8]

The Role of the IS Auditor

The role of audit in computerized information systems is vital to the continuing welfare of the organization. The high cost of investing in information technology in terms of set-up costs and its impact on achieving objectives results in an abundance of control implications. The biggest task may be to control this aspect of the organization and, if audit is kept out of these issues, its role will be relegated to minor matters only. The IS auditor may review a system (Figure 7.8), e.g. creditors, and must be able to bring into play important operational matters such as setting out terms of reference for the audit clearly:

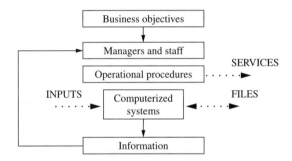

FIGURE 7.8   Business objectives and information systems.

- Start with the business objectives.
- Recognize that many controls are operational and interface with automated controls.
- Plan the computer auditor's work with this in mind.

IIA Implementation Standard 1210.A3 makes it clear that not all auditors will have specialist computing skills: 'Internal auditors should have general knowledge of key information technology risks and controls and available technology-based audit techniques. However, not all internal auditors are expected to have the expertise of an internal auditor whose primary responsibility is information technology auditing.'

There are several options for securing the necessary IS/IT skills for internal auditing:

- Use a consortium to provide the necessary skills.
- Use a small number of IS auditors (perhaps one computer expert) to assist the other auditors as they tackle computerized systems.
- Train general auditors in IS audit techniques.
- Rotate auditors between groups with one group specializing in computerized systems.
- Use consultants either to perform certain computer audit projects or to assist the general auditors.
- View computer audit as the audit of MIS and apply a wider base to computer audit projects covering managerial controls as well as computerized ones.

One model calls for the IS auditor's work to be interfaced with general auditor's work and there is a growing support for the development of all-round auditors with the requisite skills who are concerned that:

- The information should be clear, complete, relevant, consistent, sufficient, useful and timely.
- Information should be accurate and based on correct processing of data.
- Information should be secured and distributed according to defined criteria.
- It should be produced economically.
- It should be effective in meeting the objectives that have been established in the first place.
- There should be a process of continual review and adjustment.
- Someone should be responsible for the information and the above objectives.

The IS auditor will ideally have some expertise in areas such as:

- Systems development and projects.
- Computerized applications such as payroll, payments, income, performance reporting and so on.
- Information systems security standards.
- Computer assisted audit techniques.
- Systems development and project management.
- Disaster recovery and contingency planning.
- E-business and Internet design and security.
- Overall IS strategy.
- Data protection and legal requirements.
- Specialist technical areas such network management and database management systems.

Some of these areas are briefly covered below. One way of distinguishing the roles of general and IS auditors is by breaking down the audit universe as in Figure 7.9.

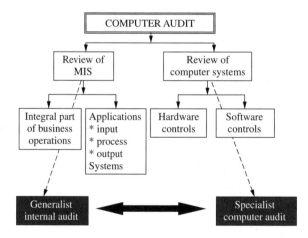

FIGURE 7.9 Analysing the computer audit approach.

Computerized systems affect the applied audit approach and there are many control features. General systems auditing can be used for any activity and depends on an understanding of the system being reviewed. As already mentioned, the IS audit role has moved towards the IS audit format and in one sense has moved closer to the general auditor's role as the two dimensions become increasingly blurred.

7.7 The Consulting Approach

Internal auditors have toyed with providing a form of internal consulting service for many years. The IIA standards now make it crystal clear that internal audit may provide consultancy as well as assurance work to an organization. The IIA's handbook on Implementing the Professional Practices Framework suggests six types of consulting work:

1. formal engagements—planned and written agreement.
2. informal engagement—routine information exchange and participation in projects, meetings etc.
3. emergency services—temporary help and special requests.
4. assessment services—information to management to help them make decisions, e.g. proposed new system or contractor.
5. facilitation services—for improvement, e.g. CSA, benchmarking, planning support.
6. remedial services—assume direct role to prevent or remediate a problem, e.g. training in risk management, internal control, compliance issues drafting policies.[9]

It is important to make clear exactly what constitutes consulting work since IIA Implementation Standard 1000.C1 says: 'The nature of consulting services should be defined in the charter.' One difficulty is type one consulting which consists of a formal engagement with a planned and written agreement. The IIA handbook series goes on to distinguish between optional consulting work and mandatory assurance services:

Assurance—adequacy of entity internal control, adequacy of process or sub-entity internal control, adequacy of ERM, adequacy of governance process, compliance with laws or regulations.

Consulting—improvement in efficiency or effectiveness, assistance in design of corrective actions, controls needed for new systems design, benchmarking.

A model of consulting investigations has been developed by the author and consists of a procedure involving ten basic steps as shown in Figure 7.10.

[1] INITIAL TERMS OF REFERENCE FOR THE WORK

[2] PRELIMINARY SURVEY

[3] ESTABLISH SUPPOSITIONS

[4] AUDIT PLANNING AND WORK PROGRAMME

[5] DETAILED FIELD WORK

[6] DETERMINE UNDERLYING CAUSES OF PROBLEMS

[7] DEFINE AND EVALUATE AVAILABLE OPTIONS

[8] TEST SELECTED OPTIONS

[9] DISCUSS WITH MANAGEMENT

[10] REPORT

FIGURE 7.10 Performing consulting investigations.

[1] Initial terms of reference for the work

- Key manager briefing and discussions on the review.
- Outline symptoms and main problem areas.
- Management success criteria established.
- Brief history of events relevant to the issue in hand documented.
- Indication of specific constraints acknowledged by management.
- Management policy on unacceptable solutions, e.g. staff cuts or major restructuring.
- Indication of future plans that management has set for short and medium terms.

We establish a framework for the exercise, scope of the review and an indication of management need.

[2] Preliminary survey

- Committee/board minutes that impact on the review.
- Brief discussions with staff to assess general consistency with key problems.
- Performance indicators.
- Analyse symptoms and capture 'what is really wrong'.
- Internal reports and budgets.
- Relevant published research that relates to the particular field of work.
- Visits to the location.

We define in detail the problem and establish outline suppositions based on these problems (i.e. a range of possible causes).

[3] Establish suppositions

- Effects of the problem on performance, quality and value for money.
- Materiality of the problem.
- Hierarchy of suppositions, the most significant ones first.
- Indications of how the suppositions may be tested to establish whether they are correct or not.
- Likely causes of problems (based around the suppositions).
- Overall extent of the problem.

We should agree with management what the problems are, their likely causes and how they will be tackled in the review.

[4] Audit planning and work programme

- Number of auditors required and time budgets.
- Levels and types of expertise required.
- Supervision of staff assigned to the project; how often and how this will be done.
- Guidance on testing.
- Review arrangements covering audit work as it is performed.
- Reporting arrangements.
- Programme of work (much will consist of research and testing).
- Time available and deadlines. For longer projects it is good practice to set milestones with defined products and progress review points.
- Administrative arrangements including travel, expenses, accommodation, computers, etc.

It is possible to set a clear progress checklist of underlying tasks and dates that can be monitored over the duration of the project.

[5] Detailed field work

- Programmed interviews.
- Available research that will have to be secured and taken on board.
- Re-performance of specific tasks if required.
- Independent expert opinion where appropriate.
- Inspection.
- Cause-and-effect analysis.
- Statistical analysis.
- Questionnaires.
- Construction of new performance indicators if required.
- Other specific testing routines.

The aim is to establish whether the original suppositions are correct. This means securing sufficient reliable evidence.

[6] Determine underlying causes of problems

- Detailed discussions with management.
- Review of managerial structures.
- Review of existing managerial practices.
- Determination of the extent of influence of the external environment.
- Level of managerial control and guidance available to staff.
- Establishing a clear relationship between problems and causes.
- Distinguishing between symptoms and these underlying causes.

We will find out why these problems arose in the first place without necessarily assigning blame.

[7] Define and evaluate available options

- Extensive research in isolating suitable options.
- Ideas from managers and staff.
- Textbook solutions can form a starting place.
- Model building.
- The application of creative thinking.
- Determination of relevant best practice elsewhere that is transferable.

The more options available the better, so long as they are feasible.

[8] Test selected options

- Defined benefits.
- Staff expertise available and required.
- Actual financial costs.
- Resource implications generally.

- Motivational aspects and impact on work flows.
- Timetable for implementation.
- Political aspects.
- Knock-on effects for other systems.
- Incremental improvements or the more risky 'big bang' approach.
- Overall impact on 'the problem'.
- Whether it complies with the fundamental 'rules' of successful change management.

We should remember that there is no 100% solution.

[9] Discuss with management

- Constraints that confront management, including practicalities.
- Agree factual content of report.
- Bear in mind the costs of the audit and the need to provide a defined benefit.
- Watch the psychology of negotiations—e.g. seek partial compromise where necessary.
- Keep in mind managerial objectives and their real success criteria.
- Consider level of work carried out and the extent to which we can be sure of our position.
- Consider overall acceptability of the audit work.

It is best practice to provide an oral presentation to top management where there are major implications from the review and the associated recommendations.

[10] Report

- Report needs to be formally cleared for final publication.
- It should ideally be an extension of the oral presentation.
- Make sure report is factually correct.
- All managerial input should be properly reflected.
- Report structure should be good and well written.

The required management action should be wholly clear and we would hope to have passed responsibility over to management and sold our ideas to them by the time the report is issued. A standard report structure may appear as Figure 7.11.

INTRODUCTION
the party commissioning the work
the fact that it is consultancy, the difference between VFM and systems

BACKGROUND TO THE OPERATION
this will normally include:
the main activities, brief history, previous reviews, main suppositions

MAIN FINDINGS
for each of the suppositions

RECOMMENDATIONS
options should be defined—stating, where appropriate, any quantified
savings and the effect on official budgets

APPENDICES
may consist of performance indicators

FIGURE 7.11   Standard report structure.

7.8 Compliance

Compliance is an issue for the internal auditor and during the audit an assessment will be made of the extent to which the business is adhering to laws, regulations and control standards. The Implementation Standard 2210.A2 confirms that: 'the internal auditor should consider the probability of significant errors, irregularities, noncompliance, and other exposures when developing the engagement objectives'. While compliance and issues relating to regularity and probity are generally incidental to the main audit objective in assessing significant risk and controls, there are times when internal audit may need to launch into an investigation into specific associated problems. In many developed countries a failure to demonstrate compliance with anti-money laundering can lead to the possible closure of the business, the seizure of assets or the revocation of operating licences. Some audit teams have compliance reviews built into their official terms of reference.

There are many banks, financial services companies, large retail outfits and other organizations that are either highly regulated or consist of hundreds of branded branches using the same basic operational and financial systems. The main worry from the board is that parts of the organizations are out of step with requirements and the internal audit team is charged with carrying out compliance reviews as a main way of tackling this high-level risk. Automated data analysis enables such audit teams to target high-risk areas of those with possible problems of non-adherence. However, the value-add proposition is that compliance reviews are the main thrust of the internal audit work. Management must establish operational procedures and suitable standards of financial management for all operations particularly for remote locations and decentralized activities. They must also check on the extent to which these standards are being applied. A formal programme of probity visits may be commissioned and effected, possibly on a spot-check basis. Internal audit would recommend that management makes these visits as part of the systems of control over these decentralized operations. It is not necessarily the primary role of internal audit to carry out these probity checks. It may be that the audit function is required to operate a series of compliance checks as part of their role in the organization. A procedure for carrying out probity audits is:

1. The work will be agreed with senior management and this may involve a one-off visit or a series of programmed visits.
2. The appropriate line manager should be contacted and a date set for the visit. It is possible to distribute an audit information brochure in advance of this visit.
3. It is possible to apply standardized documentation to this programmed audit work. Probity visits should not be allowed to consume excessive audit resources and the approach will be to apply junior staff wherever possible and work to tight budgets of up to, say, a week. This will depend on the type of audit.
4. Visits to remote establishments/operations should include:
   - A cash-up.
   - Vouching a sample of transactions from the banking arrangements.
   - Inventory checks covering all valuable and moveable items.
   - A check on a sample of local purchases and tests for compliance, integrity and effect on the cost centre.
   - A programme of tests applied to all areas that may be vulnerable to fraud or irregularity.
   - Verification of a sample of returns made to head office.
   - Other checks as required or agreed with management.
5. The work undertaken will have to meet the standards set out in the audit manual and any appropriate documentation, and report format should be agreed with the audit manager.

6. The standards of review should comply with the audit manual, and supervisory review and performance appraisal documents should be used by audit management.

7.9 Value for Money

Part of the scope of internal audit involves evaluating the adequacy and effectiveness of arrangements for securing value for money (VFM). These arrangements consist of controls that should be established by management to ensure that their objectives will be met, and are based on promoting the managerial control system. They should involve management in a continual search for efficiencies that may result in a level of savings. It is not internal audit's responsibility to identify these savings, and our performance measures should not include the amount of money saved through implementing audit recommendations. This point must be understood and may be restated in that we would expect our audit recommendations to place management in a position to identify areas where they may make savings. An example would be recommending that better information systems are installed. As part of our testing procedures we may be able to estimate any resultant savings, but this is not the primary role of the audit. Our duty is to get management to implement improvements in systems of control where required. It is possible to resource as part of our consultancy services VFM reviews that are designed to lead to savings for management. There are two views of VFM: VFM in its true sense is about the way management organizes and controls its resources to maximum effect. The narrow view sees VFM as ad hoc initiatives that result in defined savings and/or a greater level of service/output. VFM is about:

- **Economy:** resources required to perform the operation are acquired the most cost-effectively.
- **Efficiency:** resources are employed to maximize the resulting level of output.
- **Effectiveness:** final output represents the product that the operation was set up to produce.

For efficiency reviews a systems-based approach to an efficiency review would consider the standards, plans, direction and type of information that management applies to controlling their operations. The investigative approach, on the other hand, concentrates on specific methods by which efficiency may be improved. This may be by applying best practice in terms of alternative operational practices, or by isolating specific instances of waste and inefficiency that may be corrected. Economy (i.e. securing the cheapest inputs) is incorporated into the wider concept of efficiency because of the intimate link between these two. Efficiency covers basic matters of economy.

7.10 The 'Right' Structure

Once a clear audit strategy of risk-based assurance and consulting work is in place, audit management must then turn its attention to the way resources are organized. This will have a crucial effect on the delivery of audit services. Furthermore, there are many options underpinning the type of structure that should be in place, which have to be considered and decided on. Some of these options are:

- Decentralized.
- Centralized.
- Service-based.
- Client-based.

- Mixed structures.
- A project-based approach.
- Consultancy-based.
- Hierarchical structures.

Summary and Conclusions

The range and possibilities for the internal auditor in terms of the services and approaches to their work are vast. This chapter has touched on some of these approaches and considered the specific issues and nuances of each approach. Internal audit work can be broken down into assurance-based and consulting-based. A systems-based approach to assurance work can be related to reviewing higher-level systems such as the corporate governance system, the risk management system and the resulting systems of internal control. Moreover, assurance work can focus on various aspects of the control spectrum such as information systems, compliance issues, value for money and systems for protecting the corporate resource from fraud and abuse. Consulting work can also relate to each of the above areas, in that it can be geared to helping an organization set up its corporate governance arrangements including risk management and control. Consulting can also be used to drill down into these arrangements and can involve facilitating risk events and workshops.

Chapter 7: Multi-Choice Questions

Having worked through the chapter the following multi-choice questions may be attempted. (See Appendix A for suggested answer guide and Appendix B where you may record your score.)

1. **Which is the least appropriate item?**
   There is a number of concepts that underpin systems theory:
   a. Disconnected components.
   b. Affected by being in a system.
   c. Assembly of components does something.
   d. Assembly identified as being of special interest.

2. **Which is the most appropriate sentence?**
   a. CRSA is a management tool that the CAE wishes to apply to the audit process and the views of the corporate body.
   b. CRSA is both a management tool and audit technique depending on what the CAE wishes to apply to the audit process and the views of the corporate body.
   c. CRSA is an audit technique the CAE may wish to apply to the audit process and the views of the corporate body.
   d. CRSA is both a management tool and audit technique depending on what the CAE wishes to apply to the audit process.

3. **Which is the least appropriate sentence?**
   While in practice there are numerous types of CRSA events, we can suggest four basic approaches:
   a. Process. Here CRSA is used to review typical controls found in a business process with a view to checking whether the controls are robust and complied with.

    b. Projects. These CRSA events will be part of the standard risk assessment and preparation of risk registers that most project management methodologies recommend.

    c. People. Some CRSA workshops try to address incompetence issues as the main driver.

    d. Preparedness. This type of workshop is growing in popularity and consists of considering the types of risks that could impact the integrity of the corporate resource.

4. Insert the missing word(s):

The IIA define fraud as: 'Any illegal acts characterised by deceit, concealment or . . . .'.

    a. violence.

    b. violation of trust.

    c. fabrication.

    d. lying.

5. Which is the least appropriate sentence?

Fraud is an act of deceit to gain advantage or property of another with four main components:

    a. Motive. There should be a motive for the fraud.

    b. Attraction. The gain or advantage secured must have an attraction for the perpetrator.

    c. Opportunity. There must be adequate opportunity to justify the fraud.

    d. Concealment. In contrast to theft, fraud has an element of concealment.

6. Which is the least appropriate sentence?

In terms of fraud detection Practice Advisory 1210.A2-2 makes clear the difference between management and internal audit's roles:

    a. Management and the internal audit activity have differing roles with respect to fraud detection.

    b. Management has responsibility to establish and maintain an effective control system at a reasonable cost.

    c. A well-designed internal control system should not be conducive to fraud.

    d. Good internal auditors should have extensive expertise in forensic work.

7. Insert the missing words:

Computer audit tends to be known as . . . ., as we move from the idea of auditing computers to the view that we are helping to turn raw data into a reliable and secure platform for decision making.

    a. computer systems auditing.

    b. information systems auditing.

    c. information processing auditing.

    d. information technology auditing.

8. Which is the least appropriate sentence?

There are several options for securing the necessary IS/IT skills for internal auditing:

    a. Use a consortium to provide the necessary skills.

    b. Use a small number of IS auditors (perhaps one computer expert) to assist the other auditors as they tackle computerized systems.

    c. Train general auditors in IS audit techniques.

    d. Give audit work to staff from the organization's IS section.

9. Insert the missing words:

It is important to make clear exactly what constitutes consulting work since IIA Attribute Standard 1000.C1 says: 'The nature of consulting services should be defined in the . . . .'.

a. charter.

b. engagement terms.

c. audit manual.

d. audit committee report.

10. Which is the least appropriate item?

Furthermore, there are many options underpinning the type of structure that should be in place, which have to be considered and decided on. Some of these options are:

a. Decentralized or centralized.

b. Service-based or client-based.

c. Mixed structures or project-based approach.

d. Consultancy-based with no assurance work performed.

References

1. O'Connor, Joseph and McDermott, Ian (1997) *The Art of Systems Thinking*, Thorsons.
2. IIA, *Internal Auditing Alert*, May 1998, 'Validating CSA—a "how to" interview with James Roth'.
3. IIA, *Professional Practices Pamphlet*, 98-2, 'A perspective on control self-assessment'.
4. The White Paper, *Journal of The ACFE*, 2002 Report to the Nation—The Wells Report.
5. Whitehead, Mark 'Research into fraud points finger at middle managers'. *People Management*, 14 Jan. 1999.
6. 'Cybercrime Survey 2001', Confederation of British Industry, *Internal Auditing and Business Risk*, p. 20.
7. The White Paper, *Journal of The ACFE*, 2002 Report to the Nation—The Wells Report, 'CFES indicate fraud rate may be stable', p. 31.
8. McCollum, T. 'Cyber-crime still on the rise'. *Internal Auditing*—Loose, June 2002, pp. 16–17.
9. Anderson, Urton and Chapman, Christy (2002) 'The IIA Handbook Series' in *Implementing The Professional Practices Framework*, IIA, p. 21.

Chapter 8

SETTING AN AUDIT STRATEGY

Introduction

The previous chapters of *The Essential Handbook* have reflected the major challenges that face internal auditors as they seek to add value to their employers. The 'value add' proposition is a main driver for the audit services and choices need to be made in terms of what is delivered by internal audit and how this task is achieved. The IIA's Performance Standard 2000 (Managing the Internal Audit Activity) reinforces this concept by stating that: 'The CAE should effectively manage the internal audit activity to ensure it adds value to the organisation.' The most important factor in this equation is the audit strategy that is set to achieve added value. The CAE will succeed or fail on the basis of the adopted audit strategy. With this in mind we cover the following aspects of getting to a suitable audit strategy:

8.1 Risk-Based Strategic Planning

There are many reasons why a CAE would want to develop a formal audit strategy and clear objectives is the starting place for internal audit strategies. Directing resources towards accepted objectives sets the frame for success. The factors that impact on the process of setting clear audit objectives are noted in Figure 8.1.

There is no one way of defining audit objectives as they result from the changing influences of competing forces. This sounds straightforward but clarity of objectives is not always present. A discussion of scope creates an opportunity to agree on the important distinction between audit's role in contrast to management's. There are various forces that impact on the final model adopted. These range from the CAE's views, the needs of management and the type of staff employed.

FIGURE 8.1   Setting audit objectives.

The Corporate Risk Strategy

A cornerstone of audit strategy is the corporate assessment of business risk. This establishes an organization's control needs. A risk survey necessitates discussion with middle management and involves:

- A definition of the audit unit.
- An assessment of the relative risks inherent in each unit.
- Research into the type of problems units attract.
- Risk ranking related to resources subsequently assigned via an audit plan.

1. Risk assessment   We should construct a methodology that caters for different activities being associated with different types and levels of risk. IIA Performance Standard 2010 makes it clear that: 'The CAE should establish risk-based plans to determine the priorities of the internal audit activity, consistent with the organization's goals.' There is no universal formula but we need to ensure:

- The methodology is accepted by the organization.
- It is applied to the audit universe in a consistent fashion.
- It is based on the corporate risk assessment and ongoing operational risk reviews.

The organization would have to be broken down into auditable units and one approach in *Brink's Modern Internal Auditing* suggests three options for identifying audit units:

1. by function—accounting, purchasing payroll.
2. by transaction cycle—cash receipts, production.
3. by geography.[1]

2. Management participation   A further aspect of audit strategy relates to the need to involve management in the process. Management participation includes:

- Explaining that audit operates to a risk-based strategy.
- Ensuring that this strategy is based primarily on addressing organizational risk and control needs.
- Publicizing the link between risk and resource allocation.
- Keeping management informed as to changes to the existing strategies.
- Securing avenues whereby relevant information may be imparted to and from management.
- Clarifying the agreed cut-off points between management and internal audit's roles.
- Retaining a degree of independence that gives audit the final say in strategy and planning.

Successful Strategic Implementation

Strategic development is getting auditors to work together proactively to drive the audit service forward in the right direction. The need to rally round a clear goal is fundamental to the success of any strategy. A chain may be established by the CAE that represents the flow required for successful strategic implementation, as in Figure 8.2.

FIGURE 8.2   Successful strategic flow.

This is an important factor for audit management to acknowledge since it is based on strong leadership that drives a powerful message throughout the audit function.

8.2 Resourcing the Strategy

Resource management and human resource management (HRM) are major components of the strategic management process. The IIA Performance Standard 2030 makes it clear that: 'The CAE should ensure that internal audit resources are appropriate, sufficient, and effectively deployed to achieve the approved plan.' Audit management must ensure that HRM issues are adequately considered and dealt with. This sets the stage for defining management's role as one of managing (not performing) the audit work in larger audit shops. There are potential complications, since managers may find it hard to stop auditing and start managing. The fact that the type of work that auditors tend to handle can be very sensitive provides a convenient excuse for audit managers not to refer the work down to their staff. The position we need to reach is where audit managers appreciate the need to employ staff whom they can trust and rely on to discharge the audit role. They need to ensure the staff are properly developed and directed so that they are able to perform to accepted standards. The only way that this can be achieved is through the application of suitable HRM techniques. A further complication is that HRM matters must be set within the overall framework of the organization's own HRM policies. Audit management is restricted by the autonomy it has in the application of policies specific to internal audit. Having said this, everything that auditors do or fail to do is the direct responsibility of audit management and ultimately the CAE. Practice Advisory 2000–1 on managing the internal audit activity provides more detail and recommends that: 'The CAE is responsible for properly managing the internal audit activity so that: Audit work fulfils the general purposes and responsibilities described in the charter, approved by senior management and the board. Resources of the internal audit activity are efficiently and effectively employed. Audit work conforms to the IIA Standards.'

8.3 Managing Performance

Staff appraisal is a management control that audit would tend to recommend when undertaking an audit where staffing is included in the terms of reference for the work. As such one may argue that we, as auditors, should apply this technique to the management of the internal audit function. However, staff appraisal schemes can be positive motivators or complete demotivators depending on how they are designed and implemented. The theory of staff appraisals is based on telling people what is expected of them and then telling them how far they are achieving these standards, as a way of motivating them. The other benefit is the positive steps that may be taken where performance is not on par. Appraisal schemes also underpin career development programmes that again may be used to direct the activities of staff and ensure there is good progression so that good staff are retained and poor staff improved. This may be illustrated by a simple diagram in Figure 8.3.

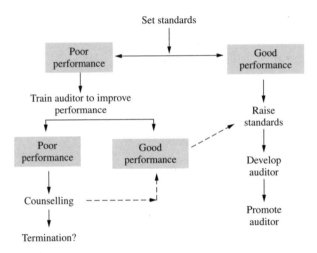

FIGURE 8.3   The auditor appraisal process.

An alternative approach to the appraisal process is to separate performance appraisal from procedures for dealing with unacceptable poor performance and particular problems. The latter would come into operation where there are obvious flaws in performance which cannot be addressed through traditional training and development programmes. Figure 8.3 is based on the organization distinguishing between different management procedures for dealing with a variety of performance-related issues. As such where the auditor breaches procedure, this is dealt with through the disciplinary procedure. Where the employee is often sick the frequent sickness procedure comes into action; and poor performance is handled by special action that may result in dismissal of the auditor in question. In this way the performance appraisal scheme can be operated in a positive mode at all times. Special staffing problems are handled by distinct and separate arrangements outside performance appraisal. Special attention will be directed towards the auditor and this will not wait for or be dependent on the performance appraisal programme. In this way these types of problems can be fast-tracked before they get out of hand. Meanwhile the appraisal scheme may continue in its positive mode. The words 'performance, development, advancement, excellence and quality' may each promote a positive environment. The counterargument is that this positive environment has to be firmly in place before any performance appraisal can be planned. Whatever the view, it is essential that auditors are appraised in a positive fashion. This in turn depends on:

1. Keeping the accent on praise.
2. Not using the appraisal scheme to criticize but using it to develop.
3. Using performance appraisal to engender good communications and listening skills.
4. Seeking to promote a win/win environment where all sides gain.

It is possible to set performance targets for each auditor based around the annual/quarterly plans. This will be based on completing defined audits, keeping within budgets, performing special tasks such as the audit manual and achieving a percentage of chargeable to non-chargeable hours. Where these targets flow from the overall organizational/departmental targets, a form of management by achievement ensues and hierarchies may be developed so that goals cascade downwards. Examples of some specific and team and overall unit performance targets may be listed:

- Absenteeism rate.
- Amount of alteration as a result of management review.
- Currency of time-monitoring information.
- Currency of timesheets submitted and authorized.
- Degree to which auditors keep within the budget hours for each audit.
- Extent of audit automation.
- Extent to which audit objectives have been met.
- Extent to which desks are kept clear.
- Extent to which developmental plans have been achieved.
- Extent to which files hold all relevant information.
- Extent to which follow-up audits find that recommendations from previous reports have been implemented.
- Extent to which the annual and quarterly plan has been achieved.
- Extent to which work plan has been completed.
- Level of absences from work.
- Level of audits within time budget.
- Level of complaints.
- Level of compliance with the audit manual.
- Level of draft reports requiring rewrites.
- Level of involvement of auditee in the audit terms of reference.
- Level of managerial agreement to audit risk criteria.
- Level of positive comments from clients via satisfaction questionnaire.
- Level of problems found during work reviews.
- Level of recoverable hours to non-recoverable hours charged in the period.
- Level of satisfaction from the clients.
- Level of staff grievances against management.
- Level of suggestions from audit staff to audit management.
- Number of aborted audits.
- Number of audit reports issued.
- Number of auditors passing professional exams.
- Number of audits completed on time.
- Number of audits delegated by the audit manager.
- Number of improvements to the audit manual.

- Number of recommendations agreed.
- Rate of production of audit products.
- Regularity of group and departmental meetings.
- Staff turnover.
- The percentage of recoverable hours charged.
- The percentage of staff with poor timekeeping.
- Time taken by auditors to get access to audit management.
- Time taken to find specific files.
- Time taken to issue audit reports after completion of the audit.
- Time taken to respond to management requests for assistance.

Productivity is a fairly simple concept that suggests inputs produce outputs via a suitably controlled process. One measure of the effectiveness of this control is to set standards for the output, based on the defined level of inputs. These standards become targets and so long as mechanisms for measuring the work have been installed, productivity can be assessed in terms of the extent to which these targets have been achieved. Career development uses performance measures as one way of measuring the way the auditor is developing and productivity factors are one feature of such a system. In this way audit management may gauge an auditor's progress through quantifiable factors as well as more subjective considerations. We must always appreciate the limitations of productivity measures, which may appear scientific, but are based on underlying (and subjective) principles that have been agreed by management. The only real feature is that they may promote a degree of consistency across staff if they are applied in a systematic fashion. They may also provide a sense of direction for development plans by highlighting some of the targets towards which we are seeking to develop staff. The standard SMART test applied to target setting is based on the following model (subject to variations):

S:	**S**pecific
M:	**M**easurable
A:	**A**chievable
R:	**R**esults oriented
T:	**T**ime based

8.4 Dealing with Typical Problems

Perfection is impossible to achieve although inefficiency should be contained within acceptable levels and controlled. Audit management is responsible for developing strategies for resolving problems in internal audit. Turning a blind eye to poor practices and not demanding relevant control information are practices that impair good service delivery and some of the typical problems include:

- Excess hours charged.
- Inadequate working papers.
- No follow-up procedure.
- Low pay.
- Inadequate audit manual.
- Poor planning.
- Inadequate supervision.
- Lack of continuing professional education.

- No career development.
- Reporting delays.
- Lack of professionalism.
- Financial emphasis.
- Performing line functions.
- No defined approach.

8.5 The Audit Manual

The topic of audit manuals touches upon a number of subsidiary issues including standardization, procedures, controlling creativity and audit approaches, and underpins professional standards for delivering the adopted audit strategy. *Brink's Modern Internal Auditing* has described the role of the audit manual: 'Audits need to be managed, and the best tool for audit management is an audit manual. An internal audit manual is an in house guide to the contents of an audit; it is a reference book which can be consulted when an audit question arises.'[2]

This section brings together the main topics that should be dealt with via the audit manual as well as discussing some models that help illustrate this all-important technique.

The Role of the Audit Manual

It is necessary to establish the role and objectives of the audit manual before considering appropriate models. Publications on internal audit procedures and performance bear on the topic and so a wide range of material has been considered. The IIA Practice Advisory 2330–1 addresses the need to record information and comments that: 'The CAE should establish working paper policies for the various types of engagements performed. Standardised engagement working papers such as questionnaire and audit programs may improve the efficiency of an engagement and facilitate the delegation of engagement work.' Our definition of the audit manual is:

> A device that involves the accumulation and dissemination of all those documents, guidance, direction and instructions issued by audit management that affect the way the audit service is delivered.

The manual is a mechanism for channelling guidance for the auditor. The available material provides comments from many different sources and will give insight into the various issues that surround the design and implementation of audit manuals. Manuals fulfil the following roles:

- Defining standards and methods of work.
- Communicating this to auditors.
- Establishing a base from which to measure the expected standards of performance.

Standardized Forms

One issue is the concept of standardized documentation and the associated role of the audit manual. Before we touch on the topic of standard forms it should be clearly established that our definition of audit manuals is as a managerial vehicle for directing auditors. This means that standardized procedures form part of the formal standards that have to be achieved. To have documentation standards as ad hoc forms without co-ordinating them as a manual will necessarily cause inconsistency and inefficiencies in their application. There is an abundance of material on the advantages of standardization and a number of features can be highlighted:

1. The most familiar standardized procedures are in the form of internal control questionnaires and audit programmes that are developed by many audit departments.
2. Flowcharts should follow a uniform pattern that should be consistently applied throughout the audit department.
3. Standardization leads to consistency and report writing can have a 'house style.'
4. Standardization can lead to auditors giving less attention to format and procedures and more attention to the actual objectives of the task at hand.
5. Standardization can constitute a vital control over each audit assignment that stops people from drifting aimlessly if the audit objectives are not held in mind.

The position we have reached in defining a model audit manual is that all moves to standardize procedures should be channelled through the audit manual. This might be the biggest single benefit from resourcing the implementation of a comprehensive and up-to-date manual. Lastly the task of progressing an audit automation strategy depends largely on having standardized procedures that might be automated and a formal vehicle for implementing these procedures, i.e. an audit manual.

Audit Approach and Methodology

We are concerned with the manual as a projection of the audit personality or the voice of the director of auditing on the basis that, in practice, auditing can be performed in a variety of ways. The IIA standards recognize this issue and have framed their requirements in a generalized way with two main implications. First, differences in audit approaches and methodology are seen as inevitable and second, it is not enough simply to declare that a certain set of standards is being adopted. The precise audit philosophy must be agreed and documented for application throughout the audit department. The point that we are moving towards is that experienced as well as new auditors need firm direction on what is expected from them in terms of discharging the particular audit role. In this respect, the audit manual is the ideal device for placing the agreed solution on record. Each audit department must offer a defined product that is the result of the 'contract' struck between audit and the organization. The ability to engage in less structured activities and move freely from project to project can be developed with a carefully thought-out methodology. This may be set out in the audit manual but not from the generalized set of audit procedures found in audit textbooks.

Impact on Creativity

There appears to be a direct conflict between the extent of direction and standardization that a comprehensive audit manual provides, and the auditor's professional autonomy. Both are essential for enhancing audit productivity. This conflict is akin to the perennial problem of reconciling managerial control and autonomy, where autonomy is defined as the freedom to succeed or fail. Auditors cannot perform if they are unclear as to what is considered successful performance while at the same time little commitment can be achieved within a bureaucratic straitjacket. Audit manuals must recognize this inherent conflict. There is a contradiction in the underlying objectives of the manual in providing direction throughout the audit function, and the need to maintain professional autonomy. The greater the degree of guidance provided, the more the auditor's efforts are restricted by standardized audit procedures. It is necessary to reconcile the two opposing forces of autonomy and control. The model in Figure 8.4 sets out the relationship between these two main factors.

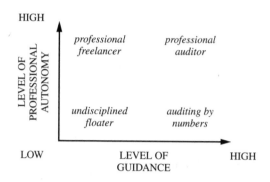

FIGURE 8.4   Autonomy versus control.

The point that we must arrive at is where auditors retain their professional flair and imagination but direct effort in the way that is required by the chief internal auditor, in line with the existing audit strategy and organizational culture. In this way we would move towards the target position shown in the far right-hand corner of Figure 8.4 by developing the 'professional auditor':

1. Ensure that more comprehensive guidance is only provided where it is required.
2. Leave general reference material outside the main audit manual.
3. Indicate whether a particular procedure is optional.
4. Explain why a procedure has been selected.
5. Allow departures as long as they are documented and justified.
6. Encourage all auditors to participate in improving the manual and consider rotating the task of maintaining it.
7. Do not appoint an auditor until the approach and standards are explained and he/she can work within them.
8. Where a requirement in the manual has been overridden consider whether an amendment is required.
9. Ensure that auditors who refuse to perform to the requirements of the manual are moved out of the audit department.
10. Test each section that is drafted to ensure that it is not unnecessarily cumbersome and bureaucratic.
11. Watch out for auditors who appear demotivated and investigate underlying reasons.
12. Ensure that there is a continuous programme to search for and amend all faults.

Structuring the Audit Manual

As with other features of a manual the structure and content depend on the particular circumstances, although it is possible to set out a four-tier model for structuring the manual in Figure 8.5.

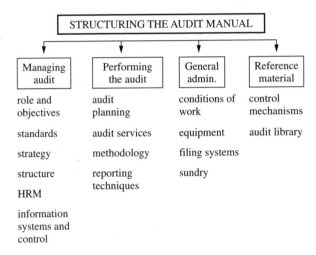

FIGURE 8.5   Structuring the manual.

1. It is generally better to have a few main sections as with the model in Figure 8.5 so as to generate some degree of form and structure.
2. Keep basic reference material outside the audit manual.
3. Maintain an extensive up-to-date audit library and cross-reference this to the audit manual.
4. Ensure that all the topics mentioned in Figure 8.5 are fully dealt with in the manual so as to promote a complete and worthwhile document.

Note that the relevant material may be held on CD, laptop or the corporate network.

8.6 Delegating Audit Work

Audit management should delegate work to more junior staff. This can be a powerful way of not only increasing overall efficiency, but also developing auditors. There are pros and cons, although delegation needs to be understood and controlled. The delegation process involves conferring authority to perform defined tasks. Overall responsibility remains with management, which is accountable for the outcome. One view of delegation is shown in Figure 8.6.

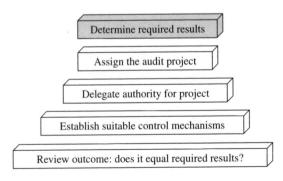

FIGURE 8.6   The delegation process.

Delegation in Internal Audit

We differentiate technical and practical delegation. In technical delegation the CAE is ultimately responsible for the activities of the internal audit department. Audit managers are likewise responsible for the activities of staff under their control. Delegation allows auditors to perform day-to-day work unimpeded, around audit plans where each internal auditor has defined responsibilities. A restricted definition of delegation is when what are normally management tasks are given to auditors in addition to, or in place of, their normal workload. These extra and more demanding tasks/projects must be carefully controlled. An example is the audit manual whose maintenance is the responsibility of the CAE but may be assigned to an experienced auditor. Other examples are:

Audit brochures	Marketing logos and web-based material
The annual report	Client presentations
Special projects	Internal reviews of audit files
Quality assurance programmes	The audit charter
Auditing standards	Staff training and development

Delegation is not abrogation of responsibilities. The CAE must be involved in matters that have a major impact on the audit services and delegation must be used with care. This includes sensitive topics such as confidential audit marketing plans, managing the audit budget, auditor discipline, the audit committee, material complaints against auditors and reviews of audit strategy. Advantages are the positive effect on staff and getting work done. Key benefits are:

- Auditors may be able to do a better job than their managers.
- Auditors themselves learn to delegate.
- New ideas may be generated.
- It acts as a communication device between managers and staff.
- It promotes trust across the internal audit department.

Delegation forces management to set clear objectives and define scope. Senior auditors may spend hours on an obscure project that provides no end product. Delegation creates the drive for the audit manager to define and communicate exactly what is to be achieved. It must be based on trust between parties each with differing needs, as in Table 8.1.

TABLE 8.1   Manager/subordinate requirements.

Manager	Subordinate
Wants good results	Enjoys the challenge
Wants to look good	May make mistakes
Wants to save time	Needs support
Wants no problems	Wants it to work out

The audit manager must allow mistakes and this is part of letting go of some managerial authority. Management should reward increased performance in taking on more difficult work. Delegation stimulates enhanced performance through opportunities provided. Problems result where additional pressures create stress and lower the auditor's ability to live up to the challenge.

It is better to use the extra effort to accelerate progress of the auditor's career development, which is why a policy on internal promotions can be useful. There must be real benefits.

8.7 Audit Information Systems

The computer has major implications for audit work. Effects range from impact on the audit field to the way audit work is performed to how audit itself uses computers to improve productivity. This section provides an introduction to the impact of computers in developing internal auditing strategy (Figure 8.7).

FIGURE 8.7   Impact of information.

Management should be undertaking a constant search for ways that information technology (IT) can be used to improve the audit service. This may mean employing computer personnel to promote IT skills through the department. An information systems strategy should be developed to ensure that efficient information systems are developed to support the overall audit strategy. The strategy should also be geared into developing overall computer literacy so that auditors may be confident in the way they approach automated systems. This may allow a step into computer audit whereby advanced computing skills may eventually be acquired. Public systems such as the Internet may be accessed and form an almost limitless database of reference information. In-house information databases may be built up over time as a complement to the audit library. In fact, it is difficult to explain how an audit department could prioritize systems-based auditing without developing a database on available control mechanisms. Direct information links between the auditor and the audit office can arise via the PC laptops, which can send files to the audit manager for review. It is then possible to promote the freelancing auditor whose motto is 'Have laptop; will travel.' Furthermore time-monitoring systems can account for audit hours and be linked into a planning and control system. In addition they can be used as a billing and accounting system.

Time Monitoring Systems

Time management systems will tend to feature in most internal audit units and this will be an important information-based system. This should enable audit management to receive regular reports on the way their staff are working. It will be used to support performance measures that relate to a variety of performance targets that would ideally have been set for both auditors and audit teams. They should cover each of the defined information needs that derive from the management of audit time. This will involve periodic reports as well as specially requested items. The reports should revolve around the time frame, types of work, auditors, audit groups and the entire audit unit. As such it should report on:

- Time spent on audits.
- Audits over budget.
- Non-recoverable time charged (such as training).
- Breakdown between assurance work and consultancy engagements.
- Audits that should have been completed.
- And so on.

The inputs of a suitable time monitoring system may be illustrated in Figure 8.8.

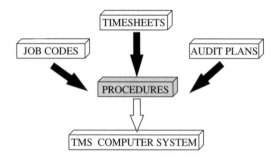

FIGURE 8.8   Time monitoring system inputs.

The various roles of time management information should be duly recognized and catered for. Here we would expect any such systems to cover the following functions:

1. A method of charging time to specific audit jobs.
2. A way of identifying variances from planned to actual hours though incorporating budgeted hours to each chargeable job.
3. A method of charging clients for work carried out and generating the supporting schedules and covering invoice if needs be. Accordingly, it is important to identify a client for each job that is set up on the system.
4. A method of establishing the status of each job. Suitable booknote messages may be used in any good system to compile a form of database of audit jobs, which will provide summary information. This may range from terms of reference, assigned auditor, special features, stage indicators (say planning, field work or reporting) and so on.

The time management system will typically be a computerized package that performs the function of recording and reporting auditors' time. There are three main components that must enter the system for it to work. This is the auditor's weekly timesheet, the job coding (and clients) and the planned hours. This may be illustrated in Figure 8.9.

As such it is not just a matter of buying a time management system and installing it on a PC or network. The underlying procedures must be carefully thought through and addressed before a suitable reporting system can come on-line and be of any use to audit management. Building

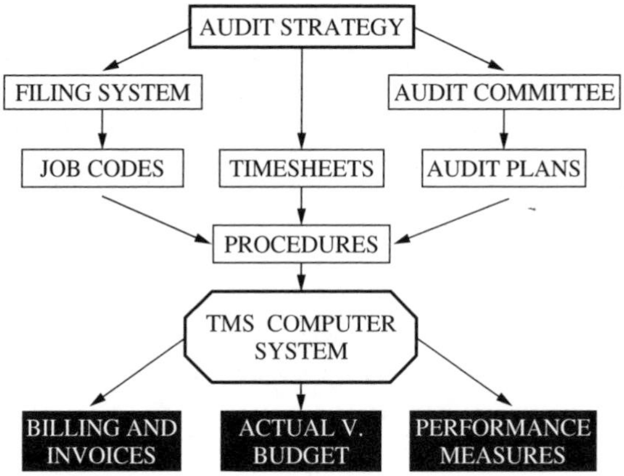

FIGURE 8.9   The audit time monitoring system.

on the point mentioned above, it is as well to resource any time management work as a proper systems development project. Here the task is not just left to the audit administration officer but is assigned a high profile and given the status of a formal computer project. To this end, for larger audit units, we may designate the following key officers:

- A systems controller.
- A systems manager.
- The data owner.

Time management should be a regular feature of audit management meetings and a key concern of the CAE. We have suggested that the job code structure is seen as a separate consideration before the computer system is established. Ideally this should reflect the way the systems-based approach and investigations role are perceived in terms of audit work and audit consultancy respectively. Any coding system must be based on clear rules which will vary between different audit sections. We may, however, make some general observations:

1. Code the work in line with the adopted reporting framework. The audit committee may have a view on this. In this way we may secure reports that feed naturally into our monthly, quarterly and annual reporting structures.
2. Do not allow auditors to set up individual codes for small jobs that will mean the system becomes overloaded. A general code of 'advice and information' may be used to record these one-off tasks. We may set a time standard and require jobs under, say, one or two days' long to go to this code. If this approach is adopted it is important that timesheets record full details of the work and are retained for later review, if there is a query from the client.
3. Following this line it is as well to have small number of fixed codes for non-recoverable (or non-chargeable) time such as annual leave, training, sickness and so on.
4. Have strict rules on who can set up codes and budget hours. This should be restricted to senior staff (say audit manager or the CAE in smaller audit units).
5. Activity reports should be checked by the audit managers on a regular basis.

We may set out an example of a coding structure where systems and investigations work have been separated (Table 8.2).

Managers rely on the progressive use of information technology and this means more computerization. This is also true for the internal audit department and suitable standards must

TABLE 8.2 Job coding system.

Description	Job code range
Recoverable	
A. Assurances—systems	
1. Corporate and operational	1,001 — 1,500
2. Financial systems	1,501 — 2,000
3. Systems development	2,001 — 2,500
4. Computer audits	2,501 — 3,000
5. Risk management	3,001 — 3,500
B. Assurances—investigations	
1. Management investigations	3,501 — 4,500
2. General probity audits	4,501 — 5,500
3. Fraud investigations	5,501 — 6,500
4. Other investigations	6,501 — 7,000
C. Consultancy services	7,001 — 8,000
D. Audit professional advice	(8,001 – 8,020)
1. Department A	8,001
2. Department B	8,002
3. Department C, etc.	8,003
E. Non-recoverable	(8,021 – 8,041)
General management	8,021
Audit admin.	8,022
Audit strategy, plans and risk appraisal	8,023
Activity reports	8,024
Client relations and marketing	8,025
Audit meetings	8,026
IT strategy and enhancements	8,027
Seminars, etc.	8,028
Professional training	8,029
IT training	8,030
Non-audit training	8,031
Other training	8,032
Delivery of training	8,033
Staffing issues	8,034
Recruitment of auditors	8,035
Performance appraisal	8,036
Audit manual, procedures and quality assurance	8,037
Audit library	8,038
Liaison with external audit	8,039
Non-audit work	8,040
Other	8,041
F. Absences	(8,042 – 8,049)
Annual leave	8,042
Sick leave—certificated	8,043
Sick leave—uncertificated	8,044
Hospital, doctor and dentist	8,045
Bank holidays	8,046
Special leave	8,047
Unauthorized absences	8,048
Miscellaneous	8,049

be applied to controlling these developments in line with organizational policies. Automation is a fact of life and the audit department must have the same level of controls that it expects from the departments it audits.

8.8 Establishing a New Internal Audit Shop

Legislation and/or internal pressures can lead to a demand for internal audit where this has not existed before. Calls for enhanced corporate governance can make secure systems of control an organizational issue to be addressed through establishing an audit committee. Research has shown that the audit committee, even where primarily concerned with external audit, will mature and concentrate more on internal audit. The situation where a newly formed internal audit function has to be developed is not unusual and we cover this. Issues include:

1. The audit charter   This sets out the role and objectives of internal audit and is at the core of the delivery of audit services.

2. Audit standards   The CAE has to decide on two types of standards before the new audit function can be developed—professional and operational standards.

3. The code of conduct   Another consideration when setting up a new audit service is whether to set standards of conduct before recruiting staff.

4. Recruitment and selection   It is essential that the 'rounded person' is acquired with a whole package of attributes. Training can only go so far, and we are not talking only about formal qualifications and experience.

5. Training   A training budget is essential for the newly formed internal audit unit.

6. The business risk assessment   This is an important part of the development of a new audit function.

7. Information systems (IS) audit   One matter that should be high on the agenda for the CAE when designing the new internal audit service relates to IS audit.

8. Fraud work   There is a need to define a clear policy on the detection and investigation of fraud and irregularities.

9. Business planning   The new CAE should devise and publish a business plan that covers the internal audit unit.

10. Assurance and consulting services   One question to be tackled early on in the life of the newly formed unit is related to the type of services that will be provided by internal audit. It is incumbent upon the CAE to decide the best way to discharge the audit role and which services will be provided and to which degree. It is possible to break down the audit role into two:

1. Risk-based assurance-based audit of all services: financial, operational, strategic and auto-mated systems.
2. Consultancy projects requested by management into regularity, compliance, VFM, management development and others.

11. Budgets   While the CAE must seek to negotiate an adequate budget, there is little scope to secure extensive funding at the outset.

12. The launch of the new service   The new service must be introduced to the organization. All the well-known devices that this entails should be applied.

13. The audit manual   Most of the matters mentioned above will be documented in a section of the audit manual and there is nothing wrong with allowing this document to grow as the audit unit develops.

8.9 The Outsourcing Approach

The internal audit strategy tells the organization what it will get from its in-house audit team. Progressive management knows what it can get from its audit shop and has very demanding expectations. Where the in-house team cannot meet these expectations without help from outsiders, then the outsourcing question rises. The IIA recognize that internal auditing may be provided through a variety of different arrangements. Their glossary contains reference to the external sourcing and says that an external service provider is:

> A person or firm, independent of the organization, who has special knowledge, skill, and experience in a particular discipline. Outside service providers include, among others, actuaries, accountants, appraisers, environmental specialists, fraud investigators, lawyers, engineers geologists, security specialists, statisticians, information technology specialists, external auditors, and other auditing organizations. The board, senior management, or the CAE may engage an outside service provider.

The IIA has also provided a perspective on outsourcing of the internal audit function, and selected extracts are summarized below:

> Research shows that effective internal auditing departments are interwoven into the fabric of their organizations. The work of these departments is integral to the efforts of management. The effectiveness of internal auditing begins with a vision statement, which is based on and linked to the overall organizational vision, and is implemented through a strategic plan. An internal auditing department with vision is:
>
> - **Proactive:** It establishes itself as a change agent throughout the organization. It identifies new initiatives to add value to the organization while retaining a clear focus on traditional audit areas such as internal control exposure and potential ethical issues.
> - **Innovative:** The innovative internal auditing department searches out the most valuable use of its resources, questions the value of routine audits, and creates opportunities to increase the value of the function. The department invests in technology, people, and the organization and partners with an external provider if it enhances the value of its services.
> - **Focused:** Auditing must be responsive to the organization it serves. It must understand and focus on management and audit committee priorities.
> - **Motivated:** A motivated auditing staff has a sense of mission, teamwork, and organizational pride. They are open to constructive suggestions and seek input on continuous improvement. They measure user satisfaction and are not resistant to change.
> - **Integrated:** Technology should be used to enhance audit productivity and teamwork. Investments should be made in technology that will assist the organization in continuous monitoring of transactions and identifying potential fraudulent transactions.

Many of the above attributes are obtained with a strong department housed within the organization. External providers may also rank highly on all of these attributes. It is up to management, the audit committee, and the board to assess the various factors and choose the right vision for their organization.[3]

The challenge has been set. Standards have been published that are miles away from the sleepy image of past day audit teams that churned out reams of mindless reports that were ignored or just tolerated. While this drive has lifted the audit profile immensely, it has also raised the bar and created a potential stumbling block for those who have not positioned themselves properly. Outsourcing, co-sourcing and partnering are always options either as part of the internal audit strategy or because of failure of the strategy to make a mark. Using outsiders has to be managed properly and selected extracts from Practice Advisory 1210.A1-1 (Obtaining Services to Support the Internal Audit Activity, make several suggestions in this respect:

> The IA activity should have employees or use outside service providers who are qualified in disciplines such as accounting, auditing economics, finance, statistics, IT, engineering, taxation, law, environmental affairs etc.... each member need not be qualified in all disciplines. An outside service provider may be engaged by the board, senior management or the CAE. Service provider used in (for example)—IT, valuations, physical conditions, measurement, fraud, actuaries, interpretation of laws/regulations, mergers, evaluating the internal audit quality assurance program. CAE should assess the competence, independence and objectivity of the outside service provider. The CAE should assess relationship with IA and the organization to ensure independence and objectivity. If it involves the external auditor—make sure the work does not impair the external auditor's independence. CAE should review with the service provider:
>
> * objectives and scope of work.
> * matters in engagement communication.
> * access issues.
> * procedures to be employed.
> * ownership of working papers.
> * confidentiality issues.

8.10 The Audit Planning Process

Planning is fundamental to successful auditing and should involve the client in defining areas for review via the assessment of relative risk. Long-term planning allocates scarce audit resources to the huge audit universe and it is impossible to audit everything. Auditors must be seen to be doing important work. The worst-case scenario is where they are unable to perform sensitive high-level investigations on management's behalf while at the same time appearing to be involved in routine low-level checking in insignificant parts of the organization. A professional audit service tends to rely more on senior auditors tackling serious high risk issues. Overall planning allows the audit to be part of a carefully thought-out system. This ensures that all planned work is of high priority and that audit resources are used in the best possible way. The main steps in the overall planning process are found in Figure 8.10.

Some explanations follow:

* **Organizational objectives.** The starting place for audit planning must be in the objectives of the organization. If these objectives are based on devolution of corporate services to business units, then the audit mission must also be so derived. Management must clarify goals

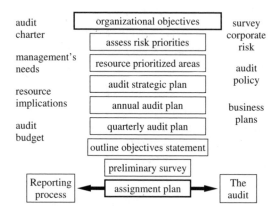

FIGURE 8.10   The planning process.

and aspirations before plans can be formulated and this feedback can be achieved by active liaison and communication.

- **Assess risk priorities.** The relative risks of each audit area must be identified, with reference to the corporate risk database.
- **Resource prioritized areas.** Suitable resources for these areas must be provided.
- **Audit strategic plan.** A plan to reconcile workload with existing resources should be developed. This should take on board the various constraints and opportunities that are influential now and in the future. The strategic plan takes us from where we are to where we wish to be over a defined time frame, having due regard for the audit budget.
- **Annual audit plan.** A formal audit plan for the year ahead is expected by most audit committees.
- **Quarterly audit plan.** A quarterly plan can be derived from the annual plan. Most organizations experience constant change making the quarter a suitable time-slot for supportive work programmes.
- **Outline objectives statement.** Audit management can make a one-line statement of expectations from an audit from work done so far in the planning process.
- **Preliminary survey.** Background research requires thought on key areas to be covered in an audit. This ranges from a quick look at previous files and a conversation with an operational manager to formal processes of many days of background work involving a full assessment of local business risks.
- **Assignment plan.** We can now draft an assignment plan with formal terms of reference, including budgets, due dates and an audit programme.
- **The audit.** Progress should be monitored with all matters in the terms of reference considered.
- **The reporting process.** Planning feeds naturally into reporting so long as we have made proper reference to our plans throughout the course of the audit.

Audit plans will then flow naturally from the organization's strategic direction while the underlying process should be flexible and, as strategies alter, planned reviews be reassessed. The flow of planning components should be kept in mind as we consider each aspect of audit planning. The internal audit world has and will continue to change at a pace that many find uncomfortable. New demands create new challenges for the CAE. Audit planning is one area where we need to respond in a positive and dynamic manner. The well known approach to planning audit work involves defining a risk index consisting of appropriate factors (e.g. materiality, impact on reputation, state of control risk and management requests). These are applied to the defined audit universe (all systems within the organization) to produce a risk-assessed plan of work for the next three to five years. A summary will look like this:

FACTOR	SCORE	WEIGHT?
Materiality (how big is the system?)	1–10	
Impact on reputation (does it matter?)	1–10	
State of control (anything going wrong?)	1–10	
Management (have they asked for help?)	1–10	
Score for the system	4–40	

So high-scoring audits receive early attention, although we may look at everything on a cyclical basis over the three years. We may also perform detailed transactions-testing of key financial systems through the year. A more advanced method revolves around the corporate governance framework. Here we concentrate audit resources on key areas such as:

- Boardroom arrangements and accountabilities.
- Remunerations committee.
- The role and impact of audit committee.
- The impact of NEDs on the board accountability.
- Factors that encourage financial misreporting.
- Reliability of audit committee and external audit coverage (and independence).
- Control framework in use.
- Reporting on internal controls.
- Risk assessment and risk management arrangements.
- Ethical standards and staff awareness.
- Anti-fraud policies and whistleblowing arrangements.
- Project management (including change programmes).
- Control activities—and performance management.
- Information systems (security and integrity).
- Communications—across and up/down the organization.
- Control assurance reporting—and underlying evidence such as CRSA.
- Control environment—and ethics and tone at the top.
- Compliance teams and routines. Fraud policies and security.
- Accreditation systems such as ISO 9000, EFQM, IiP.
- HR policies such as staff training, competencies, vetting and learning programmes.
- Financial systems and validation routines by financial controller.

In this way the internal auditor seeks to 'quality assure' the governance framework established by the board. It takes a hands-off approach and seeks to review whether the above high-level systems are in place and are working for the year in question to promote good corporate governance. An alternative audit planning process may be based on a risk-based approach where we promote risk assessment and review areas of particular concern. This would involve:

- Corporate board level risk assessment—identify and classify key risks (top ten risk policy).
- Risk management—assign these risks to responsible managers and ensure they establish a risk management framework (avoid, accept, transfer, insure, contingency plans and/or controls).
- Operational level CRSA programmes—where risks are identified and associated controls reviewed by work groups (for action planning).

- Discussion—talk to management about their risk assessment and key controls that they are dependent on.
- Risk database—prepare a risk database and isolate areas of high risk and controls that are crucial to business success, based on the organization's risk management process in operation.
- Discuss the results with the audit committee and allow corporate and operational risk assessment to drive the annual audit plans for assurance and consulting work.

So we focus on helping the board and management establish good risk management practices and then review the areas of continuing concern (i.e. high residual risk)—or simply review key areas deemed critical to business success. The internal audit plan reflects a combination of the supporting role in helping establish risk management (consulting services) and audits of high risk areas (assurance-based) that have been identified by the board and senior management through their risk register. We have a number of options for planning audit work within the context of corporate governance and risk management. The main guidance suggests that each organization will adopt its own solution that takes on board its risk appetite, environment and organizational culture. Audit will respond accordingly and a planning framework that represents a hybrid of the above three approaches may result (with varying emphasis). Whatever format is adopted the CAE of the future must ensure:

- It fits with the way the organization responds to corporate governance.
- It is mainly driven by the corporate risk register.
- The board/audit committee accepts that this is the best way to apply audit resources.
- It underpins and links into the annual opinion that the CAE provides on the system of internal control.
- It is dynamic, flexible and responds to the changing demands of risk management and accountability.

The IIA.UK&Ireland has issued a position statement on Risk-Based Internal Auditing that argues the following key stages to this advanced approach to audit work. Risk-based auditing is based around the need to provide independent assurance to the board that:

- The risk management processes which management has put in place within the organisation are operating as intended.
- These risk management processes are of sound design.
- The responses which management has made to risks which they wish to treat are both adequate and effective in reducing those risks to a level which is acceptable to the board.
- And a sound framework of controls is in place to sufficiently mitigate those risks which management wishes to treat.

In terms of developing long term audit plans, the risk-based process may be performed along the following lines:

- Corporate objectives.
- Identification of risks to achieving objectives.
- What is the risk appetite of the business?
- Is the risk management process a adequate and effective process for identifying, assessing, managing and reporting on risk?
- For sound processes the organisation's view on risk can be used, and where this is not the case, audit will wish to facilitate the identification of risk with management and help refine the overall risk management process.

- Determine risk universe.
- Determine scope and priority of assignments.
- Based on risks select areas for review.
- For each area, review adequacy of risk management process.
- Where risk management is largely okay, determine how management gain assurances, and provide audit assurances. Where this is not the case, facilitate improvements.

Once a suitable audit planning process has been designed the resulting plans can be scheduled as follows:

- November—start the new planning process and build in extra capacity for consulting requests for management (via a formal assessment criteria).
- December—draft risk assessment forms and review of corporate risk database. One audit team uses the following allocations of productive audit time that is assigned in outline to: 50% annual audit plan, 20% emerging risk issues, 7% special investigations, 20% special projects, 3% follow-up.
- January/February—analyse information and talk to senior management and the board, and include all agreed consulting projects in the audit plan.
- March—finalize the annual audit plan after having discussed the draft plan with the audit committee.
- End March—publish the plan and allow update facilities.
- April—plan now live.

Summary and Conclusions

Many internal audit shops have moved on from the risk assessment checklists and entered into a dialogue with the board about how the audit resource can be used to best effect, that is utilizing the corporate assessment of risks along with auditors' special expertise in risk management, control models and specific control mechanisms (and requests for consulting projects), and the way objective assessments can be used to promote accountability and help managers deliver. Moreover, we have developed a basic framework for defining three different approaches to strategic audit planning.

Chapter 8: Multi-Choice Questions

Having worked through the chapter the following multi-choice questions may be attempted. (See Appendix A for suggested answer guide and Appendix B where you may record your score.)

1. **Insert the missing words:**
   The IIA's Performance Standards 2000 (Managing the Internal Audit Activity) states that: 'The CAE should effectively manage the internal audit activity to ensure it . . . . to the organisation.'
   a. makes sense.
   b. is of assistance.
   c. is worthwhile.
   d. adds value.

2. Which is the least appropriate item?

A cornerstone of audit strategy is the corporate assessment of business risk. This establishes an organization's control needs. A risk survey necessitates discussion with middle management and involves:

a. A definition of the audit unit.

b. An assessment of the quality of staff in each unit.

c. Research into the type of problems units attract.

d. Risk ranking related to resources subsequently assigned via an audit plan.

3. Which is the least appropriate item?

IIA Performance Standard 2010 makes it clear that: 'The CAE should establish risk-based plans to determine the priorities of the internal audit activity, consistent with the organization's goals.' There is no universal formula but we need to ensure that:

a. The methodology is accepted by the organization.

b. It is applied to the audit universe in a consistent fashion.

c. It is based on the corporate risk assessment and ongoing operational risk reviews.

d. All frauds will be uncovered in the organization.

4. Which is the most appropriate sentence?

a. Strategic development is getting new auditors to work together proactively to drive the audit service forward in the right direction.

b. Strategic development is getting auditors to work separately to drive the audit service forward in the right direction.

c. Strategic development is getting auditors to work together proactively to drive the audit service forward in the right direction.

d. Strategic development is getting auditors to work together proactively to drive the audit service forward even where this is not in the right direction.

5. Which is the least appropriate sentence?

It is essential that auditors are appraised in a positive fashion. This in turn depends on:

a. Keeping the accent on praise.

b. Not using the appraisal scheme to criticize but using it to develop.

c. Using performance appraisal to engender good communications and listening skills.

d. Seeking to promote a win/lose environment where all sides gain.

6. Which is the most appropriate sentence?

Our definition of the audit manual is:

a. A device that involves the accumulation and dissemination of all those documents, guidance, direction and instructions issued by audit management that affect the way the audit service is planned.

b. A book that involves the accumulation and dissemination of all those documents, guidance, direction and instructions issued by audit management that affect the way the audit service is delivered.

c. A device that involves the accumulation of all those documents, guidance, direction and instructions issued by audit management that affect the way the audit service is delivered.

d. A device that involves the accumulation and dissemination of all those documents, guidance, direction and instructions issued by the audit committee that affect the way the audit service is delivered.

7. Which is the least appropriate sentence?

Audit manuals fulfil the following roles:

a. Defining standards and methods of work.

b. Communicating this to auditors.

c. Establishing a base from which to measure the expected standards of performance

d. Encouraging internal staff disciplinary proceedings where standards are poor.

8. Insert the missing words:

Each audit department must offer a . . . . that is the result of the 'contract' struck between audit and the organization.

a. defined product.

b. defined report.

c. audit budget.

d. CRSA service.

9. Which is the least appropriate sentence?

Delegation of audit work by the audit manager has a positive effect on staff and key benefits are:

a. Auditors will always do a better job than their audit managers.

b. Auditors themselves learn to delegate.

c. New ideas may be generated and it acts as a communication device between managers and staff.

d. It promotes trust across the internal audit department.

10. Which is the least appropriate sentence?

The time monitoring reports should revolve around the time frame, types of work, auditors, audit groups and the entire audit unit. As such they should report on:

a. Time spent on audits and audits over budget.

b. Non-recoverable time charged (such as training and audit report writing).

c. Breakdown between assurance work and consulting engagements.

d. Audits that should have been completed.

References

1. Moeller, Robert and Witt, Herbert (1999) *Brink's Modern Internal Auditing*, 5th edition, New York: John Wiley and Sons Inc., p. 494.

2. Moeller, Robert and Witt, Herbert (1999) *Brink's Modern Internal Auditing*, 5th edition, New York: John Wiley and Sons Inc., p. 497.

3. IIA.Inc., *Professional Practices Pamphlet 98-1*, A Perspective on Outsourcing of the Internal Audit Function, p. 12, Internal Auditing: The Long-Run Approach.

Chapter 9

AUDIT FIELD WORK

Introduction

We have established that there are many different interpretations of the internal audit role and many approaches to performing both assurance and consulting work. One basic approach that has been discussed is risk-based systems auditing. This involves establishing the system objectives, finding out what risks should be addressed and then developing appropriate solutions to mitigate unacceptable levels of risk. The audit can be done by the client (with help from internal audit), by the auditor but with a great deal of participation with the client, or entirely by the internal auditor (as an outsider). These perspectives form a spectrum from objective review through to facilitated self-assessment. Whatever the adopted format, the auditor should perform field work to arrive at an opinion and advice on managing outstanding risks. Apart from the self-assessment approach, which is more consultancy than anything else, the internal auditor may go through variations on several set stages in performing the audit. These set stages are covered in this chapter and include:

9.1   Planning the Audit
9.2   Interviewing Skills
9.3   Ascertaining the System
9.4   Evaluation
9.5   Testing Strategies
9.6   Evidence and Working Papers
9.7   Statistical Sampling
9.8   Reporting Results of the Audit
9.9   Audit Committee Reporting
9.10 An Risk-Based Audit Approach (RaCE)
      Summary and Conclusions
      Chapter 9: Multi-Choice Questions

9.1 Planning the Audit

The annual audit plan lists those high risk areas that are targeted for audit cover during the next 12 months. The quarterly audit plan provides more detail by setting out those audits that will be performed by specified auditors in the following three months. Before the full audit is started and resources committed, an assignment plan will direct and control these resources. Before we are in a position to formulate assignment plans, we need background information on the targeted operation. Preliminary work will be required, the extent of which will vary according to the size of the audit. This section sets out the principles behind the preliminary survey and assignment planning, although the approach and level of detail will vary depending on the policies of each individual audit department. The IIA Performance Standard 2200 deals with engagement planning and requires that: 'internal auditors should develop and record a plan for each engagement, including the scope, objectives, timing and resource allocation.'

Control Objectives

Control objectives are the positive things business managers want to happen rather than negative things they want to prevent happening and they address the risks inherent in the work being done. Control objectives are used by some auditors to represent a statement of the desired result or purpose to be achieved by the specific control procedures to ensure business objectives are achieved. Once set it is possible to start thinking about the risks to each of the defined control objectives to reinforce the performance/conformance dimensions of acceptable business practices. The drawback is that it is often difficult to sell the idea of control objectives to client management. Note that Implementation Standard 2110.A2 reinforces the scope of internal auditing and provides a framework for control objectives by requiring that:

> The internal audit activity should evaluate risk exposures relating to the organisation's governance, operations and information systems regarding the:
> - Reliability and integrity of financial and operational information.
> - Effectiveness and efficiency of operations.
> - Safeguarding of assets.
> - Compliance with laws, regulations, and contracts.

The Preliminary Survey

The preliminary survey seeks to accumulate relevant information regarding the operation under review so that a defined direction of the ensuing audit (if it goes ahead) may be agreed. The internal audit files will be the first port of call and any previous audit cover will be considered. All assignment audit files should contain a paper entitled 'outstanding matters' that will set out concerns that were not addressed via the audit at hand. The files tell only part of the story as will the resultant audit report, and it is best to talk to the auditor who last performed work in the relevant area. It is advisable to carry out background research into the area subject to the survey. This might include national research, committee papers, recent changes and planned computerized systems. Much of this information should really have been obtained via the corporate risk assessment. It is always advisable to get some basic facts before meeting with management so as to create a good impression. We can now meet with the key manager and tour the operational area. An overview of the real risks facing the manager in question can be obtained. A feel for the audit can be gathered from impressions gained from touring the work area, where the initial impression can be used to help direct the auditor towards particular problems. The preliminary survey will involve a consideration of several important matters, including:

1. Operational procedures   Recent work carried out by other review agencies should be obtained and considered, although watch out for bias where the work was commissioned for a particular reason. Reports contain natural bias set by the terms of reference. For example, a staffing review commissioned by an employee union is more likely to recommend pay rises. The preliminary survey involves assessing local business risk factors that affect audit objectives. No audit can cover all the relevant areas within a specific operation and the assignment plan states what will be done and what is not covered. It is the process of assessing local risk that allows the auditor to key into the target elements of the operational area. This is done at preliminary survey before the audit objectives and scope of the review can be finalized and agreed. The auditor must isolate the system for review and distinguish it from parent systems, subsystems, parallel systems and link systems. Systems theory states that a system is defined in line with the perceptions of the reviewer. The system selected by the auditor has to be defined before it can be audited and the preliminary survey comes to the rescue. Systems boundaries can only be determined after the necessary information has been accumulated and digested. This must happen before the assignment planning stage so that a clear plan may be documented and shown to management. The aim of the preliminary survey will be to agree the objectives and scope and timing of the audit with management. What needs to be done, how and when it will be done, will be derived from the survey as a prerequisite to the proper preparation for the full audit. It will be necessary to note areas that will not be considered as outside the terms of reference. This is important because management often feel that an audit will reveal all that is wrong with a system. A clear definition of what was not included in the audit will help to avoid this. Note that the IIA define engagement objectives as: 'broad statements developed by internal auditors that define intended engagement accomplishments'. The impact on audit work might be an issue either by redirecting resources or adjusting the scope of another audit that would be affected by the planned work. A major benefit of the preliminary survey is an understanding of the nature of the audit. This highlights the type of audit skills required, including special skills relating to automation and/or technically complicated matters such as contract law. Audit standards require audit management to ensure they can perform audits to professional standards. It is the responsibility of all managers to use their resources properly and if it is clear that an audit is too difficult for the available resources then the project should be aborted. It is a useful policy to get senior auditors or audit managers to perform the preliminary survey and then assign the full audit to more junior staff. The survey is perhaps the most difficult part of the audit process since once the terms of reference have been set and a programme of work agreed the remainder can be fairly straightforward. It means that the audit manager has a full knowledge of the audit and can supervise and review the work as it progresses. The preliminary survey should result in a programme of work that has been identified as a result of the background work. This may be in the form of a detailed audit programme or simply a list of key tasks depending on the type of audit, the approach to work and the policies of the audit unit.

2. The audit programme   As well as isolating the system for review and determining the direction of the audit, the assignment plan may result in an audit programme for use during the audit. Performance Standard 2240 mentions work programmes and says that: 'Internal auditors should develop work programs that achieve the engagement objectives. These work programs should be recorded.' And there are separate standards for assurance and consulting work that suggest:

- **2240.A1**—Work programs should establish the procedures for identifying, analysing, evaluating, and recording information during the engagement. The work program should be approved prior to the commencement of work, and any adjustments approved promptly.
- **2240.C1**—Work programs for consulting engagements may vary in form and content depending upon the nature of the engagement.

The term audit programme (or work programme) should be carefully considered since an audit programme tends to be associated with a series of predefined testing routines. This does not promote the risk-based systems approach since the direction of the testing procedures depends on the outcome of the risk and control evaluation. The IIA define the engagement work programme as: '*a document that lists the procedures to be followed during an engagement, designed to achieve the engagement plan*'. The audit programme may be seen more as an audit guide and may include:

1. Defining the various tasks that need to be performed. Here a list of key tasks should be compiled for the lead auditor that sets the direction of the audit process that will now be carried out. This is not only a useful planning tool that can be used to monitor progress on the audit, but also provides firm guidance for the auditor on work that must be completed.
2. Defining the extent of work in a particular part of the operation. For smaller audits with a standardized approach it is possible to list the various testing routines. Defining testing programmes makes the audit controllable. It is based around the required tests and in basic audits this may give the number of items that should be selected and how they are tested. Audit management can exercise firm control. This would not be appropriate for a risk-based systems approach since it is controls that are tested after they have been assessed for their impact on risks and testing is not carried out for its own sake.

The key differences between the systems and compliance/probity approaches to audit work are found in Figure 9.1.

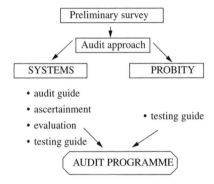

FIGURE 9.1   Systems-based approach versus probity.

This is an important distinction. Compliance and probity audits emphasize transactions testing, and the audit programme is formulated at the preliminary survey stage. For risk-based systems auditing, this detailed testing programme can only be defined after the system has been documented and assessed. The programme of work that is set for a systems audit can be described as an audit guide that determines the work required to complete the audit and this may be drafted at preliminary stage. The programme will include target dates and perhaps a progress checklist for stages of the audit. Not only is it used as a monitoring tool but as each task is carried out, the date completed and reviewed should be entered on the schedule and provides a comprehensive record of work. The audit techniques may be identified and this may affect the auditors assigned. Statistical sampling, flowcharting, interviewing, computer assisted audit techniques, product inspection, third-party circularization and other techniques may be planned where clearly required. Resourcing these techniques can be dealt with at the pre-planning stage. The audit programme should be formally signed off by the audit manager to constitute an approved work plan for the field auditor/s. Attaching the programme to the associated terms of reference and budget for the work provides a management tool for controlling the audit. The audit programme sets direction for the testing stage, but care must be taken not to suppress the auditor's initiative or responsibility for the work. There must be direction but at the same time freedom to explore key issues and form an opinion on the state of controls. For systems audits, the test programme appears after most of the crucial evaluation work has been completed. For compliance audits it is essential that the auditor uses the programme as a means to an end and not an end in itself. This means tailoring the programme to fit the audit while retaining responsibility for the end results. Where the audit is being driven by the audit programme then it is necessary to make clear the tasks that need to be carried out.

3. The preliminary survey report   It is advisable to present a formal preliminary survey report (PSR) once the work has been completed. Another consideration is that access to information and explanations is important to establish at an early stage and help is given here by Implementation Standard 2220.A1, which states 'The scope of the engagement should include consideration of relevant systems, records, personnel, and physical properties, including those under the control of third parties.' The PSR goes to the audit manager, along with a brief description of the system to be used to prepare the assignment plan. The PSR of one or two pages will cover the following:

1. An outline of the system under review including systems objectives and boundaries.
2. The work undertaken in the preliminary survey.
3. An initial opinion on the risk areas based on the key control objectives covering compliance, information systems, safeguarding assets and value for money.
4. Recommendations for the proposed assignment in terms of the nature and extent of audit cover now required.
5. An appendix with outline systems notes and a draft audit guide/programme for the full audit.

Assignment Planning

Each audit must be carefully planned as this is the only way to control it. Assignment planning takes all available information and allows the objectives, scope, direction and approach to be defined. We have considered how the preliminary survey will have been conducted before plans can be formulated and will provide much information for formulating the assignment plan. The preliminary survey report will set out the proposed objectives of the full audit stage. Factors to be addressed in the assignment plan are:

1. The terms of reference for the audit by audit management and disclosed to the client management. They guide audit work and feature in the resultant report with an audit opinion on each component. The precise terms of the audit should be given much consideration in line with Performance Standard 2220, which says: 'The established scope should be sufficient to satisfy the objectives of the engagement'.
2. The scope of work including areas for coverage and parts of the system not to be dealt with at this time. This may be referred to in a memorandum to client management publicizing the pending audit.
3. Target dates for start and completion and key stages. For larger audits, break the task down into defined stages and manageable parts that may be reported on separately. This enables the auditor to maintain a focus on the objective at hand, and report before going on to deal with the next part. For example, a corporate system, which has been devolved down to departments like personnel, budgeting, or expenditure processing, may be broken down into sections relating to each department. A separate report will be drafted for each department along with a composite report covering the corporate arrangements. Auditors can be drafted in to deal with each department if a suitable programme of work has been prepared and explained and the work programme requires extensive testing and interrogation of the corporate database. Once compiled, it can be completed by a variety of resources including temporary audit staff. Practice Advisory 2230-1 acknowledges that auditors may

have development needs and suggests that: 'Training needs of internal auditors should be considered, since each engagement serves as a basis for meeting developmental needs of the internal auditing activity.' Some assistance may be provided by audit management to address any particular problems experienced by the field auditor. This may include any problems with following up action taken on an audit report previously issued, that impacts on the current audit. The auditor will also be concerned that compliance issues have been addressed by management and Implementation Standard 2210.A2 covers this point by commenting that: 'The internal auditor should consider the probability of significant errors, irregularities, noncompliance, and other exposures when developing the engagement objectives.'

4. A full definition of the system under review including the points where it starts and finishes and interfaces with other related systems. This avoids unnecessary confusion over the duration of the audit with a clear focus on exactly what the system is. It allows the auditor to think through the associated systems and their impact on the audit.

5. Identification of high risk areas and critical points of the audit that may require special attention and/or resources. This may refer to the timing of the audit, say in relation to restructuring, a new computer system, a recruitment campaign or a new staff performance scheme. On this point, Implementation Standard 2210.A1 says that: 'Internal auditor should conduct a preliminary assessment of the risks relevant to the activity under review. The engagement objectives should reflect the results of the risk assessment.' On the other hand, consulting engagements are defined by the client and Implementation Standard 2210.C1 makes this clear: 'Consulting engagement objectives should address risks, controls and governance processes to the extent agreed upon with the client.'

6. Definition of the reporting and review arrangements including a list of the individuals who will receive draft reports. Where the audit is geographically remote, the review arrangements must be determined so that this process does not hold up the progress of the audit report.

7. Agree the confirmed audit programme (or guide) for each part of the audit and the testing regimes (for compliance reviews). The audit techniques that should be applied may also be defined along with a list of standardized documents (having reference to the audit manual) in use in the audit unit. On this point, Practice Advisory 2240-1 argues that: 'Engagement procedures, including the testing and sampling techniques employed, should be selected in advance, where practicable, and expanded or altered if circumstances warrant.'

8. The assignment plan will outline any travel and hotel arrangements along with subsistence allowances. This should recognize the need to save time and ensure efficient use of resources.

9. Identify the auditors assigned to the project and their roles. Performance Standard 2230 covers resource allocations and states that: 'Internal auditors should determine appropriate resources to achieve engagement objectives. Staffing should be based on an evaluation of the nature and complexity of each engagement, time constraints, and available resources.' The assignment planning task must identify which auditors are assigned. The audit manager or lead auditor should perform the preliminary survey so that a good insight into the audit is obtained by those directing the work. Once done, the audit proper should be assigned. A trend is for a move away from teamwork with a single auditor being given an audit to streamline resources. It fits with the development profile of auditors who, apart from trainees, should be given responsibility for whole projects. Meanwhile the IIA Performance Standard 2201 provides a list of matters to be considered when planning the audit such as:

   • The objectives of the activity being reviewed and the means by which the activity controls its performance.

   • The significant risks to the activity, its objectives, resources and operations and the means by which the potential impact of risk is kept to an acceptable level.

- The adequacy and effectiveness of the activity's risk management and control systems compared to the relevant control framework or model.
- The opportunity for making significant improvements to the activity's risk management and control systems.

Consulting engagements are more straightforward and are covered by Implementation Standard 2201.C1, which requires that: 'Internal auditors should establish an understanding with consulting engagement clients about objectives, scope, respective responsibilities, and other client expectations. For significant engagements, this understanding should be documented.'

Assigning Time Budgets to Audits

We must define an audit budget in terms of time allowed. Time is the key factor on any audit. Setting a time budget acts as a principal control over the assignment and is the single most important concern of audit management. A viable audit is achieved within budget to professional audit standards and as a full discharge of its objectives. Budgeted hours must be realistic and achievable. An alternative approach is more basic and simply states (for example):

LARGE AUDIT:	**4 WEEKS**
MEDIUM-SIZED AUDIT:	**2 WEEKS**
SMALL AUDIT:	**1 WEEK**

The extent of work done in such time frames depends on the skill and expertise of the individual auditor. A performance appraisal scheme rewards those who deliver quality reports within the time constraints. There are two different views. One seeks to perform the audit terms of reference to the full no matter how long this takes, even if budgeted hours are extended. This normally involves extensive testing and an inability to defer parts of the audit to a later stage. The other view is that audit management sets a defined number of hours according to the level of risk attached. When this budget expires the auditor must transfer to another work area, so recognizing the risks of not dealing with the next planned audit. Extensions are not encouraged as the auditor has to perform as much work as possible during the budget hours and then move on to the next job. The adopted policy must be explained and detailed in the audit manual since work done on one audit detracts from work that might be done elsewhere. One solution is to disallow budget extensions unless there is good reason such as to avoid the psychological dilemma of 'auditor attachment'. This occurs where the auditor becomes so engrossed in an operation that they see themselves as an expert who has a duty to solve all problems after mastering the system. Client managers assimilate the auditor into an executive role by constantly seeking advice on operational decisions. The auditor becomes too closely associated with the operation, asking for more and more time to spend on the audit. The correct position is to provide budgeted hours for the audit and then remove the auditor from the work once this has expired unless there are exceptional circumstances. The working file will show what work is outstanding that may be deferred to the next audit. Auditor attachment can lead to audit saturation where there has been too much time spent by the audit team on only one area of risk.

The Assignment Planning Process

The audit manager should provide all guidance in the assignment plan before the full audit commences. Objectives in the assignment plan should be achieved and the audit manager review should ensure this. Performance Standard 2100 makes clear the audit link to corporate governance and states that: 'The internal audit activity should evaluate and contribute to the improvement of risk management, controls and governance processes using a systematic and disciplined approach.' The assignment plan should also incorporate review points over audit hours charged and quality of work to judge the value of work performed. Not all requests for formal consulting projects can be accepted by the internal auditor and Implementation Standard 2220.C1 makes it clear that some projects will have to be declined by saying that: 'In performing consulting engagements internal auditors should ensure that the scope of the engagement is sufficient to address the agreed-upon objectives. If internal auditors develop reservations about the scope during the engagement, these reservations should be discussed with the client to determine whether to continue with the engagement.'

Planning Documentation

There are many versions of documents that assist audit planning to provide standards and checklists for the work and areas that should be covered in the plan, showing each task and indicating:

The audit objective	Who does what
For how long	Any particular guidance
The review arrangements	

This control will not work unless there is an inbuilt monitoring system of continual supervision and review of progress. The audit manager should provide all necessary direction via the assignment planning process. The details above are the minimum information that should be contained in audit plans before the full audit is approved by audit management. Practice Advisory 2010-1 also gives guidance on what should be included in engagement work schedules:

- what activities are to be performed, when they will be performed and the estimated time required;
- scheduled priorities;
- dates and results of last engagement;
- updated assessments of risks, risk management and control;
- requests by senior management, audit committee and governing body;
- major changes in enterprises, business, operations, programs, systems, and controls;
- opportunities to achieve operating benefits; and
- changes to and capabilities of the audit staff.

The work schedules should be sufficiently flexible to cover unanticipated demands on the internal audit activity.

9.2 Interviewing Skills

Gathering information is a fundamental part of audit work as the auditor spends a great deal of time fact-finding. The starting place for establishing facts is simply to ask, and herein lies the importance of interviewing. Some of the synonyms for interviewing are:

audience, conference, consultation, dialogue, meeting, talk, examine, interrogate, question

We take a wider view of the concept and mean it simply to refer to 'talking with' in a structured manner. The technique of interviewing should be mastered by the auditor and there is much material available on this topic that will contribute to this task. We see interviewing as a process, a task, a set structure, an audit standard and an exercise in understanding human behaviour. These components will be covered in the material below. Interviewing is based around effective communications and it is a good idea to remember the basic communications model to appreciate where things could go wrong and how communicating may be improved using Figure 9.2.

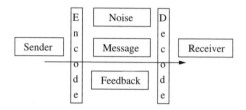

FIGURE 9.2 Communications.

The sender has to decide how to transmit the message which is then sent and decoded (rightly or wrongly) by the receiver. All this is against the background noise that consists of anything that gets in the way of clear messages being delivered and received. The positives are located in the feedback loop where understanding of the message is fed back to the giver to ensure it has been properly received and understood.

Types of Interviews

There are many different types of interviews that the auditor will undertake and within each type there may be several different categories. Most are founded on Kipling's six friends in terms of trying to find out *when, why, where, how, what, who.* One list of different types of interviews may appear as:

Initial contact with the client	Fact-finding
Corporate risk assessment survey	Post-audit
Audit marketing	Recruitment
Staff appraisal	Fraud

Structuring Interviews

Interviews are structured meetings where information is provided and obtained. Based on much that we have already discussed, we may provide an outline illustration of how we might structure a typical audit interview in Figure 9.3.
Explanations follow:

- **Introductions.** This involves introducing all parties present at the interview and explaining their role and position within the information-gathering process.
- **Objectives.** What is hoped to be achieved from the interview is then fully communicated and further clarification provided if needs be.
- **Questions and answers.** The main body of the interview should then proceed in a way that flows naturally and promotes the achievement of the original objectives of the meeting.

FIGURE 9.3   Interview structures.

- **Wind up.** The next stage is to recheck the information that has been given and any matters (such as the exchange of specific documents) that have already been agreed.
- **Closure.** An indication of next steps, further meetings and specific arrangements such as planned meetings with key staff should be given. Formal thanks (and possibly handshakes) should also be a feature of the last stage of the interview process.

Behavioural Aspects of Interviewing

What might appear a straightforward interview may go badly wrong and leave the auditor and client confused. There are many reasons why people act in an unpredictable way which generally stems from a lack of appreciation by the auditor of the behavioural aspects of audit work. The actions of one aggressive auditor who may have left many years ago may still be foremost in many managers' minds whenever the auditors call. There are many behavioural aspects that the auditor should bear in mind when conducting interviews and interviewees may possibly be asking themselves the following questions:

- What do they want from me?
- Are they human?
- Are they assessing me?
- Can I trust them?
- Should I tell them everything?
- What are they writing down?
- What about my problems?
- How can they help me?
- How will their work affect me?
- Who will be blamed if they find any errors?
- Are they going to propose drastic changes?

The auditor poses a threat in terms of the potential for making changes to the working lives of everyone they meet. People generally dislike change particularly where they cannot be sure how it will affect them. Where these changes are based on levels of unmitigated risk the auditor finds in the manager's area of responsibility, any suggested changes may be associated with negative connotations. These feelings can affect the way the interview progresses and the auditor needs to be sure that the audit objectives and how they should build into management's needs are carefully conveyed to the interviewee. The first few minutes of the interview may consist of a clear attempt by the auditor to explain the audit role and approach before a constructive dialogue may be entered into. It is also important to indicate the next steps that will be followed, after the interview is concluded. The auditor's actions must be consistent with his words and if he/she is seen as a spy for senior management, little or no co-operation will be received.

The mismatch between what the auditor says they do and management's own understanding can lead to fundamental conceptual problems. This has to be fought against at all times by the auditor to dispel myths, and build proper working relationships. Even where the auditor is involved in investigations into irregularity, there is still a view that the auditor is primarily examining the circumstances at issue and not the people concerned. Where a name can be fitted to a problem, then this should be a natural consequence of the proceedings and not a witch-hunt. One of the hardest challenges in the audit role is seeking to reconcile the assurance and consulting roles. We would hope that the image of the jackbooted 'find the transgressor' auditor does not cross over into our main role in assurance auditing and make constructive communications with management and staff impossible. Much resistance from client can be pre-empted by discussions on this point in a frank and open manner, so long as our actions coincide with our words.

Types of Questions

Some interviews go on for hours while others last a few moments and these two extremes do not necessarily coincide with the auditor obtaining full or limited information. The success of an interview is not only measured by length of time. Long discussions may be constructive but can result in inefficient use of time. The efficiency of interviews increases by the selective use of different types of questions. Interviewees are guided by skilful use of questioning so that material issues are expanded on while specifics are dealt with more quickly. Types of question include:

- **Open questions**   such as, 'Tell me about your job'.
- **Closed questions**   such as, 'Do you work in the accounts department?'
- **Probing questions**   such as, 'Tell me more about xyz'.
- **Confirmatory questions**   such as, 'Your job description refers to an xyz, is this correct?'
- **Clarification**   along the lines, 'I thought you said that you worked for Mr X?'.

In general one should not use the following types of questions:

- **Leading questions**   such as, 'Surely you check these invoices before approving them?'
- **Loaded questions**   such as, 'You appear to be more qualified than your boss'.
- **Trick questions**   along the lines, 'You say that you have worked here for three and a half years; what date did you start?'

One principle that should be applied is that constant feedback should be obtained throughout the interview and matters double-checked as far as possible. For more formal occasions the interviewee should be asked to comment on the documented interview record at the close of the meeting. Interviewing is widely used to secure audit information. Interviews intrude into the interviewee's world and may be resisted or encouraged depending on the relationship established. Experienced auditors set up interviews and secure information in an efficient and effective manner. The interview is a two-way process and the auditor must convey audit objectives clearly and convincingly. There are many barriers to good interviews and these should be recognized and carefully managed with the aid of a comprehensive audit manual and training workshops.

9.3 Ascertaining the System

Risk-based systems auditing relies on evaluating the whole system of risk management and internal control, which ensures operational objectives will be achieved. This task can only be performed where the systems that are being considered are properly understood, which in turn relies on the auditor's ability to document the system efficiently. There are several alternative methods, each with its own advantages. Some of the more popular ones are mentioned here.

Alternative Methods

The main options that the auditor has for documenting the system are:

1. Narrative notes.
2. Block diagrams.
3. Flowcharts.
4. Internal control questionnaire (ICQ).

There are different types of flowcharts which may be shown in Figure 9.4.

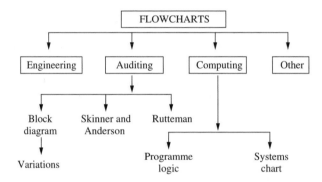

FIGURE 9.4   Types of flowcharts.

Despite clear differences between types of flowchart, there are basic principles per Figure 9.5.

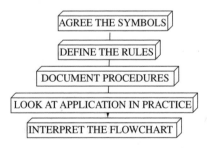

FIGURE 9.5   Basic flowcharting rules.

Narrative

Systems are set out by straightforward narrative where the main parts of the system are noted in point format. The processes are described from start to finish to convey the required information on which to base an evaluation. The bulk of these systems notes may be taken direct from the interview with the operations manager. For simple systems that do not involve much document flows, this may be sufficient. For more complicated systems it may be necessary to go on to draft a block diagram and/or a detailed flowchart. Narrative provides a useful short-cut to systems documentation and as long as it conveys the right information clearly, it is a valid technique. It should be possible to cross-reference relevant documents to the narrative and then attach them to the notes for future use. Structured narrative notes divide the operation into sections or people alongside brief notes on each activity to form a diagrammatic representation of events. This might appear as Table 9.1.

TABLE 9.1 Structured systems narrative notes.

System stage	Dept. A	Dept. B	Dept. C
1	notes xxx	notes xxx	notes xxx
2	notes xxx	notes xxx	notes xxx
3	notes xxx	notes xxx	notes xxx
4	notes xxx	notes xxx	notes xxx
etc.			

This captures the system simply on a single document without needing detailed symbols and keys.

Block Diagrams

Block diagrams fall in between detailed flowcharts and narrative. They consist of a series of boxes each representing an operation or control. It provides a simple diagrammatic representation in Figure 9.6.

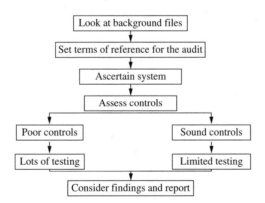

FIGURE 9.6 A block diagram.

One may show the flow of information and the organizational arrangements. The main advantage is that this technique is quick and simple, and sample diagrams can be incorporated within the audit report to aid understanding by outlining the system. For high-level work that does not require a detailed analysis of documentation this can be an efficient way of recording the system. This contrasts with flowcharting where there is an obsession with the detailed movement of documents.

The Rules of Flowcharting

Flowcharts are detailed representations of documents and information that record most parts of a defined operation. The rules that are applied to audit charts are:

1. Provide clear headings and dates so that the system dealt with is clearly identified. Do not make them unnecessarily complicated as this consumes time and may not aid the audit process.
2. Look for exception routines and note these so that a complete picture is provided.
3. Test the flowchart against the client's understanding of the system.
4. Distinguish between operations/processes and controls so that the flowchart can feed directly into the control evaluation procedures.
5. Number the events in sequential order as they may be referred to in other audit working papers.
6. Keep the narrative brief to avoid making the schedule appear cramped.
7. Show destination of all documents by not leaving loose ends.
8. Distinguish between information and documentation flow.
9. Use a convention of moving through the system—top to bottom and from left to right.
10. Apply standardized symbols and keys that are fully agreed and detailed in the audit manual.

Rutteman

The Rutteman convention is popular and tends to be used by ICAEW/ACCA trained auditors:

1. It has fewer symbols than some more detailed flowcharting conventions.
2. It has fewer operations.
3. There is less narrative in the margin.
4. Everything has to be concluded.

Some of the standard symbols used are listed in Figure 9.7.

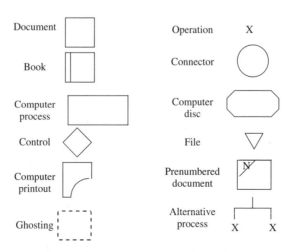

FIGURE 9.7 Standard flowchart symbols.

TABLE 9.2 Files.

	Permanent	Temporary
Alphabetic	A	TA
Numerical	N	TN
Date order	D	TD

Documents that have been processed will normally be found in temporary or permanent files. Temporary files are those awaiting further instructions or information to complete the transaction as in Table 9.2.

As a final outcome of all transactions we should find that they:

1. Are permanently filed.
2. Have left the system.
3. Are destroyed.

Ghosting is applied when multi-part documents are used and the separate parts may be subjected to different sequences of operations so that a restatement of each part may be the simplest way to depict these operations. Sequences of operations representing a subroutine may be shown on a separate chart and ghosting can be used to restate the initial document in the chart. As a brief example of this flowcharting convention refer to this narrative in Figure 9.8:

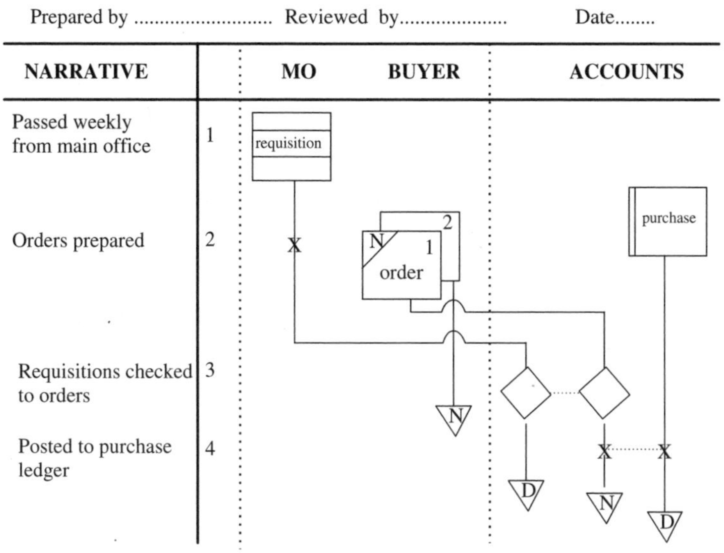

FIGURE 9.8 Ordering system—flowchart.

1. Weekly requisitions received by buyer from main office (MO).
2. Three-part order prepared by buyer.
3. Documents sent to accounts where they check the requisitions with the orders.
4. Requisitions are filed in date order.
5. Orders are entered into purchase ledger.

Pros and Cons of Flowcharting

Main advantages:
- Highlights weak controls particularly relating to a lack of segregation of duties and authorization.
- Indicates possible duplication of work where tasks are repeated.
- Permanent record of the system.
- Shows instances of formal authorization.
- A logical and systematic procedure that can be learnt and applied by all auditors.
- Ensures the complete system is ascertained. Narrative notes may not follow all documents from initiation to conclusion and only by formally charting their flow may gaps be spotted.
- Used to highlight instances of internal check.
- Allows a bird's-eye view of the system.

Disadvantages:
- Training in the techniques required for competent use.
- Time consuming as detailed operations are documented.
- Can be badly drawn and hardly understood by anyone.
- Tends not to be descriptive and suits complicated systems with lots of document flows.
- May be subject to constant change and require updating as systems change.
- Can show excessive detail and become very complicated.
- Becomes an end in itself instead of a tool to be sensibly applied as part of the overall audit process.
- Inappropriate for corporate and managerial systems with high-level controls to be explained rather than charted.

Using the Flowchart

Flowcharts may be used in the following ways:

1. Weak areas or waste of resources may be isolated so that audit attention may be directed towards these parts of the system, or problems can simply be referred to in the report.
2. One can draw a second flowchart to show proposed improvements. The relevant stages may be highlighted in 'before' and 'after' charts that form the basis of discussions with management.
3. One may use the internal control questionnaire (ICQ) in conjunction with flowcharts, expanding on areas where there may be systems weaknesses. ICQs are also a form of systems ascertainment in that they relay the control features of the area under review.
4. Walkthrough tests may be used to take a small sample of transactions through the system so that the integrity of the documentation may be determined.
5. Automated flowcharting packages may be used.

Balancing the Level of Details Required

There must be balance in the use of ascertainment techniques so that efficiency is maintained and there is perspective involved in applying flowcharting. For the best ascertainment options consider:

- **Narrative**   A simple descriptive overview gleaned directly from the interviews. It should be used wherever possible unless the level of documentation becomes too detailed to deal with in note form.

- **Block diagrams** Illustrate the main stages of a system and the relationships between components. With the growing use of graphical presentation software, there is scope for attractive diagrams that can be imported into the audit report for ease of reading. Main systems stages have to be summarized for block diagrams to be of any use although the advantage is simplicity in design and ease of use.
- **Detailed flowchart** These should be used sparingly and only where absolutely necessary. Because of time constraints and the move away from basic operational detail, they have limited use. Where a sensitive system, such as pre-signed cheque ordering, use and dispatch, must be carefully accounted for, monitored and controlled at all stages, detailed flowcharts will probably be required.

Standards on the above including appropriate conventions should be comprehensively dealt with in the audit manual. It is difficult to seek to flowchart in detail all organizational systems as this would be a momentous task and require constant updating. Having said this, Sarbanes-Oxley (see chapter two) is partly dependent on documenting internal controls and ascertainment techniques used by the auditors may also be employed by management to good effect. For internal audit work, the choice of ascertainment technique depends on the type of audit and approach adopted. There is a wide variety of available methodologies and this adds to, rather than dilutes, the auditor's skills base. The audit manual is the right vehicle for setting such standards. Some audit shops are moving away from formal flowcharting and rely more on mind maps that demonstrate conceptual links between systems, operations and other business processes, such as local, corporate and intranet based systems. Various boxes, circles and other symbols are used by the auditor to illustrate the system and how they work.

9.4 Evaluation

Evaluation may be seen as the most important stage in any audit review since this provides an opportunity for auditors to apply professional creativity to the fullest. The audit opinion and recommendations should flow from the systems weaknesses identified during the systems evaluation. Audit testing routines are carried out to confirm the original evaluation in terms of the application of controls and the effects of control weaknesses. The IIA's Implementation Standard 2120.A4 states that:

> Adequate criteria are needed to evaluate controls. Internal auditors should ascertain the extent to which management has established adequate criteria to determine whether objectives and goals have been accomplished. If adequate, internal auditors should use such criteria in their evaluation. If inadequate, internal auditors should work with management to develop appropriate evaluation criteria.

If the evaluation is flawed then all the remaining audit work will suffer. Audit recommendations will provide substandard solutions to risk exposures.

Defining the System

The preliminary survey establishes which system is being audited. The statement on scope of audit work in the assignment plan will document what is being reviewed and it is this system that will be subject to evaluation. We then have to turn to the model of the system that is being evaluated. The system may be conceived as one of several models:

The prescribed system   This perceived version of the system is laid down in procedure notes and official documents. The original systems intentions may be set out in old committee papers and formal reviews commissioned by management. The official description of the system will follow this formally agreed format. The auditor has to be concerned with this system since it may be the one that is officially approved by the organization and if it has altered, then fresh approval may have to be sought. For example, where the organization has agreed a central purchasing function then any variation to this model, where managers place their own orders, should be formally authorized. If not, we may be in breach of procedure.

The alleged system   This follows the procedures that are described by the management and staff operating the system.

The planned system   The system that management wishes to install may be called the planned system.

The emergency/contingency system   Although the system may be clearly set out and applied on most occasions, there is also an emergency system that the auditor may wish to consider. This is based on the need to 'get things done' in an emergency and may result in many overrides of official procedure.

The ideal system   Published research on systems control and value-for-money studies, by their nature, use generalizations on how defined operations may be improved. The temptation to set out ideals on systems control may be seen as part of the drive to establishing an 'ideal system'.

The auditor's preferred system   The auditor's understanding of the systems processes and control weaknesses may convince him/her that certain improvements are required. These may be seen as the auditor's version of the ideal system.

Staff's preferred system   Supervisory staff and front line employees may have a vision of the type of controls that should be incorporated.

The workable system   This is the system that works in practice and retains all the required control features. It may fall somewhere between the ideal system, management's system, audit's preferences and the procedures applied by staff themselves.

The best system   The question arises as to what is the best system. There would seem to be several interpretations. The 'best' system is able to contain risks to management's objectives, which brings into play exactly how this criterion should be applied.

   The auditor's understanding of the system should include:

1. Understanding the needs of the parties who rely on the system.
2. Understanding the adopted success criteria.
3. Understanding systems constraints.
4. Understanding the overall risk management arrangements implicit in the system.

Evaluation Techniques

The system being reviewed is the system being applied in practice in line with management's operational objectives. The evaluation applied should be based on those controls required to ensure risk to the achievement of objectives are mitigated with no great loss or inefficiency. Evaluation techniques include:

1. **Flowcharts.** These help identify systems blockages, duplication of effort and segregation of duties along with controls that depend on documentation flows and the way work is organized.
2. **Transactions testing.** By testing transactions one might pick up systems malfunctions that cause error conditions identified by the tests. Where we are able to manipulate large amounts of data, the ability to carry out a limited range of tests quickly arises. This cannot be seen as a systematic evaluation since it does not rely on a full understanding of the operation under review, but leaves matters to chance as samples are selected and examined.
3. **Directed representations.** One cannot deny the usefulness of information provided by persons who have knowledge of the system. If management states that there are unmitigated risks at the outset of an audit, one would be ill-advised to ignore this source of information. Complaints from users, operatives, middle management and third parties can provide a short-cut to the evaluation process. One would look for bias in these comments as they could not be taken without some degree of substantiating evidence.
4. **Internal control questionnaires (ICQ).** Dealt with below.
5. **Internal control evaluation system (ICES).** Dealt with below.

Recommendations should be based on dealing with problems as illustrated in Figure 9.9.

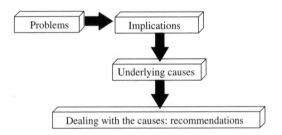

FIGURE 9.9 Evaluation.

At some stage we apply this framework against what we find in practice. This is why the evaluation stage is where the auditor's creative abilities come to the fore.

Internal Control Questionnaires (ICQ)

Internal control questionnaires (ICQ) are widely used to assist the control evaluation process and there are many standard packages. They consist of a series of questions applied to a particular operation and designed so that a 'no' answer indicates a potential control weakness. One might ask:

> Is the task of receipting income separated from the recording of this income?

The idea being that a 'no' answer may mean that official duties are insufficiently segregated. The potential weaknesses are then further explored and compensatory controls looked for before testing routines are applied. ICQs have a number of specific advantages and disadvantages:

Advantages

1. Provides a permanent record of the evaluation stage. As the schedules are completed they automatically record the response to each key point examined as a ready-made working paper.
2. A disciplined, systematic approach to evaluation not depending on the whims and fancies of the assigned auditor.
3. Helps audit supervisors as the standard of evaluation is set beforehand through compilation of the ICQ. The expectation that field auditors will ensure full coverage of the defined areas via this process provides a useful management tool for controlling the audit.
4. Provides direction to the auditor by setting out clearly the areas that are to be addressed. In this way the auditor can approach an audit armed with the necessary tools, i.e. the ICQ checklists. There is no need to rethink the control mechanisms that form part of the evaluation process as they are set out in the ICQ. The 'what should be' model is then available to be used to assess the adequacy of existing practices. Some might argue that the ICQ provides indispensable guidance.
5. It is simple to use as the questions are directed at control objectives that should be present in the operation under review.
6. The technique can be used by inexperienced auditors who should find it simple to adapt their work to provide responses to the listed questions.
7. It de-personalizes the audit by setting tried, trusted, and objective criteria for the controls in operation. The auditor can defend a charge of being too obsessed with control by referring to the ICQ standards adopted by the internal audit function and not devised in a hit-or-miss fashion.
8. ICQs promote a systems-based approach. They emphasize controls as the main source of audit attention, rather than the testing programmes that may be the main basis for the audit. Controls are deemed by the ICQ to accomplish objectives that support the main thrust of the systems approach.
9. Provides good structure and form to the audit by defining beforehand the way systems will be assessed. Planning is easier as time can be assigned to completing the requirements of the ICQ and the work has a natural start and finish in line with the control standards used.
10. It results in comprehensive cover of an area by dealing with all foreseeable points. It is impossible for an auditor to be aware of all control features within an ICQ, particularly the more comprehensive ones. Having the checklist to hand enables one to take on board many factors.

Disadvantages

1. They can lead to a stereotyped approach where each year the auditor seeks to examine a series of predetermined factors that is wholly predictable. It may engender a bureaucratic approach where detailed enquiries are repeated time and time again with little or no real inspiration from the auditor.
2. It can become mechanical as the task of completing the never-ending checklist becomes so laborious that the auditor develops a secret desire to leave the profession.
3. They may be followed blindly by an auditor whose preoccupation is to complete schedules without really understanding why. It is one thing to provide comprehensive direction on audit coverage, but simply to employ form fillers is unacceptable. Where strict time limitations are placed on completing the schedules, there may be little time to think through the actual implications.
4. Detailed ICQs may stifle initiative. The inexperienced auditor may find the detailed guidance useful whereas the more skilled may feel frustration with this mechanical process. The wish

to divert resources to new issues that may have been discussed with client management may be impaired by the fixation with the ICQ as documentation that needs to be completed. The professional auditor needs freedom to follow high-level issues to their conclusion as a way of targeting key risks.

5. Management may feel it is a cumbersome, time-consuming technique. Where the auditor is completing a checklist, which ranges from important matters to immaterial detail on insignificant parts of the system, it may appear amateurish. There will be some parts of the ICQ to be based on questions to line management and it may be tedious to seek the required responses. Some of the questions may elicit inappropriate answers and some may display poor understanding by the auditor of the systems. Most of these disadvantages arise from a misuse of the ICQ procedure which, at its worst, ends up with the auditor sending a list of 101 questions to management.

There are a several ways that the ICQ technique may be applied more efficiently and effectively:

- Tailor the standardized ICQ to the specific circumstances based on understanding of the system under review. Make each question relevant. Using automated schedules makes this task much easier where the auditor can amend the document on computer.
- Gear the questions into high risk areas as a way of interfacing them with the system. Once the risks have been agreed then the questions can be directed to the relevant control issues.

Parts of the ICQ that relate to a stores system may appear in Table 9.3.

TABLE 9.3   Control-related ICQ.

Question	Yes	No	Test no.
ORDERING SYSTEM			
CONTROL OBJECTIVE: To ensure that stores are authorized, delivered, correct, safeguarded and available.			
Q.1 Is person certifying the order independent of the storekeeper?			
Q.2 Are orders placed only with approved suppliers?			
Q.3 Does the order make reference to a purchasing contract?			
Q.4 Are stock level reports issued regularly for reordering purposes?			

Do not give them to the manager to complete but use them for fact-finding discussion. The ICQ should be completed by using all available sources of information from interviews, observation, initial testing, documents, manuals, representations, and past audit files. It is compiled as the audit progresses taking on board a wide range of information.

Internal Control Evaluation System (ICES)

The internal control evaluation system/schedule (ICES) is partly a conceptual model linked directly into the systems-based approach and partly a mechanism for setting out the evaluation process in matrix format. Unlike ICQs it involves setting out the components of good evaluation in a schedule (or matrix) format so that a systematic series of steps can be undertaken before testing, conclusions and recommendation are made. The main headings may appear at the top of the schedule as:

- Systems objectives.
- Control objectives (if this approach is being applied).
- Risks to the achievement of objectives, rated for impact and likelihood.
- Available control mechanisms.
- Existing control mechanisms.
- Initial evaluation of the adequacy of controls.
- Testing strategy required.
- Test results.
- Conclusions on overall risk management arrangements.
- Recommendations.

The entire audit process is established in a formal systematic fashion, although this technique tends to be used by more experienced auditors with a full understanding of the system. Note that this format appears very similar to the risk registers that are prepared through the CRSA process. An example of this audit evaluation approach applied to an audit of a local authority small business grant approval system in Table 9.4.

There are several advantages to this approach:

1. It treats controls as part of the process of mitigating risks to achieving objectives therefore it starts with what management is trying to achieve (i.e. the systems objectives). The entire audit process is seen to flow from this start point.
2. The auditor does not possess a pat answer to controls as suggested by the ICQ approach. It is a question of working out what control objectives are relevant (having regard to the systems objectives) and then seeking to determine what control mechanisms should be in place. This technique is more difficult to master as it requires a commitment to systems auditing. Instead of being armed with a list of questions, the auditor is armed with a database of control mechanisms that fit various risk scenarios.
3. The ICES requires the auditor to analyse the system and break it down into logical components as it flows from input, process through to the final output in chronological order.
4. The ICES deals with risk and exposures as an extension of the evaluation procedure. This requires a considered understanding of the activities under review. A good appreciation of risk enables the auditor to direct control mechanisms at the right parts of the system.
5. The ICES flows naturally into the testing routines as after compliance has been reviewed, the poorer parts of the system are then subject to substantive testing.
6. The ICES forms a record of control weakness to be placed in front of management and discussed before the draft audit report is prepared. We are able to provide a full audit process encapsulated within the ICES schedules. This contains details of objectives, how existing controls compare with desirable ones, the test results obtained, final opinion and recommended improvements derived from resolving weak controls that were confirmed by tests applied.
7. The ICES means a move away from the old audit programme approach where a list of basic tasks is given to the auditor to work through. This method leads to creative, thinking auditors who can operate more at strategic levels.
8. An even better format may be an integrated audit approach where the business advice would embark on a risk workshop to get to the key risks that would then be used to drive the

TABLE 9.4 Business advice service control evaluation.

System aim— I. to encourage business regeneration through local grants

Process stage and control objective	Inherent risks	Desirable controls	Existing controls	Initial assessment	Testing strategy ref; and results	Audit recommendations
GRANTS AVAILABLE I.A awareness of grant	little appreciation of grant availability	wide publicity	word of mouth only	inadequate	I.A.I survey of local businesses Result—awareness poor	I. need to launch scheme properly
ELIGIBILITY ESTABLISHED I.B objective eligibility criteria	many ineligible businesses applying	information package	new comprehensive leaflet and website in use	very comprehensive material	I.B.I check that applying businesses receive info Result—OK	n/a audit assurances provided
BUSINESSES APPROVED I.C meet criteria	wrong businesses approved	formal assessment	subjective selection	open to abuse	I.C.I check whether wrong approvals made Result—poor	2. prepare formal assessment criteria
GRANTS PAID I.D pay the correct person	cheques going astray	ID and collection	posted out	can go astray	I.D.I check that ID system adhered to I.D.2 cheques received by businesses Result—no fraud	n/a audit assurances provided
BUSINESSES GROW I.E effects of grants known	grants have no impact on local community	database follow-up	not done	VFM not assured	I.E.I examine failure rates of aided businesses Result—poor	3. monitoring and new tracking system required

resulting audit. They would then resume to work through ways forward (rather than audit recommendations) before the audit report and agreed management action plan was prepared and issued in draft.

Evaluation as a Continuous Process

This section has commented on some of the techniques that auditors use when evaluating systems. Although formal evaluation is a clear component of the audit process, it is also a function that can occur continuously throughout the audit. The final audit opinion will be derived from many factors and information that the auditor uncovers during the audit:

- As flowcharts and systems notes are formulated they indicate systems weaknesses in high risk areas. These should be separately noted for future reference when developing a testing programme. It is possible to get an initial impression when, say, touring the location and this adds to the auditor's understanding. If an auditor finds files and documents scattered, these initial impressions may be tested by checking the whereabouts of a selected sample.
- Matters connected with the economy, efficiency and effectiveness of the operation may arise at any time during the audit. They may suggest that management has not taken reasonable steps to ensure they are providing value for money. These are all findings relating to the overall state of controls that may appear in the audit report.
- Systems control objectives will have to be carefully defined in line with management views since this will have a fundamental bearing on the controls that are assessed. Where management has failed to set clear objectives there is little hope that they will have any success in discharging their responsibilities. If there are objectives but they fall out of line with organizational policies then this is a finding in its own right. We can go on to suggest that 'auditing through business objectives' brings the auditor closer to the high-level issues than any other audit procedure. The success criteria and risk management strategy that management apply will guide the auditor in deciding whether the controls are working.
- The objectives of the system and management perception on what is being achieved have to be fully appreciated before controls can be reviewed. This requires the auditor to have a good understanding of the system under review and means management has to be fully involved in the auditor's work.
- An understanding of the available control mechanisms again will assist the evaluation process. Imagine an auditor who has been given a laptop that contains the full text of the audit manual. In addition a comprehensive library of control mechanisms would also sit on the hard disk. Having been given terms of reference for the audit and budgeted hours for the job, we would expect that the library of control mechanisms (used in conjunction with the audit manual) would guide the auditor in the most important task of control evaluation.
- The level of existing controls should be assessed as a package that together forms a system of internal control which in turn has to be checked for compliance. The act of obtaining information on the proper functioning of these controls must occur throughout the audit and not just during control evaluation. We would hope that formal control evaluation would provide an opportunity to bring the findings together so that an actual opinion on controls may be provided. One way of summarizing these findings is to relate operational risk to the four key control objectives of reliability and integrity of financial and operational information; effectiveness and efficiency of operations; safeguarding of assets; and compliance with laws, regulations, and contracts.
- Fraud is usually an indicator of poor control and where this has occurred in the past, the evaluation should be carried out with a view to preventing similar control breaches that might

facilitate fraudulent activity. As such, matters relating to past frauds should be brought into play when considering the adequacy of the entire system of internal controls.

- Compensating controls may be used by operatives where formal controls are inadequate in containing risk or are not used in practice. They may be organic in nature and if formally adopted, may be more effective than official procedures. Key controls are fundamental control mechanisms that have to be in place as opposed to less material optional control features. An example of a key control is regular feedback for managers on operational performance.

- The whole control environment including the operational culture will have an impact on the way control mechanisms are defined and adopted. If the auditor ignores this then the evaluation will be substandard. An ICQ approach is better able to deal with assessing the control environment while the ICES copes better with assessing risk in systems and processes that can be broken down into clear stages.

During control evaluation the auditor's judgement is perhaps the single most important factor and this will be based on experience and training. The whole process of reviewing the system will arise throughout the audit and the formal evaluation techniques may be used to confirm the auditor's initial opinion. Control findings have to be tested. First, they must be checked to see if controls are being applied as intended. Second, the effects of weaknesses must be established and quantified as Figure 9.10 demonstrates.

FIGURE 9.10   Evaluation confirmation cycle.

9.5 Testing Strategies

Testing is the act of securing suitable evidence to support an audit. It confirms the auditor's initial opinion on the state of internal controls. It is a step in control evaluation, although many auditors test for the sole purpose of highlighting errors or non-adherence with laid down procedure. It depends on the audit objective. The IIA Practice Advisory 2240-1 requires audit procedures to be planned: 'Engagement procedures, including the testing and sampling techniques employed, should be selected in advance, where practicable, and expanded or altered if circumstances warrant.'

The Testing Process

Practice Advisory 2310-1 underpins the need for good information to support the audit process and states that:

> Sufficient information is factual, adequate and convincing so that a prudent, informed person would reach the same conclusions as the auditor. Competent information is reliable and the best attainable through the use of appropriate engagement techniques. Relevant information supports engagement observations and recommendations and is consistent with the objectives for the engagement. Useful information helps the organization meets its goals.

The testing process may be noted below:

- Define the test objective.
- Define the testing strategy.
- Formulate a series of audit testing programmes.
- Perform the test.
- Schedule the evidence.
- Interpret the results.
- Determine the impact on audit objectives.
- Determine the next step.

The Four Types of Tests

Walkthrough   This involves taking a small sample of items that are traced through the system to ensure that the auditor understands the system. It occurs during the ascertainment stage of the audit and may lead into further tests later. The client may be asked to refer to named documents representative of the transaction cycle that will be cross-referenced to the interview record to assist this process of 'capturing' the system.

Compliance   This determines whether key controls are adhered to. It uncovers non-compliance or unclear procedures. If key controls are not being applied, and this is not compensated for by the system, they become reclassified as weak controls. Note that compliance testing is implicit in IIA Implementation Standard 2120.A3. 'Internal auditors should review operations and programs to ascertain the extent to which results are consistent with established goals and objectives to determine whether operations and programs are being implemented or performed as intended.'

Substantive   These determine whether control objectives are being achieved. Weak controls imply objectives will not be achieved and substantive tests are designed to confirm this initial audit view on the impact of residual risk. Substantive tests may isolate risks that materialize in the form of error, poor information, direct loss or poor value for money.

Dual purpose   This is not a test but a recognition of the practicalities of testing controls where one may wish to combine compliance and substantive testing. An example is to examine an invoice that is certified for payment (compliance test) and is valid (substantive test). It would be impractical to select this invoice twice for two different tests to be separately applied.

The important tests are deemed to be compliance or substantive as these are the two main techniques used to support audit work. The relationship between the four tests is shown in Figure 9.11.

We summarize our discussion:

- Walkthrough tests seek to determine how the system's objectives are achieved.
- Compliance tests seek to determine whether control mechanisms are being applied.
- Substantive tests seek to determine whether control objectives are being achieved.
- Dual purpose tests check for both compliance and actual error, abuse or inefficiency.

Comparing Compliance and Substantive Tests

There are key differences between the two main types of test. We restate the systems-based approach to auditing and how these tests fit into the audit process in Figure 9.12.

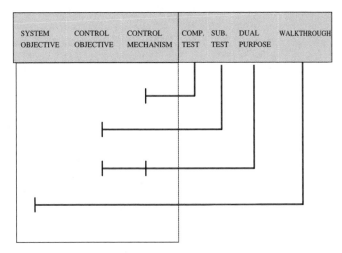

| SYSTEM OBJECTIVE | CONTROL OBJECTIVE | CONTROL MECHANISM | COMP. TEST | SUB. TEST | DUAL PURPOSE | WALKTHROUGH |

FIGURE 9.11 The various test patterns.

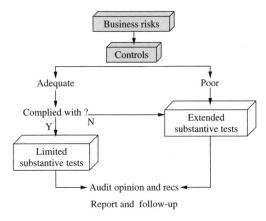

FIGURE 9.12 Compliance and substantive tests.

We look first for compliance with key controls then review results. Substantive tests are then directed towards outstanding residual risk, including those where key controls are not being observed or revealed through compliance testing.

Testing Considerations

The decision on what to test and the extent of testing will be based on factors revolving around evaluation of the systems of internal control. The internal auditor will need to secure sufficient information to complete the audit and Practice Advisory 2310-1 suggests that:

Sufficient information is factual, adequate and convincing so that a prudent, informed person would reach the same conclusions as the auditor. Competent information is reliable and the best attainable through the use of appropriate engagement techniques. Relevant information supports engagement observations and recommendations and is consistent with the objectives for the engagement. Useful information helps the organization meets its goals.

Testing considerations include:

The relative risks	Management needs
Previous audit cover	The auditor's own experiences
The level of managerial support for the audit	The availability of evidence
The audit objectives	The level of materiality of the item reviewed
The time available for the tests	The assessment of internal control

Testing Techniques

There are many ways that one can gather the necessary evidence to support the testing objective. The number and types of techniques are limited only by the imagination of the auditor.

Re-performance   Rechecking a calculation or procedure can give evidence as to its reliability. This enables the auditor to comment directly on the accuracy by which transactions are processed although it does depend on the auditor being able to perform the necessary task.

Observation   This is a useful method of information gathering since it is obtained first-hand by the auditor.

Corroboration   Having facts from one area confirmed by reference to another party is a good way of verifying the accuracy of these facts.

Inspection   Inspection is a formal way of observing physical attributes against a set criterion.

Reconciliation   The process of balancing one set of figures back to another is based mainly on the principle of double-entry bookkeeping that ensures the accounts balance at all times.

Expert opinion   This is less a technique and more a source of assistance linked to another technique.

Interviews   More often than not the best way to find something out is simply to ask and much useful information can be obtained through the interview forum.

Review of published reports/research   Another source of supportive evidence is to be found in reports that impact on the area under review.

Independent confirmation   An obvious source of evidence is to get someone to independently agree defined facts.

Receiving the service as a client   Most operations that produce goods or services recognize the key concept of client care that means there must be a net value from what is being delivered. If we were going to audit McDonald's Restaurants, the first thing to do would be to purchase a meal from the outlet.

Mathematical models   The auditor may construct a model that may be used to gauge particular features of an operation.

Questionnaires   Formal surveys can be used to assist the audit process.

Comparison   Vouching comes under this heading in that we can seek to check one item against another one which has an associated factor.

User satisfaction surveys   Obtaining direct feedback from persons who use the service/product delivered by the operation under review can provide an insight into the success or otherwise of the operation.

We have already suggested that there is an open-ended list of testing techniques, although whatever techniques are applied it is important to record all results carefully. Clearly, testing is not just limited to basic financial systems but can be applied in any environment. For some of the more sensitive ones such as the client satisfaction survey, the auditor should make it clear to management that the exercise is being undertaken. Copies of the pro forma documentation that is being used for the purpose should also be provided. Whatever the approach we must beware appearing to be spies, performing some type of undercover work, as this will probably impair the audit image.

Achieving Control Objectives

Tests check that control objectives are being achieved. This helps confirm the auditor's view of those controls that need improving and helps quantify the extent of the problem. Control objectives ensure that the systems objectives are achieved with regard to:

- The information systems.
- The extent of compliance.
- Safeguarding assets.
- Value for money.

When applying test results to determine if control objectives are achieved the auditor should consider:

The success criteria management is applying   There is often a conflict between factors the auditor would look for when judging the success of a system. These range from timeliness, accuracy, presentation, client feedback, to performance targets. Not all these will be achieved at the same time. More important is the view of management success. Tests that highlight whether business objectives are being met must bear in mind the different interpretations of objectives. There is little point reporting that 2% of timesheets are not reviewed when management feels it so immaterial as not to be worthy of attention. The auditor should ask the important question whether the control objectives promote management systems objectives.

Any systems constraints   There are always constraints over how a system operates. This may relate to resource levels, the availability of information, unforeseeable circumstances, and computer downtime.

The extent of achievement   The auditor should recognize there is no such thing as 100% perfection in any business system. All systems have some imperfection that results in 'error conditions' discovered through audit testing. These errors may not have a significant effect on the performance of the operation and can be tolerated by management.

The need to secure good evidence for an audit opinion   Testing provides direct material that can underwrite the audit report and conclusions that are contained therein. We would take findings, draw general conclusions, then provide suitable recommendations based on the wider picture in Figure 9.13.

The idea is to gather the test findings into control issues in a compartmentalized manner, so that we may form a view not on the testing itself, but more on the underlying control implications.

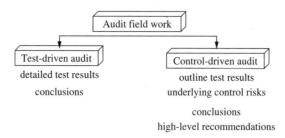

FIGURE 9.13   Putting testing into perspective.

A lack of clear operational standards may lead to inconsistent work that promotes errors and oversights by staff. Rather than discuss how each error may be corrected, we may deal with the root problem.

9.6 Evidence and Working Papers

Audit testing results in much material that should support the reported audit opinion and associated recommendations. The test results along with other material gathered throughout the audit process will constitute audit evidence and this will be held in suitable audit working papers. Standards of working papers and documentary evidence are a topic that all auditors come across in the course of their work and generally there is a view that good standards are a prerequisite to good control. There are various IIA performance standards that address the need for proper records of each audit engagement that has been carried out:

- **2330**—Recording Information: Internal auditors should record relevant information to support the conclusions and engagement results.
- **2330.A1**—The CAE should control access to engagement records. The CAE should obtain approval from senior management and/or legal counsel prior to releasing such records to external parties, as appropriate.
- **2330.A2**—The CAE should develop retention requirements for engagement records. These retention requirements should be consistent with the organization's guidelines and any pertinent regulatory or other requirements.
- **2330.C1**—The CAE should develop policies governing the custody and retention of engagement records, as well as their release to internal and external parties. These policies should be consistent with the organization's guidelines and any pertinent regulatory or other requirements.

Note that the external auditor may be sued where their work may have been performed negligently and their working papers may be used in any defence to this charge. Here we look at some of the requirements for internal auditors' working papers and filing systems.

Evidence Attributes

The evidence the auditor uses for the audit opinion should be:

Sufficient   This is in line with materiality, level of risk and the level of auditors' knowledge of the operation. Sufficient means it should be enough to satisfy the auditor's judgement or persuade management to make any changes advocated by audit.

Relevant   This ensures that evidence is directed to the control objectives.

Reliable   The information should be accurate, without bias and if possible produced by a third party or obtained directly by the auditor.

Practical   One would weigh up the evidence required, the cost and time taken to obtain it and sensitivity.

9.7 Statistical Sampling

All auditors need knowledge of statistical sampling and it is advisable to adopt a clear policy regarding its use. We summarize popular ways statistical sampling may be applied, although a specialist textbook will provide a fuller understanding. Statistical sampling has a clear role and auditors make a decision during systems audits in Figure 9.14.

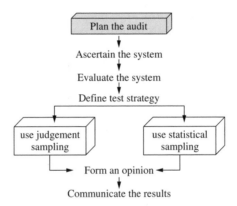

FIGURE 9.14   Role of sampling.

An auditor has to decide whether statistical sampling will be used based on knowledge and an appreciation of the technique and its application.

The External Audit Perspective

Most auditing textbooks have a chapter on sampling and so it might appear to be mandatory. One must consider the differences between the internal and external audit objectives before assessing the relative value to be derived. The external auditor is primarily concerned with:

1. Whether accounts show a true and fair view. Decisions may range from disagreement, qualification, through to a level of uncertainty and as such invite a yes/no response.
2. The reliance that can be placed on underlying financial systems of internal control. As a short-cut to checking all the figures in the final accounts there may be some reliance placed on controls, although there must be some direct testing to secure evidence to support the audit opinion.
3. Whether the level of errors found by examining selected transactions has a material effect on the accounts in terms of influencing the audit opinion. Materiality is a firm external audit concept that places emphasis on the impact of problems on the reliability of the final accounts.

4. Whether the level of testing carried out means that they have discharged their professional responsibilities. Substantive testing is fundamental to the external audit and the need for a defendable choice is uppermost. A method to determine sample size is useful. There are tests that can be applied to 100% of a database although this gives a long list of items for further manual investigation, which will take time. The need to restrict the number of items examined remains.

The internal auditor is more concerned about:

1. Whether examining selected transactions confirms initial opinion on the systems of risk management and internal control. Samples are selected and examined to see whether the results coincide with the initial audit opinion.
2. Whether their findings are sufficient to convince management to act. Where management agrees that problems exist there is little point in extensive testing. It may be necessary to get an idea of the scale of the problems, although the main objective is to get management to act. The internal auditor will use a consultancy-based approach that emphasizes the solutions and not the detailed errors that fall within a test-based model. The audit report will then be based around the proposed changes.
3. Whether the risk of any losses or deficiencies may be quantified. This is where statistical sampling comes to the fore. This would apply more in investigative work than in systems auditing.

In conclusion, the external auditor is primarily concerned about accepting or rejecting a financial statement while internal audit work is geared to encourage management to act on defined control weaknesses. It is the external auditor who is more concerned with the use of statistical sampling in financial audits, although it does have a role in internal audit.

Reasons why statistical sampling may not be used   There are many internal auditors who do not use statistical sampling and audit departments that have no firm policy. There are many reasons why it may not be used:

1. Staff lack awareness and have had no training. This means that Figure 9.14 suggests that the auditor does not necessarily make a conscious choice between statistical and judgemental sampling because of the lack of knowledge. The fact that statistical sampling can be complicated may discourage its use. It can be time consuming to master and cumbersome to use.
2. One needs knowledge of the population and this requires time-consuming research. It may be difficult to tell exactly what is contained in the sample because of the nature of the audit. It is still advisable to analyse the populace as this gives an insight into an operation.
3. It may stifle the 'audit nose' by not allowing the auditor to be guided by years of experience. Statistical sampling relies on randomness and does not allow the auditor to choose individual transactions. The auditor's 'intuition' can be suppressed.
4. Quoting figures and probability ranges may not convince non-numeric managers to act. It depends on the perceptions of the client for the work, which vary. Some managers appreciate this approach while others feel intimidated. This factor should be balanced so as not to produce an audit report resisted by management although much depends on the terminology used by the auditor.
5. Statistical sampling is not readily applicable to small unusual populations. The real benefits come where population sizes are larger and samples relatively smaller.

Advantages of Statistical Sampling

Results may be defended against bias   Bias conjures up images of the auditor being subject to favouritism, narrow-mindedness, one-sidedness and partiality. Samples selected for no justifiable reason may foster accusations of auditor bias. Where there is a scientific method of defining sample sizes and selecting items we can assume the more appropriate stance of being objective, detached, dispassionate, fair, unemotional and above all, just.

A defined sample size is provided   A close examination of statistical tables brings out the feature of larger populations requiring only relatively small increases in sample size to meet set parameters. A judgemental sample of, say, 5% becomes more difficult to handle for larger systems with thousands of accounts. Statistical methods permit smaller samples that are statistically valid.

One may safely extrapolate the results and apply them to the wider population   This is a moot point in that there are many auditors who extend sample results to the entire data field when the sample has not been obtained using statistical sampling. Although this prediction is usually accepted by management this is technically improper. The only professional prediction is one that sets the statistically significant results within the set parameters (e.g. 95% of cases will tend to fall within a defined range).

The technique is repeatable and one would expect a similar result from any repetition   The exercise of tossing 100 coins will tend to produce around 50% heads and 50% tails each time. With statistical sampling we would expect on average to find similar results each time the test procedure is applied.

It forces one to define and consider the attributes of the population   We set as a disadvantage the need to research the data being tested from a holistic viewpoint and this is also seen as an advantage. The more that is learnt about an area, the better will be the auditor's ability to direct the audit. Unfortunately time is now seen as the most important component of the audit function that must be controlled and this does not promote extensive pre-planning. The balance to this last point is the growing trend whereby whole databases are downloaded and explored on a regular basis. This not only encourages a greater familiarization but also allows one to generate global figures concerning the total number of records and other key facts.

Computers make statistical sampling more convenient to use   It is simple to ask the computer to generate random numbers. Many interrogation packages have in-built statistical tables.

The level of confidence may be predefined   Statistical sampling allows one to define predetermined risk parameters that the final opinion may be set within. This is factual and cannot be challenged as it states that a probable number of selections will follow a set pattern, but not all of them. This is a comfortable position for the auditor as it allows an authoritative opinion that in terms of logical presentation cannot be refuted, even if the precise interpretation may be.

Judgement, Haphazard and Statistical Sampling

Judgement sampling   The auditor uses knowledge of systems and people to select items more likely to exhibit certain features. The sample is purposely biased by the auditor to take on board matters that the auditor is aware of. For example, we may be concerned about our ordering system where an individual who left some months ago was known to be medically unwell and made known errors. We may look at orders he processed and skew the sample.

Haphazard sampling   This allows the selection of items at random but is not based on any defined statistical formula. The intention is to secure an unbiased sample, although because the sample size is not mathematically based, it is not possible to formally extrapolate the results. The selected sample size may be too small or too large. It is best applied to smaller populations, say under 100 items, since statistical sampling is of no use at these levels.

Statistical sampling   The auditor has to define the population and set confidence levels. A predetermined sample size will be provided and one may indicate how reliable and accurate the results are. The results secured from testing the sample may be extrapolated to draw quantified conclusions about the population.

The Normal Distribution

The bell-shaped curve represents the normal distribution. The shape of the curve is determined by the mean and the standard deviation (SD) of the underlying values whereby the greater the range of values the flatter the curve. This feature is used in statistical sampling to allow the area under the curve to equate to 1. If the mean is seen as 0 then we can calculate that each SD from the mean will cover a defined portion of the normal distribution curve. This appears in Figure 9.15.

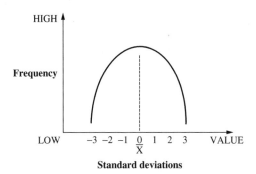

FIGURE 9.15   The normal distribution.

Area under the curve:

$$+ \text{or} - 1 \text{ SD} = 68.3\%$$

$$+ \text{or} - 2 \text{ SD} = 95.4\%$$

$$+ \text{or} - 3 \text{ SD} = 99.7\%$$

The relationships between the values and the SDs have been translated into statistical tables. These may be used to form conclusions about the population that are derived from an examination of a sample of the population. This is based on the theory that the mean of a distribution of sample means is equal to the mean of the population from which the sample is drawn. It is important to know the SD of the sample that is used and a formula may be used to calculate this figure. This is not reproduced here but it should be noted that the smaller the range of values the smaller the SD while the greater the range (i.e. variation from the mean) the larger the SD.

Applying Statistical Sampling to the Audit Process

It is important that statistical sampling is considered in terms of its actual role in the audit process. It is used when performing the testing routines required to confirm or otherwise the initial evaluation of internal controls. To this end the samples and ensuing tests may be used for:

Quantifying the effects of control weaknesses   Substantive testing reveals the implications of a lack of control. This is where statistical sampling may be used to allow a generalist comment based on the results of a predetermined number of transactions. We have already agreed that one can only give an overall opinion on the entire database where the sample has been statistically prepared.

Getting management to act on audit recommendations   Ensuring that internal audit recommendations are supported by indicating the extent of risk in failing to take remedial action encourages management to adopt them. So where we find excessive levels of non-compliance with a key control, this must be quantified and set against the corresponding recommendation.

Highlighting implications of failure to act on identified control weaknesses   We use statistical sampling to predict the extent of uncontrolled error. This need not be in terms of one-off examples that give no indication of the scale and extent of the problems as in some audit reports. Scientific sampling can result in matrix boxes in the report where the type of errors found can be given global values based on extrapolation, to increase the impact of the findings.

Statistical sampling is a means to an end. It assists in achieving defined test objectives, without examining the entire population. The role of statistical sampling within the testing routine is described in Figure 9.16.

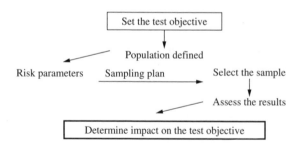

FIGURE 9.16   Testing using statistical sampling.

Sampling Techniques

There are two main aspects to statistical sampling. One is how the number of items to be examined is defined. The other relates to the methods used to extract the required information. The latter is called the sampling method or selection technique. Methods used to define numbers tested are called sampling plans. This section deals with sampling methods and these may be set out as:

Random sampling   This technique is used to select samples such that each item in the population has an equal chance of being chosen. Random number tables may be used to choose the required items and these may be generated by an appropriately programmed computer.

Stratified sampling   If we recall that the normal distribution places values in the shape of a bell, then a skewed distribution will not appear symmetrical. This may mean that the auditor can divide the population into several segments that may consist of, say, a small number of high value invoices for revenue contracts and a large number of small value ones for one-off supplies. The auditor may wish to pay more attention to high value items and in so doing can split the population into two and apply statistical sampling plans with different confidence levels to each one. The auditor may have decided that payments to overseas agents are not adequately controlled and there is a significant risk that many such payments may fall foul of anti-corruption legislation and may wish to examine a sample of these payments. The population of payments to 1,755 overseas agents may be divided into the strata in Figure 9.17.

Stratification:

£ Amount	Number	£ Total amount
0 – 9,999.99	1,400	2,800,000
10,000 – 19,999.99	150	2,000,000
20,000 – 29,999.99	65	1,500,000
30,000 – 39,999.99	35	1,200,000
40,000 – 79,999.99	45	2,500,000
80,000 and over	60	20,800,000
	1,755	30,800,000

FIGURE 9.17   Stratified sampling.

The auditor may wish to examine all 60 payments over £80, 000 and then extract a sample of 100 further payments using three value-based strata:

Stratum	£ Range	Total amount	Initial sample
1	0–9,999.99	2,800,000	28
2	10,000–29,999.99	3,500,000	35
3	30,000–79,999.99	3,700,000	37
	80,000 and over	20,800,000	___
		30,800,000	100

The initial sample of 100 items distributed per value:

$2.8 + 3.5 + 3.7 = 10$ which gives $2.8/10 \times 100 = 28$ $3.5/10 \times 100 = 35$ $3.7/10 \times 100 = 37$

and then all 60 that are over £80,000.

Cluster sampling   This is a convenient way of selecting items for testing where once the number of transactions has been defined, they are then taken from one filing area. This may be a single drawer of a filing cabinet and is based on simple working practicalities.

Interval sampling   Here the population should be homogeneous, with no cyclical bias or missing items. If we divide the population size by the sample size then the sampling interval is obtained and every nth item is chosen for testing. One might imagine a computer being asked to select, say, every 20th item from a particular file.

Automated sampling   This may be seen as a selection technique where the auditor uses sampling software to set parameters, determine the number for testing, access the relevant file and then download the selected items into a separate spreadsheet for later analytical testing by the auditor.

Setting Risk Parameters

Statistical sampling is based on probability theory and as such one must set upper and lower limits within which the results may be placed. It is similar to saying that on average a die will fall on the number six on 1/6 occasions. With statistical sampling one has to set the criteria within which the results should be evaluated and this falls under three basic parameters:

Error rate   This is the level of error that one may expect from the population being tested. Error may be seen as, for example, the number of invoices that are incorrect. This is normally set at 5% and most statistical sampling tables are based on this figure. If the actual error rate is different then a revision to the quoted risk boundaries has to be made. The rate is determined by the auditor and is based on pilot studies, discussions with management and the results of previous audits.

Confidence   Confidence is the degree to which the results derived from the sample will follow the trend in the actual population. A 95% confidence means that 95 out of every 100 items examined will reflect the population. The position on confidence levels is in Table 9.5.

TABLE 9.5   Confidence levels.

Level	Perception
Below 90%	is too low to be of any real value.
90%	is where the auditor knows a lot about the population but wishes to convince management.
95%	is the level that is generally used and is high enough to satisfy the auditor and management.
99%	is too high and will result in most of the population being selected.

Precision   This shows the margin within which the results can be quoted and defines the degree of accuracy that is required. It may be in terms of the quoted error being expressed as a figure taken from testing the sample plus or minus the degree of precision, say 2%. The real result relative to the population will be somewhere within the lower and upper levels. If one needs to be accurate to 2% one may find an error in the sample of, say, £100, this may be quoted for the population as between £98 and £102. The level chosen will depend on the objective of the test and how the results are used.

Extrapolation   This is when results taken from a sample are grossed up and applied to the whole population. The average result from the sample is multiplied by the value of the population to give the estimated total error. Risk parameters are set by the auditor and depend on the test objective. It is practice to use 5% error rate tables, with 95% confidence at plus or minus 2% precision. Using these standards, most statistically extrapolated results will be accepted by management.

Audit Testing and Statistical Sampling

The two main types of audit testing are compliance and substantive testing although one may perform some walkthrough tests during the ascertainment stage. Note the following:

- **Compliance tests.** Here one is testing the existence or otherwise of a particular control. The test is of a yes/no nature where an attribute (i.e. control adherence) is either present or does not exist. An example may be a test to determine the number of purchase invoices that have not been authorized by a designated officer before being paid.
- **Substantive tests.** These tests are carried out to establish the extent to which the implications of a control weakness may be quantified. We may be concerned to discover the total value of purchase invoices incorrectly posted to the wrong year due to poor cut-off procedures.

These two testing conventions require different statistical sampling plans geared into the objectives of the tests. Compliance testing is concerned with specific attributes so that a frequency may be quoted. Substantive testing looks for variables and enables the auditor to quote a range of values from the test results. The sampling plans mentioned below may be placed in Table 9.6.

TABLE 9.6   The sampling plans.

Compliance testing	Substantive testing
Attribute sampling	Variable sampling
Stop-go sampling	Difference estimates
Discovery sampling	Monetary unit sampling

Compliance testing requires variations of attribute sampling, while substantive testing is based on variations of variable sampling. These plans are expanded below.

The various sampling plans   Each of these sampling plans will be briefly dealt with. It is important to appreciate where each plan may be applied in determining the number of items to examine. Graham Westwood (from unpublished course notes from a Masters degree programme, City University Business School, 1991) has suggested a criterion for selecting the most appropriate plan:

Quantitative features (substantive tests):
- Is the book value of the population available?
- If no—use variable sampling.
- If yes—do we expect a difference?
- If no—use MUS.
- If yes—use difference estimates.

Qualitative features (compliance tests):
- Is fraud suspected?
- If yes—use discovery sampling.
- If no—do we expect a low error rate?

- If no—use fixed attribute sampling.
- If yes—use stop-go sampling.

Substantive Testing Sampling

Variable sampling   This plan enables one to take the average result from the sample and extrapolate this to arrive at an estimated error rate that applies to the entire population. A preliminary sample of 50 items is taken and the error rate calculated along with the SD from the sample. The error rate divided by the SD gives a proportion that can be used to determine sample sizes from the table for various confidence levels. For additional items the SD is recalculated.

Difference estimates   Where the book value (BV) is available one may take the difference between the BV and actuals for a preliminary sample of 100 items. The resulting SD is used to calculate the new sampling error rate that may be compared to the original. This technique provides a short-cut and can be very convenient. If there are many missing items then the differences may actually be bigger than the BV.

Monetary unit sampling (MUS)   This plan is used by external auditors and incorporates an assessment of the strength of the particular internal control system. The poorer the internal controls the greater the degree of reliability required which in turn makes the sample size larger. One assumes that the population consists of a series of values and in so doing the larger (and more material) items are naturally selected once the sampling interval is determined. One is looking for an over- or understatement of monetary values so that the auditor can decide whether the account may be accepted or not in an audit opinion. Accordingly one is able to sample, say, the debtor's figure and examine all the larger items before deciding if the balance sheet figure is correctly stated (i.e. not overstated). An MUS plan may give the result that out of a population size of £100,000, 60 items should be examined which are selected at intervals of £1,667.

There are **advantages** to this plan:

1. One only needs the value of the population and not the actual number or the SD.
2. The confidence level is determined by the reliability of the system of internal control.
3. High value items are always included in the sample.

There are also several **disadvantages**:

1. It is biased towards high value items that may in fact be better controlled than lower value ones.
2. No error can be defined for the population.
3. It will ignore nil-value items.
4. It is only used for accept/reject decisions.
5. One needs to know the total value of the population.
6. A low confidence level will dilute the results.
7. It is a complicated technique to apply in practice.

Compliance Test Sampling

Attribute sampling   One needs to set an error rate, confidence levels and precision limits. This may be a 5% error at 95% confidence plus or minus 2%. The error rate determines which statistical sampling table is used and this table will give the required sample size at a glance. When one determines the actual error rate then the precision is recalculated for errors over the set rate. Additional error rate tables are used with the new error rate for the revised precision levels.

Stop-go sampling   This is an incremental sampling plan that starts with smaller samples to save time once one sets an acceptable probability level. The plan assumes that all populations over 2,000 are the same. The sample will give a maximum acceptable error rate of, say, 5% and if the actual results are higher, then further samples are taken until the results are acceptable and within the set limit.

Discovery sampling   Discovery sampling is based on the notion of determining how many items must be examined if one has a fair chance of discovering a suspected fraud. The plan gives the sample size required to find the error and is useful for planning purposes, although no conclusions may be drawn about the population itself. As with all sampling plans one must set a probability within which fall the chances of discovering the fraud with the sample size that the table provides.

Testing secures material to support the audit findings and that can be of use when formulating the audit report. The results are used to confirm or not the auditor's opinion in a way that can be communicated to management. Compliance tests can be quite straightforward as long as one understands the control that is being tested. Substantive tests may pose problems. The auditor may set up as an expert in determining whether something has been successful. Care is required and the auditor should remember the overriding objective of securing adequate management action to solve real and material control weaknesses that affect the success of the operation/organization. Working papers hold the documentation that results from the testing process which is why it is included here. The audit manual should establish standards for documenting audit work and retaining necessary information. There should be defined disposal dates for what will eventually be confidential waste. It is essential that these standards are high and contribute to the overall efficiency of the audit process. Moreover, the CAE should establish suitable reviewing mechanisms to ensure that these standards are being properly adhered to throughout the audit department. Janet L. Colbert has provided some advice on the use of audit sampling:

> Before becoming enmeshed in performing sampling procedures, internal auditors should step back and first consider whether this technique is appropriately suited to the task at hand. In certain circumstances, sampling is simply not the best approach; and depending on other information gathered for a particular area, performing a sample may not be necessary. Sampling also affects the reliability of results; whereas an examination of 100 percent of a population produces results with high reliability, sampling decreases reliability. In addition, auditors produce different types and amounts of work-paper documentation depending on whether sampling, or another approach, is utilised. As with any examination procedure, sampling should be used judiciously, as a poor decision can lead to inaccurate results. Auditors need to make sure that the target population meets the necessary criteria for conducting a sample before applying this technique. When used appropriately, sampling can add significant value to the audit process by increasing efficiency and effectiveness of testing procedures.[1]

Statistical sampling is not a mandatory technique although it should not be ignored by the auditor as it can be used to comment on a system through the use of a relatively small sample. The audit department should define a clear policy on the use of this technique and where and how it should be applied, and this should appear in the audit manual. The use of automated statistical sampling via a suitable software package assists getting auditors to use statistical sampling. If judgement sampling is, in the main, being applied this should be stated as clear policy having reviewed the applicability of statistical sampling.

9.8 Reporting Results of the Audit

Some auditors argue that the audit report is the fundamental end product of any audit and IIA Performance Standard 2400 states that: 'Internal auditors should communicate the engagement results.' In reality the impact of the audit should be the actual changes that are created as a result of the investment of audit resources and here the report forms just part of this process. Whatever the view, the fact is that audit reporting is one of those fundamental techniques that must be mastered by the auditor. Sawyer has made clear that: 'Reports are the auditor's opportunity to get management's undivided attention. That is how auditors should regard reporting—as an opportunity, not dreary drudgery—a perfect occasion to show management how.'[2]

There are many components and principles that underlie audit reporting, the most important of which is the quality of audit work that has been carried out prior to the reporting stage. Reporting is important and a useful phrase to express this importance comes from the IIA Handbook Series: 'an auditor's greatest idea or discovery is only as effective as his or her ability to express the concept to others and elicit the desired response'.[3]

Interim Audit Reports

Before the full audit report is produced one would expect interim reports particularly on larger projects. These have three main uses:

1. They force the auditor to build the report as work is progressed.
2. They keep the audit manager up to date and allow interim reviews of work performed.
3. In this way they may be given to the client and so act as a continuous report clearance device as well as bringing the client into the audit process itself.

Audit Assignment Reports

This is what most auditors think of when considering the topic of audit reports and it is dealt with below:

1. Executive summaries   A two or three page summary can be attached to the front of the report or issued as a separate document. It provides a concise account of objectives, main conclusions and the steps that management should be taking. This recognizes that managers are busy and wish to take a short-cut in getting to grips with any material issues that may result from an audit.

2. Follow-up reports   All audit work should be followed up and it is possible to establish a standardized reporting format to check on outstanding audit recommendations. These audits tend to be simple to perform but sensitive in nature. They involve forming a view on whether management has done all it promised to.

3. Fraud investigation reports   These reports detail the allegations, the work carried out and why, as well as the main findings.

4. Oral reports   Auditors are charged with reporting the results of audit work and this may be in an oral format. Oral reports are designed to save time and can have a more direct impact on the recipient. They also allow the audit client to provide instant feedback to the lead auditor.

The Reporting Process

Audit reports are not simply published documents but are the result of a comprehensive audit reporting process that may be summarized in Figure 9.18.

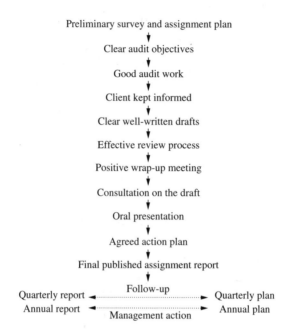

Preliminary survey and assignment plan

Clear audit objectives

Good audit work

Client kept informed

Clear well-written drafts

Effective review process

Positive wrap-up meeting

Consultation on the draft

Oral presentation

Agreed action plan

Final published assignment report

Follow-up

Quarterly report ← .... → Quarterly plan

Annual report ← .... → Annual plan

Management action

FIGURE 9.18   Audit reporting process.

Preliminary survey and assignment plan   The audit report actually starts with a plan that sets the framework for the ensuing audit.

Final published assignment report   A final report should be prepared along with a clear definition of reporting lines and people who should be given copies. There are many audit units guilty of producing 'draft' reports that remain in circulation without a final version, much to the confusion of all involved with this document. Where there are problems with the accuracy of the final report these should be corrected. The IIA Performance Standard 2421 sets a direction here: 'If a final communication contains significant error or omission, the CAE should communicate corrected information to all individuals who received the original communication.' It may also be an idea to consider any developments that have occurred since the completion of the audit field work and refer to them in the final report if appropriate. Meanwhile, two IIA Implementation Standards address the publication of audit reports to external parties: 2201.A1—When planning an engagement for parties outside the organisation, internal auditors should establish a written understanding with them about objectives, scope, respective responsibilities and other expectations, including restrictions on distribution of the results of the engagement and access to engagements records; 2410.A3—When releasing results to clients or other parties outside the organization, the communication should include limitations on distribution and use of the results.

If the internal audit activity meets the conditions for use, reference should be made that 'the engagement was conducted in accordance with the Standards for the Professional Practice of Internal Auditing.'

Follow-up   The process is still not complete until we have set up a follow-up routine in line with best audit practice. These standards can be mentioned within the report or the accompanying letter.

Quarterly reports   The audit report should feed into the quarterly reporting cycle that seeks to summarize what has been found and reported on in the relevant three-month period. Reference to the quarterly plan makes this a dynamic process that is linked to a defined reference point.

Annual report   The above is equally true for the annual reporting cycle that again should be set within the context of the plan for the year in question.

Management action   We arrive at the true audit product in terms of management action based on the audit report. All else is simply to set a foundation within which this action may be stimulated by the auditor. The objective of the reporting process is to get management to act on audit's advice. A report that suggests no action is required is just as significant as one that asks for many changes. Assurances (of good control) allow management to channel resources into riskier areas. The reality of corporate life is that there are many reports and other types of communications that bombard managers.

It is essential that the entire reporting process is carefully managed and controlled since a failing in any one component will impair the impact of the report. Note that the final result of this process may be defined as 'management action' to secure changes and improvements to the way the organization designs, implements, seeks compliance with and reviews its systems of internal control. There are auditors who complain that managers fail to implement audit recommendations and that they should be disciplined accordingly. In practice, however, most of the blame can be placed on a failure by audit management to implement a suitable reporting process based on the concepts set out above. An apt comment from the late Joe Morris made in 1997 is still relevant today: 'An internal audit report that talks about yesterday is no good at all.'[4]

Objectives of the Audit Report

Extensive audit resources may be spent on performing an audit and the client may see as the end product a published audit report. It is therefore important that the objectives of this final document are clearly established and the four main functions of the audit report are:

- To **assure** management that business risks are well controlled.
- To **alert** them to areas where this is not the case and there are defined risk exposures.
- To **advise** them on steps necessary to improve risk management strategies.
- To support **action** plans prepared by client management.

Underlying Components of Action

The audit report is the result of a comprehensive process and is a means to an end. There are several clear parts of the audit process that directly impact on the audit report: this working paper is called an internal control evaluation schedule (which records the results of the internal control evaluation system—see page 231) and contains details of each major control weakness that appears as an audit finding in the published report. The aim is to lead the auditor into creative thinking so that problems may be solved. A logical foundation will have been built, which these ideas can be founded on. The ICES will form the main reference document for the wrap-up meeting where material issues will be discussed with the auditee. This working document will also feed directly into the draft audit report in that it will set out what was done, what was found, what it means and what now needs to be done. The stage at which the ICES appears in the report drafting process may be illustrated in Figure 9.19.

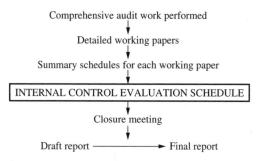

FIGURE 9.19 Internal control evaluation schedule.

The ICES should form a high-level summary of the working papers (properly cross-referenced), which lends itself to being fed directly into the audit report itself. Moreover relevant material, which will enter into the report's standards, findings, conclusions and recommendations, will be found in the ICES that promotes a structured approach to drafting the formal audit report. (Also see Table 9.4.)

Formulating the Audit Opinion

As well as identifying control weaknesses the auditor is charged with forming and publishing an opinion based on the audit work performed. This part of the audit report may be based on:

- The results of control evaluation.
- The existing control culture.
- Outstanding risk.
- The underlying causes of basic problems.
- Whether controls are adhered to.
- Whether controls work.
- The practicalities of available remedies.
- Management's efforts to improve.
- The effects of any future changes planned.
- Overall impressions on management's ability and willingness to address residual risk.
- Findings from unofficial sources.

Formulating Recommendations

It is not enough to point out problems without providing guidance on required action. This is the positive part of the audit report and when formulating recommendations, we should consider:

- The available options.
- The need to remove barriers to good risk management and control.
- The exercise of creative thinking.
- Value-for-money (VFM) points.
- The resource implications of recommended controls.
- Any bad management practices that impair control.
- The ideal solution.
- The costs of poor control in terms of unmitigated risk.
- Practical workability.

The auditor should point management in the right direction and stimulate effective management action. It is possible to adjust the tone of audit recommendations and choose from:

- We recommend...
- We strongly recommend...
- It is advisable for management to...
- It is essential that management...
- Management needs to urgently address...
- Management should consider...

Auditors may make many recommendations and these should be structured for maximum impact, the most important first. There should be a few enabling steps that management should take and these should be detailed in the opening part of the recommendations. They should be designed to place management in a position to effect the various recommendations. This would also appear in any executive summary and should not consist of more than two or three items in discussion mode. The remaining recommendations should follow in order of priority. One useful approach is to document a series of recommendations for each main section of the report and then repeat them as the final part of the executive summary (cross-referenced to the main report). Recommendations should be presented to create maximum impact. There are many busy executives who are primarily interested in what is being recommended, and why.

The Review Process

Audit work should be reviewed before a report is published and this should occur on two levels. First, there should be a supervisory review of the underlying working papers where all audit findings should be supported by sound, evidenced audit work. The second level concentrates on the audit report and the way the work, conclusions and recommendations are expressed. The review should look at the quality as well as quantity of work. If work is reviewed as it progresses the draft report will not be delayed awaiting the audit managers' review. The report review may look for:

The structure	What the findings are based on
How they are expressed	The tone of the report
Any gaps	The terminology used
Spelling and grammar	Whether the house style has been applied

The Clearance Process

The draft audit report, once reviewed, has to be cleared and management given the opportunity to comment on the contents. The findings should not come as a surprise to management and it is advisable to bring them to the manager's attention as they arise. Regular progress reports (probably oral) and a brief meeting at the end of each week will assist this process. A wrap-up meeting with the line manager should be held at the end of the audit where the main findings are discussed. The reviewed draft should be sent to the line manager (only) and an informal meeting held to discuss this as soon as possible after completion of the work. Factual matters should be dealt with and the auditor may well revise the draft as a result. The auditors' conclusions will only change where the factual corrections materially affect audit findings. Once this has occurred a further draft should be formally sent to those affected by the work including the next tier of management. Formal written comments will be taken on board and a final report published. This is a useful technique for involving the actual operational manager as the report will be more reliable and we would have hopefully secured this officer's full support before it goes to a wider audience. Note that where management accepts without question all audit recommendations, this may mean they are not particularly interested in the results and wish to get rid of the auditor. Effective action normally starts with close discussions with management on each audit recommendation. Again see the section below on change management for a different perspective on this issue. Management is entitled to choose not to follow audit recommendations and in this instance it is the auditor's responsibility to ensure they understand the implications and are prepared to assume the associated risk. Management will then assume full responsibility for this documented decision and this issue may be brought to the attention of the audit committee.

Formulating the Action Plan

It is a good idea to form an agreed action plan with management based on the audit. This allows management to take over the audit recommendations and so be fully involved in implementing them. An action plan may be devised during the drafting procedure and once agreed may be included in the published report. Where management is allowed to form its own action plan, this becomes a very efficient way of getting audit recommendations implemented, although we would expect a degree of negotiation by both sides. Accordingly the auditor should work out which recommendations should be pursued and which may be partly given up for a greater good. The best solution is to include the action plan within the executive summary as part of the agreed solution and we would look for items such as work required, by whom, deadlines and reporting lines as a way of ensuring that the recommendations will come about. Once complete the action plan should belong to management as it seeks to embark on the necessary workload.

Supportive Evidence

Recommendations must be based on sound evidence and the extent of this supporting material depends on the importance of establishing the effects of control weaknesses. Where internal auditors are required to attend management working parties which publish reports and make recommendations without comprehensive research then their views should be qualified as not being derived from the normal audit process. The formal audit reports in contrast must be based on sound evidence that has been derived from the audit process.

Change Management

Many auditors become demotivated when their audit reports are more or less ignored by the client. Some feel that line managers should be disciplined through failure to act on audit recommendations while others simply feel less enthusiastic about their work as a result. Where reports are not actioned there is always an underlying reason. Occasionally this is because management is acting negligently and against the best interest of the organization. More often, it is because they can see no good reason to obey unrealistic recommendations made by people who do not understand the operation in question. Audit recommendations generally form part of a change process in that they tend to ask for something that is not already being done. As such they lead to some of the tensions that change itself creates and this in turn affects the client. Moreover the auditor may also be a source of management stress. When performing an audit the auditor should recognize the implications of the change process and ensure that where necessary these are taken on board particularly at the reporting stage. At this stage (there is a separate chapter on change management) it should be noted that on receipt of a draft audit report the client may exhibit some of the following reactions:

- What does this mean?
- Will I lose out?
- Will I benefit at all?
- How should I play this?
- Will this lead to something bigger?
- Can I use this to get something?
- Is the auditor manipulating me?
- Is there a hidden motive behind all this?
- What are the costs of getting these recommendations actioned?
- Can I afford to ignore this report?
- Will my boss support me?

Where these questions are left unanswered, the client may feel threatened and react negatively. If the audit has been professionally carried out with a clear understanding of management's systems objectives along with its close involvement at all stages of the review, then these fears may be reduced.

Logical Presentation

The flow of information contained in an audit report should follow a logical path that takes the reader through the audit process itself. The logical flow may appear as in Figure 9.20.

SUBJECT

SCOPE

PLANNED COVER

ACTUAL COVER

MODE

EXISTING DEFICIENCY

UNDERLYING CAUSE

EFFECT/IMPLICATION

ENABLING STRUCTURE

REQUIRED CHANGES

FIGURE 9.20   Logical presentations.

There are many ways that this information may be presented, although the principle of providing a logical flow of problems, causes, effects and required action should stand.

Structuring the Audit Report

A defined structure for audit reports should be implemented by the CAE and this should be followed when drafting audit reports. This will vary from department to department depending on the nature of the work that is carried out and the type of individuals who will be receiving the audit report. One example is in Table 9.7.

TABLE 9.7   Report sections.

Section	Coverage
One	This will contain the executive summary to the report.
Two	This will outline the objective, scope, approach and work done.
Three	This will contain a background to the area under review.
Appendices	Restrict these to the minimum.

The CAE should adopt a suitable policy on responses from the client and they may be:

- Incorporated into the report.
- Built into a management action plan.
- Included as an appendix.

Some audit departments send the draft for consultation without the executive summary and formulate recommendations after the client has been able to comment on the findings. The participative approach comes into its own where the auditor forms joint recommendations with the client after discussing the findings. This agreed action plan is then reported in the executive summary. Note that where there has been close co-operation throughout the audit, problems with formal responses will probably not arise.

Ongoing Drafting

Most auditors are very efficient when performing the field work and by working hard can give a good impression to clients. Back at the office, there is a tendency to slow down and spend much time on drafting the audit report and this may lead to delays in publishing the report. One solution is to encourage auditors to write reports as they carry out the audit and the outline structure may be drafted as soon as the audit is started. Laptop PCs are essential to this process and as drafting occurs, any gaps may be spotted before the auditor leaves the client. Where a reporting structure has been agreed via the audit manual then one will be able to complete an outline when the audit is started. The terms of reference part of the report may be drafted from the assignment plan while a section on background to the operation will be available in the early part of the audit. It is not acceptable to produce reports weeks after the audit and the reporting standard should set clear deadlines on this topic.

The One-Minute Manager

Research has shown that a typical manager will spend only a few minutes on each item of business before turning to another matter. Auditors who cannot identify with this point will find their work for all intents and purposes ignored. Managers may speak of the 'audit books' to describe the detailed reports sent out by the audit department that are full of what appears to be insignificant facts and endless testing results. As well as using executive summaries, the auditor is well advised to give oral presentations to bring home audit points and in so doing save management much time and effort. The manager may need quickly to know:

What are the risks?	What caused these risks to arise?
What are the implications?	What is the best solution?
What action should I take?	What happens if I do nothing?

An auditor who anticipates and answers all of these questions in, say, a brief meeting/presentation will be well received by senior management. Note that the formal comprehensive audit report should still be provided. The key is to anticipate unanswered questions and resolve them. If this does not happen then the impact of the audit report is lessened and a tendency not to act on the findings will arise. One only makes changes where there is a clear impetus based primarily on sound justifications and clear benefits. The realities of working life mean that management does not have time to deal with anything that fails this basic test. The audit manual should contain a specimen audit report. Having this on disk assists preparing audit reports and saves time. It may be necessary to have a number of specimens, for short reports, for longer ones and for reporting the results of fraud investigations. Another useful standard is to insist that each paragraph in the report is attached to a unique paragraph number from one onwards, for ease of reference. There are several Practice Advisories that give advice on audit reporting and possible communications criteria:

2410-1:   Although the format and content of the engagement final communications may vary by organization or type of engagement, they should contain at a minimum, the purpose, scope, and results of the engagement... Less significant observations or recommendations may be communicated informally. Engagement observations and recommendations emerge by a process of comparing what should be with what is:

- **Criteria**—standard, measure, expectations...
- **Condition**—factual evidence found during the audit...
- **Cause**—reason for the difference...
- **Effect**—risk or exposure as a result of the condition...

Conclusions (and opinions) are the internal auditor's evaluations of the effects of the observations and recommendations on the activities reviewed... A signed report should be issued after the engagement is completed...

2420-1:   Accurate communications are free from error and distortions and are faithful to the underlying facts... Objective communications are fair, impartial, and unbiased... Clear communications are easily understood and logical... Concise communications are to the point and avoid unnecessary elaborations, superfluous detail, redundancy, and wordiness... Constructive communications are helpful to the engagement client and the organization and lead to improvements where needed... Complete communications are lacking nothing that is essential... Timely communications are well timed, opportune and expedient.

Audit reporting procedures play a crucial role in the success of audits. The reporting mode should be geared into the culture of the organization and the needs of management. We have set out the minimum information that the auditor needs to consider when acquiring expertise on communicating the results of audit work as required under audit standards. We should also refer to the internal audit department's own reporting standard which will reflect the audit role agreed with the organization.

An Approach to Audit Clearance Procedures

One approach is to use audit presentations as part of the report drafting procedure to involve management and get an interactive response from them:

1. Complete field work with ongoing discussion with management on findings as they arise.
2. Draft a report that sets out work done, findings and recommendations.
3. Hold a presentation where the report is discussed, concentrating on the outline recommendations as the most important part. Give out the draft report at this meeting and 'sell the ideas'.
4. Ask management to consider the detailed report and meet again for its response. An action plan should then be formulated.
5. Review the report to take on board any matters that management has brought to your attention.
6. Send the report out for wider consultation with all who feature.
7. Prepare final report for formal publication.

There is no point in convening a presentation where the relationship between internal audit and the client is impoverished or has broken down. The presentation then becomes point scoring with little constructive work possible. There is nothing to be gained from a presentation where the underlying audit has not been professionally done. Where findings are flawed, recommendations unworkable and/or the auditor has not been objective, the work cannot be defended in a presentation.

9.9 Audit Committee Reporting

Activity reports are produced periodically by the CAE to formally report the activities of the internal audit department. These would typically go to the audit committee and may be based around an annual report and four separate quarterly reports. There are two key Practice Advisories on reporting on internal control and selected extracts follow:

2120.A1-1: ...The challenge for internal audit is to evaluate the effectiveness of the organization's system of controls based on the aggregation of many individual assessments—gained from internal audit engagements, management's self assessments, and the external auditor's work... (para. 7)

...The opinion section of the report is normally expressed in terms of negative assurance... If the control deficiencies or weaknesses are significant and pervasive, the assurance section of the report may be a qualified or adverse opinion, depending on the projected increase on the level of residual risk and its impact on the organization's objectives. (para. 9)

...The value of the report may be enhanced by including major recommendations for improvements and information about current control issues and trends... (para. 10)

Ample evidence exists of an 'expectation gap' surrounding the internal audit activity's work in evaluating and providing assurances about the state of control processes... (para. 11)

2060-1:   The CAE should submit activity reports to senior management and to the board at least annually. (para. 1)

Significant engagement observations (in the activity report) are those conditions that, in the judgement of the CAE, could adversely affect the organization—e.g. irregularities, illegal acts, errors, inefficiency, waste, ineffectiveness, conflicts of interest and control weaknesses. (para. 2)

...Senior management may decide to assume the risk of not correcting the reported condition... (para. 3)

Activity reports should also compare—actual performance of internal audit, expenditures v budgets—explain variances and action taken. (para. 5)

Quarterly Reporting Cycle

The quarterly reports will tend to include:

- Planning and control matters for the audit department.
- An outline of audit's performance for the quarter
- Statistics on types of work performed and departments charged.
- Brief summary of reports issued.
- Details of staff turnover.
- Overall productivity per output within time budgets.

Many are now seeking to assess internal audit's performance in terms of outcomes rather than outputs. For example, some people feel that an organization should measure the state of its control environment (through surveys and assessment) and assess the extent to which it is improving. If audit is contributing to a better understanding of internal control, compliance and the management of risks generally throughout the organization then targets may be set and considered in respect of these matters.

Annual Reporting Cycle

As well as recording the work carried out over the last year, reference will be made to the annual plan that will also be submitted for the coming year. As auditors we will be aware that reports can act as key controls so long as they are linked to a reference point in terms of expectations, that is a form of plan. There is a timing problem in that the planning period will start before the report can be available and this gap has to be dealt with through interim measures. The main point is that the report will discuss the risk and control issues of the organization, while the plan will seek to address any continuing deficiencies. The current audit strategy and how far audit plans, based on this strategy, have been accomplished will therefore be a feature of the report. There are several interesting points that can be noted regarding the annual audit report:

- The annual report must be received by the highest levels of the organization, ideally a suitably constituted audit committee.
- All comments relating to particular audits should be based on final audit reports, i.e. not uncleared drafts that management has not yet been able to respond to.

- Where the annual reporting period has expired then the current position must be available in outline to members of the audit committee so that the information that is provided is up to date.
- A view on the overall state of risk management and internal controls should be expressed along with the main implications of any material weaknesses and how these might then be tackled.
- A suitable format for the annual report should be decided beforehand
- The annual report will be formed more at an overview level
- The results are used as the basis of the annual audit opinion, which is one of the key supporting documents to enable the board and the executive chairman to sign the Statement of Internal Control and other disclosure documents with confidence. The risk and assurance programme, which has been in use since audit testing, gives assurance that the system of internal control is operating effectively.
- Problem areas encountered over the year.
- Pensive thoughts on the current state of the audit function and barriers to good performance.
- Performance data covering internal audit should be based around comparing actual results to planned targets.

9.10 A Risk-Based Audit Approach (RaCE)

One possible approach (developed by the author), albeit fairly general, is to frame the audit work around a model that we have called ICE, internal control evaluation. It is better referred to as risk and control evaluation (RaCE) and as a model can be applied to many different approaches to audit assurance and consulting services. Our RaCE model appears in Figure 9.21.

RISK and CONTROL EVALUATION						
A. Business area						
B. Corporate risk database		AUDIT APPROACH				
C. Control environment		←———————————————→				
D. Business risk awareness AUDIT REVIEW				VALIDATION		
E. Business objectives		FACILITATION				
F	G	H	I	J	K	L
RISKS	RISK RATING	CONTROL STANDARDS	KEY CONTROLS	RaCE AND TESTING	RISK OWNER	INTEGRATED ACTION PLANS
Comments..						

FIGURE 9.21   The RaCE approach.

The model is an interpretation of an audit approach that does not start with the need to 'catch people out'. It is based on adapting the approach to the context in question, and moving between the extremes of *audit review, facilitating* the client's assessment to simply *validating* the current self-assessment process. A useful quote on the concept of audit findings comes from Larry D. Hubbard who wrote:

> The term 'finding' is actually a misnomer. If a problem exists, auditors are not usually the ones who discover or identify it. Instead, it's more likely that the workers or management in the area already knew of the problem but just haven't addressed it yet. Calling this a finding suggests that our clients were hiding the problem and that we found it—a 'hide and seek' game between auditors and clients that organizations don't need to play. I prefer to label the issues encountered during an audit as either 'ineffective controls' or 'risks that have not been addressed'. . . A good audit report entails positive news for our clients. Or, as management might say, 'the best audit report is no audit report at all'.[5]

Using the alpha references A to L, the RaCE is explained in outline:

A: First identify exactly what business area is in the annual audit plan. This may be a section, team, project, process, change programme, local office, establishment, contract, business unit or whatever is deemed to be a distinct auditable area.

B: The next step is to find out where the business area (BA) stands on the corporate risks database in terms of relative risk in the organization. This should have been done to form the basis of the annual audit plan.

C: It may then be possible to assess the control environment in the BA. COSO and CoCo each have assessment questions and guidance that can be used to judge whether the BA is on a sound footing in terms of having an environment that reflects the corporate position in a trustworthy and reliable manner.

D: The next stage is to assess the extent to which risk and control assessment is understood and practised in the BA. Where there is a developed risk assessment procedure and good appreciation by managers, supervisors and staff generally, then we can start to judge where the BA stands in terms of having a robust risk management process in place and reliable risk registers.

E: This is simply isolating the agreed business objective of the BA in question.

Armed with the knowledge secured from the assessments A to E above, the audit approach may be determined. This may entail performing a standard audit (Audit review) where the control environment and level of risk appreciation is such that it is not possible to rely on a facilitated self-assessment review. Where the BA has a good control environment but is not equipped to carry out the risk assessment, then a facilitated (Facilitation) approach may be provided by the audit team to help the client get up to par. Where both the control environment promotes integrity, compliance and competence and self-assessment is being applied then audit may simply validate (Validation) the self-assessment already used by the BA, and concentrate on key controls that have been deemed important in managing the more material risks.

F: Risk to the achievement of business objectives are defined and updated to reflect current changes. For well-performing BAs the risk assessment will be based more on the future strategy, since the current position is already successfully managed.

G: Risk rating is simply the degree of materiality and likelihood that forms the basis for most risk assessment models.

H: Control standards are mechanisms that may be applied to managing the business risks that have been isolated in G.

The tasks F to H may be performed by the auditor (for the Audit approach), a convened workshop of client staff facilitated by the auditor (Facilitated approach) or through an examination of the current risk assessment already carried out by the client management (Validation audit approach).

I: This involves identifying the key controls in use.

J: The evaluation stage comes next where the key controls are considered in terms of whether they are sufficient to manage the risks, as compared to the control standards developed in H. Testing is carried out using the audit approach, while audit effort will focus on judging whether the client is able to assess compliance under the current arrangements. Where the RaCE is found to be sound on a self-assessed basis then the auditor may focus on validation and may perform some limited independent testing to check that controls are working properly.

K: Each risk assessment should be assigned to a risk (or process) owner so that it is clear where responsibility and accountability lie.

L: This part of the RaCE simply states that action required to manage risks is integrated within the current performance management arrangements. The way this is done is entirely up to the manager so long as the risks in question are dealt with in an efficient and effective manner in line with the corporate risk policy and defined risk appetite.

Where the auditor captures the above information in the RaCE, this process can drive the audit so that ascertainment is about identifying the system and risk (e.g. the flowchart and interview record), evaluation features in column J cross-referenced to the auditors' records and testing schedules are referenced to the lines in column J. Audit recommendations are based around findings from the evaluation and test results and feature in the final column L. The audit report is then a representation of the RaCE and describes the system, the risks, how they are managed and anything more that needs to be done to help ensure business objectives can be achieved. Where the RaCE has been performed by the client staff and facilitated by the auditor it becomes a joint effort between audit and client with some formal testing performed by the auditor. Where the RaCE has already been recently performed by the client, the auditor validates the work, updates the RaCE, performs selective testing and then is able to provide assurances on the adequacy of risk management and the underlying systems of internal control. The RaCE process depends on all parts of the organization embracing the risk management concept and using internal audit to assist this task with a mixture of assurance and consulting input depending on which approach best suits the business area in question. In this way the auditor:

- Recognizes that some business areas can be relied on to self-assess their systems and audit only needs to validate (and check) the arrangements in place.
- Helps those business areas that need to develop their risk assessment practices and so assesses their progress at the same time.
- Reviews areas where there are obvious problems and makes recommendations to improve the control environment and get risk management practices put in place. Audit will be concerned that the integrity and competence of people within the business area is properly developed.

In this way, audit field work may then be performed in a way that is both flexible and dynamic and makes sense to the client manager, board and the audit committee.

Summary and Conclusions

This chapter has provided an introduction to audit field work, from planning through to performing and reporting the engagement. We have mentioned interviewing, and the wider task of ascertaining the system, evaluation, testing techniques and communicating the results. In one sense, we have tried to write about something that is impossible to capture in one idea, that is the combination of risk-based systems audits, reviews, investigations, consulting projects and short exercises that typifies the internal auditors' work. Moreover, there really is no such thing as generic audit field work. There are only different types, and approaches to audit work to suit different contexts and challenges.

Chapter 9: Multi-Choice Questions

Having worked through the chapter the following multi-choice questions may be attempted. (See Appendix A for suggested answer guide and Appendix B where you may record your score.)

1. **Insert the missing words:**
   The annual audit plan lists those high risk areas that are targeted for audit cover during the next 12 months. The quarterly audit plan provides more detail by setting out those audits that will be performed by specified auditors in the following three months. Before the full audit is started and resources committed, an . . . . will direct and control these resources.
   a. audit team.
   b. audit report.
   c. audit manual.
   d. assignment plan.

2. **Insert the missing words:**
   The preliminary survey seeks to accumulate relevant information regarding the operation under review so that a defined direction of the ensuing audit (if it goes ahead) may be agreed. The . . . . will be the first port of call and any previous audit cover will be considered.
   a. audit committee.
   b. internal audit files.
   c. chief auditor.
   d. internet.

3. **Which is the most appropriate sentence?**
   a. We must define an audit budget in terms of time allowed. Time is the key factor on any audit. Setting a time budget acts as a principal control over the assignment and is the only concern of audit management.
   b. We must define an audit budget in terms of time allowed. Time is the key factor on any audit. Setting an audit travel expenses budget acts as a principal control over the assignment and is the single most important concern of audit management.
   c. We must define an audit budget in terms of time allowed. Time is the key factor on any audit. Setting a time budget acts as a principal control over the assignment and is the single most important concern of audit management.

d. We must define an audit budget in terms of time allowed. Interviews are the key factor for any audit. Setting up interviews acts as a principal control over the assignment and is the single most important concern of audit management.

4. Insert the missing words:

Gathering information is a fundamental part of audit work as the auditor spends a great deal of time fact-finding. The starting place for establishing facts is simply to ask, and herein lies the importance of . . . .

a. interviewing.
b. planning.
c. analysing.
d. testing.

5. Which is the least appropriate sentence?

Based on much that we have already discussed, we may provide an outline illustration of how we might structure a typical audit interview:

a. Introductions. This involves introducing all parties present at the interview and explaining their role, relative importance, status and position within the information-gathering process.
b. Objectives. What is hoped to be achieved from the interview is then fully communicated and further clarification provided if needs be.
c. Questions and answers. The main body of the interview should then proceed in a way that flows naturally and promotes the achievement of the original objectives of the meeting.
d. Wind up. The next stage is to recheck the information that has been given and any matters (such as the exchange of specific documents) that have already been agreed.

6. Which is the least appropriate item?

The main options that the auditor has for documenting the system are:

a. Narrative notes.
b. Block diagrams.
c. Flowcharts.
d. Surveillance.

7. Which is the least appropriate item?

Flowcharts may be used in the following ways:

a. Weak areas or waste of resources may be isolated so that audit attention may be directed towards these parts of the system, or problems can simply be referred to in the report.
b. One can draw a second flowchart to show proposed improvements. The relevant stages may be highlighted in 'before' and 'after' charts that is presented to management as the new system designed by the auditors.
c. One may use the internal control questionnaire (ICQ) in conjunction with flowcharts, expanding on areas where there may be systems weaknesses. ICQs are also a form of systems ascertainment in that they relay the control features of the area under review.
d. Walkthrough tests may be used to take a small sample of transactions through the system so that the integrity of the documentation may be determined.

8. Which is the least appropriate item?

The system being reviewed is the system being applied in practice in line with management's operational objectives. The evaluation applied should be based on those controls required to ensure systems objectives are achieved with no great loss or inefficiency. Evaluation techniques include:

a. Flowcharts. These help identify systems blockages, duplication of effort and segregation of duties along with controls that depend on documentation flows and the way work is organized.

b. Transactions testing. By testing transactions one might pick up systems malfunctions that cause error conditions identified by the tests.

c. Directed representations. One cannot deny the usefulness of information provided by persons who have knowledge of the system. If management states that there are defined systems weaknesses at the outset of an audit, we will tend to ignore this source of information.

d. Internal control questionnaires (ICQ) and Internal control evaluation system (ICES).

9. Which is the most appropriate sentence?

a. The ICQ should be completed by the chief audit executive using all available sources of information from interviews, observation, initial testing, documents, manuals, representations, and past audit files.

b. The ICQ should be completed by the auditor using all available sources of information from interviews, observation, initial testing, documents, manuals, past audit files but not representations made by managers.

c. The ICQ should be completed by the client manager using all available sources of information from interviews, observation, initial testing, documents, manuals, representations, and past audit files

d. The ICQ should be completed by the auditor using all available sources of information from interviews, observation, initial testing, documents, manuals, representations, and past audit files.

10. Insert the missing words:

During control evaluation the . . . . is perhaps the single most important factor and this will be based on experience and training.

a. auditor's instincts.

b. auditor's likes and dislikes.

c. auditor's judgement.

d. auditor's analytical software.

11. Which is the least appropriate item?

The four types of tests:

a. Walkthrough: This involves taking a large number of items that are traced through the system to ensure that the auditor understands the system.

b. Compliance: This determines whether key controls are adhered to.

c. Substantive: These determine whether control objectives are being achieved.

d. Dual purpose: This is not a test but a recognition of the practicalities of testing controls where one may wish to combine compliance and substantive testing.

12. Which is the most appropriate sentence?

The internal auditor will need to secure sufficient information to complete the audit and Practice Advisory 2310-1 suggests that:

a. Sufficient information is factual, adequate and convincing so that a prudent, informed person would reach the same conclusions as the auditor. Competent information is reliable and the best attainable through the use of appropriate engagement techniques. Relevant information helps the organization meet its goals. Useful information supports engagement observations and recommendations and is consistent with the objectives for the engagement.

b. Sufficient information is reliable and the best attainable through the use of appropriate engagement techniques. Competent information is factual, adequate and convincing so that a prudent, informed person would reach the same conclusions as the auditor. Relevant information supports engagement observations and recommendations and is consistent with the objectives for the engagement. Useful information helps the organization meet its goals.

c. Sufficient information helps the organization meet its goals. Competent information is reliable and the best attainable through the use of appropriate engagement techniques. Relevant information supports engagement observations and recommendations and is consistent with the objectives for the engagement. Useful information is factual, adequate and convincing so that a prudent, informed person would reach the same conclusions as the auditor.

d. Sufficient information is factual, adequate and convincing so that a prudent, informed person would reach the same conclusions as the auditor. Competent information is reliable and the best attainable through the use of appropriate engagement techniques. Relevant information supports engagement observations and recommendations and is consistent with the objectives for the engagement. Useful information helps the organization meet its goals.

13. Which is the least appropriate item?

There are various IIA performance standards that address the need for proper records of each audit engagement that has been carried out:

a. 2330—Recording Information: Internal auditors should record relevant information to support the conclusions and engagement results.

b. 2330.A1—The CAE should control access to engagement records. The CAE need not obtain approval from senior management and/or legal counsel prior to releasing such records to external parties.

c. 2330.A2—The CAE should develop retention requirements for engagement records. These retention requirements should be consistent with the organization's guidelines and any pertinent regulatory or other requirements.

d. 2330.C1—The CAE should develop policies governing the custody and retention of engagement records, as well as their release to internal and external parties. These policies should be consistent with the organization's guidelines and any pertinent regulatory or other requirements.

14. Which is the least appropriate item?

The evidence the auditor uses for the audit opinion should be:

a. Sufficient: This is in line with materiality, level of risk and the level of auditors' knowledge of the operation.

b. Relevant: This ensures that evidence is directed to the control objectives.

c. Reliable: The information should be accurate, without bias and if possible produced by a third party or obtained directly by the auditor.

d. Practical: One would weigh up the evidence required, regardless of the cost and time taken to obtain it, all sound evidence should be secured.

15. Which is the least appropriate item?

Statistical sampling has a clear role and auditors make a decision during systems audits. The internal auditor will be concerned about:

a. Whether examining selected transactions confirms initial opinion on the systems of risk management and internal control.
b. Whether their findings are sufficient to convince management to act.
c. Whether the risk of any losses or deficiencies may be quantified.
d. Whether their tests can be extended to include 100% of system transactions.

16. Which item is incorrect?

With statistical sampling one has to set the criteria within which the results should be evaluated and this falls under three basic parameters:

a. **Error rate:** This is the level of error that one may expect from the population being tested. Error may be seen as, for example, the number of invoices that are incorrect. This is normally set at 5% and most statistical sampling tables are based on this figure. If the actual error rate is different then a revision to the quoted risk boundaries has to be made. The rate is determined by the auditor and is based on pilot studies, discussions with management and the results of previous audits.
b. **Confidence:** Confidence is the degree to which the results derived from the sample will follow the trend in the actual population. A 95% confidence means that 95 out of every 100 items examined will reflect the population.
c. **Precision:** This shows the margin within which the results can be quoted and defines the degree of accuracy that is required. It may be in terms of the quoted error being expressed as a figure taken from testing the sample plus or minus the degree of precision, say 2%. The real result relative to the population will be somewhere within the lower and upper levels. If one needs to be accurate to 2% one may find an error in the sample of, say, £100, this may be quoted for the population as between £88 and £112. The level chosen will depend on the objective of the test and how the results are used.
d. **Extrapolation:** This is when results taken from a sample are grossed up and applied to the whole population. The average result from the sample is multiplied by the value of the population to give the estimated total error. Risk parameters are set by the auditor and depend on the test objective. It is practice to use 5% error rate tables, with 95% confidence at plus or minus 2% precision. Using these standards, most statistically extrapolated results will be accepted by management.

17. Insert the missing words:

There are many components and principles that underlie audit reporting, the most important of which is the . . . . that has been carried out prior to the reporting stage.

a. degree of detailed work.
b. quantity of audit work.
c. time spent on testing.
d. quality of audit work.

18. Which sentence is least appropriate?

Before the full audit report is produced one would expect interim reports particularly on larger projects. These have several main uses:

a. They force the auditor to build the report as work is progressed.
b. They keep the audit manager up to date and allows interim reviews of work performed.

    c. In this way they may be given to the client and so act as a continuous report clearance device as well as bringing the client into the audit process itself.

    d. They allow a detailed document of everything that happened during the audit to be prepared and presented.

19. **Which sentence is least appropriate?**

This is what most auditors think of when considering the topic of audit reports and it is dealt with in some detail below:

    a. Executive summaries: A two or three page summary can be attached to the front of the report or issued as a separate document.

    b. Follow-up reports: All audit work should be followed up and it is possible to establish a standardized reporting format to check on outstanding audit recommendations.

    c. Oral reports: Auditors are charged with reporting the results of audit work and this may be in an oral format which avoids the need to prepare a written report.

    d. Fraud investigation reports: These reports detail the allegations, the work carried out and why, as well as the main findings.

20. **Which sentence is least appropriate?**

Extensive audit resources may be spent on performing an audit and the client may see as the end product a published audit report. It is therefore important that the objectives of this final document are clearly established and the four main functions of the audit report are:

    a. To support action plans that are prepared by the auditor for client management.

    b. To alert them to areas where this is not the case and there are defined risk exposures.

    c. To advise them on steps necessary to improve risk management strategies.

    d. To assure management that business risks are well controlled.

References

1. Colbert, Janet L. 'Audit sampling'. *Internal Auditor*, Feb. 2001, pp. 27–29.
2. Sawyer, Lawrence B. and Dittenhofer Mortimer A. assisted by Scheiner James H. (1996) *Sawyer's Internal Auditing*, 4th edition, Florida: The Institute of Internal Auditors.
3. Anderson, Urton and Chapman, Christy (2002) in The IIA Handbook Series in *Implementing The Professional Practices Framework*, IIA, p. 167.
4. Morris, Joe, *Internal Auditing*, Sept. 1989, p. 19.
5. Hubbard, Larry D. 'What's a good audit finding?' *Internal Auditor*, Feb. 2001, p. 104.

Chapter 10

MEETING THE CHALLENGE

Introduction

This short chapter considers some of the challenges for the profession based on comments from writers from the internal audit community and beyond. The areas that are touched on include:

10.1 The New Dimensions of Internal Auditing
10.2 Globalization
10.3 The Changing Auditor
10.4 Meeting the Challenge
10.5 Ten Little Maxims
    Summary and Conclusions
    Chapter Ten: Multi-Choice Questions

10.1 The New Dimensions of Internal Auditing

We accept that internal audit must deliver added value to the organization and this is defined by the IIA as:

> Organisations exist to create value or benefit to their owners, other stakeholders, customers, and clients. This concept provides purpose for their existence. Value is provided through their development of products and services and their use of resources to promote those products and services. In the process of gathering data to understand and assess risk, internal auditors develop significant insights into operations and opportunities for improvement that can be extremely beneficial to their organisation. This valuable information can be in the form of consultation, advice, written communications or through other products all of which should be properly communicated to the appropriate management or operating personnel.[1]

Against this measure is the changing context of internal auditing which is summed up in the IIA's work on the context for internal auditing competency frameworks, in Chapter 5 of the IIA Handbook Series on 'Implementing the professional practices framework':

Past Focus	Additional Focus
hard controls	soft controls
control evaluation	self-assessment
control	risk
risk	context
risk threats	risk opportunities
past	future
review	preview
detective	preventive
operational audit	strategy audit

auditor	consultant
imposition	invitation
persuasion	negotiation
independence	value
audit knowledge	business knowledge
catalyst	change facilitator
transaction	processes
control activities	management controls
control	risk
consciousness	consciousness[2]

This sets the new dimensions of internal auditing as the concepts on the right-hand side become a benchmark for each chief audit executive to consider.

10.2 Globalization

One real development in internal auditing coincides with the way business (and public services) are becoming increasingly internationalized. Physical location is no longer an issue as buying activity is moving away from the local high street as it launches into hyperspace through the Internet. The IIA has grasped this new thinking and is developing the profession into a global internal auditing organization whose broad business objectives include:

- Establishing global standards for the practice of internal auditing.
- Promoting the professional certification of internal auditors worldwide.
- Fostering the development of the profession around the globe.
- Representing and promoting internal auditing across national borders.
- Facilitating the timely sharing of information among Member associations.
- Searching for globally applicable products and services.[3]

10.3 The Changing Auditor

Philip Sainty has described a survey conducted by the institute in the wake of the WorldCom debacle, concerning the way the internal auditing profession has moved away from traditional financial auditing towards risk-based auditing. Four groups were described in terms of attitudes towards this change in focus:

- **The Evangelist**   Some 48% of respondents fell into this group. They believed that the move towards risk-based auditing has not had a negative impact on the traditional work of internal audit and should continue unfettered.
- **The Doomsayer**   Some 24% of respondents fell into this group. They believe that the move towards risk-based auditing has damaged the traditional work of internal audit and should not continue.
- **The Pragmatists**   Some 18% of respondents fell into this group. They felt that the move to risk-based auditing had changed the traditional work of the internal audit, but said that the trend should continue nonetheless.
- **The Doubters**   Some 5% of respondents fell into this group. They felt that the move to risk-based auditing had not damaged the traditional work of internal audit but said that the trend should not continue.[4]

We said at the start of *The Essential Handbook* that it is important not to throw the baby out with the bathwater. Professor Andrew Chambers has warned about the dangers of getting swept away on the tide of consulting styles and not retaining a semblance of our original role, by suggesting that:

> I am a bit of a traditionalist. Rather than looking for some jazzy, sexy new horizon to strive for (as has been internal auditors' wont since the start) my view is that the pendulum may swing back. Someone has to provide the good old fashioned assurance through control assessment (including detailed testing) comprehensively covering all the affairs of the enterprise over time. When will managements and internal auditors learn! Boards are already convinced, I think—they know the importance of assurance.

10.4 Meeting the Challenge

All countries to a greater or lesser extent are coming to recognize the great value from an internal audit service. It is hard to think of any particular corporate service that is enshrined in laws and regulations and which carries the burden of the societal expectations that we have mentioned. In August 2002, LeRoy E. Bookal, chairman of IIA.Inc., wrote that:

> With our unique viewpoint as independent but inside observers, internal auditors play a vital role within governance processes by keeping the board, senior management, and external auditors aware of risk and control issues and by assessing the effectiveness of risk management... Audit committees and boards are facing skyrocketing liability costs and ever-increasing workloads. It's no wonder that liability costs are rising—boards have to meet more governance challenges each year, but their resources for information about their increasingly complex organisations are limited. In the post-Enron era, it is surprising that boards of directors for any publicly held companies would choose to do without internal auditing. It is also surprising that investors, liability insurers, and other stakeholders have not questioned the decision to do without internal auditing more often... There is no simple checklist showing everything internal auditors can do to add value, because, at times, techniques for adding value are as unique and personalized as the organisations for which we work.[5]

10.5 Ten Little Maxims

There is much that internal audit is expected to contribute and much that can be done to make this contribution. We have featured the words of Larry Sawyer in the Handbook and there is no reason not to include something in the final chapter. Many years ago Sawyer wrote out Ten Little Maxims for the internal auditor:

1. Leave every place a little better than you found it.
2. You can't stomp your foot when you are on your knees.
3. Know the objectives.
4. Nothing ever happens until somebody sells something.
5. Every deficiency is rooted in the violation of some principle of good management.
6. Never believe what the first person tells you.
7. The best question is, 'Mr or Ms Manager, how do you satisfy yourself that... ?'
8. Politics and culture will usually win over rules and regulations.
9. When you point your finger, make sure your finger nail is clean.
10. Murphy was an optimist.[6]

Summary and Conclusions

The IIA.Inc has prepared a note on their web site that considers 'Internal Auditing: Adding Value Across the Board' in which they suggest:

> One does not have to sit in the boardroom or occupy the CEO's chair to recognize the rapid-fire changes going on in today's corporate environment. The business pages regularly contain reports of mergers, acquisitions, and other organizational restructurings; electronic commerce and other information technology breakthroughs; privacy invasions; and plain old-fashioned frauds. And things are likely to get even more frenetic. The challenges of today's changing world introduce great opportunities for management and the board and point to the necessity for competent internal auditing. Especially in these times of constant change, internal auditing is critical to efficient operations, effective internal controls and risk management, strong corporate governance, and in some cases, the very survival of the Organization.

My view of the changing world of the internal auditor is quite simple, and it is summed up in the following dimensions that move through stages 1–7; from old- to new-look contexts:

1. We're here to check on you
2. We're here to check your controls
3. We're here to check your risks
4. We're here to check your risk management system
5. We're here to help you establish risk management
6. We're here to help you achieve success
7. We're here to help you prove you can be trusted to take care of our business

Chapter Ten: Multi-Choice Questions

Having worked through the chapter the following multi-choice questions may be attempted. (See Appendix A for suggested answer guide and Appendix B where you may record your score.)

1. Which is the most appropriate sentence?
We accept that internal audit must deliver added value to the organization and this is defined by the IIA as:

a. Organizations exist to create value or benefit to their owners, other stakeholders, customers and clients. This concept provides purpose for their existence. Value is provided through their development of audit reports and their use of resources to promote those reports.

b. Organizations exist to create money for their owners, other stakeholders, customers and clients. This concept provides purpose for their existence. Value is provided through their development of products and services and their use of resources to promote those products and services.

c. Organizations exist to create value or benefit to their owners, other stakeholders, customers and clients. This concept provides purpose for their existence. Professionalism is provided through their development of products and services and their use of resources to promote those products and services.

d. Organizations exist to create value or benefit to their owners, other stakeholders, customers and clients. This concept provides purpose for their existence. Value is provided through their development of products and services and their use of resources to promote those products and services.

2. Insert the missing word:

The IIA has grasped this new thinking and is developing the profession into a . . . . internal auditing organization whose broad business objectives include:

- establishing global standards for the practice of internal auditing.
- promoting the professional certification of internal auditors worldwide.
- fostering the development of the profession around the globe.
- representing and promoting internal auditing across national borders.
- facilitating the timely sharing of information among Member associations.
- searching for globally applicable products and services.
  - a. good.
  - b. dynamic.
  - c. global.
  - d. important.

3. Which is the most appropriate sentence?

In August 2002, LeRoy E. Bookal, chairman of IIA.Inc., wrote that:

a. There is no simple checklist showing everything internal auditors can do to add value, because, at times, techniques for adding value are as unique and personalized as the organisations for which we work.

b. There is a simple checklist showing everything internal auditors can do to add value, because, at times, techniques for adding value are as unique and personalized as the organisations for which we work.

c. There is no simple checklist showing everything internal auditors can do to add value, because, at times, techniques for adding value are common and personalized as the organisations for which we work.

d. There is no simple checklist showing everything internal auditors can do to add value, because, at times, techniques for adding value are personal to the auditor and not the organisations for which we work.

4. Insert the missing words:

The IIA.Inc has prepared a note on their web site that considers "Internal Auditing: Adding Value Across the Board" in which they suggest:

. . .The challenges of today's changing world introduce great opportunities for management and the board and point to the necessity for competent internal auditing. Especially in these times of . . . ., internal auditing is critical to efficient operations, effective internal controls and risk management, strong corporate governance, and in some cases, the very survival of the Organization.

a. constant change.
b. confusion and chaos.
c. political uncertainty.
d. economic growth.

5. Which is the most appropriate sentence?

My view of the changing world of the internal auditor is quite simple, and it is summed up in the following dimensions that move through stages 1–7; from old- to new-look contexts:

a. We're here to check on you and we're here to check your controls.

b. We're here to check your risks and we're here to check your risk management system.

c. We're here to help you establish risk management and we're here to help you achieve success.

d. We're here to make sure you can be trusted to take care of our business.

References

1. IIA Standards—Glossary.
2. Chapman, Christy and Anderson, Urton, IIA 2002 'Implementing the professional practices framework', p. 91, in The IIA Handbook Series.
3. Global IIA, The Case For Globalization, 1 Oct. 2001 (www.theiia.org).
4. Sainty, Philip, 'Breaking out'. Internal Auditing and Business Risk, Sept. 2002, pp. 19–20.
5. Bookal, Leroy E., Chairman of IIA.Inc. 'Internal auditors—integral to good corporate governance'. Internal Auditing, Aug. 2002, pp. 44–49.
6. Sawyer, Lawrence B., 'An internal audit philosophy'. Internal Auditor, Aug. 1995, p. 46.

Appendix A

SUGGESTED ANSWERS

Trainers may detach the answer guide from each copy of the book before handing it out to participants.

CHAPTERS	1	2	3	4	5	6	7	8	9	10
QUESTION										
1	b	b	c	a	d	a	a	d	d	d
2	c	d	b	d	a	d	b	b	b	c
3	d	a	d	b	b	d	c	d	c	a
4	a	d	a	a	a	b	b	c	a	a
5	c	c	c	b	d	a	c	d	a	d
6		b	b	d	d	c	d	c	d	
7		d	c	d	c	b	b	d	b	
8		d	c	c	d	a	d	a	c	
9		b	b	a	a	d	a	a	d	
10		a	a	a	a	b	d	b	c	
11									a	
12									d	
13									b	
14									d	
15									d	
16									c	
17									d	
18									d	
19									c	
20									a	

Appendix B

CANDIDATE'S ANSWERS

Please insert your answers in the table below and then add up the number of correct answers achieved. Note that there are 100 questions—the total score will therefore represent a percentage.

CHAPTERS	1	2	3	4	5	6	7	8	9	10
QUESTION										
1										
2										
3										
4										
5										
6										
7										
8										
9										
10										
11										
12										
13										
14										
15										
16										
17										
18										
19										
20										
CORRECT SCORES										
TOTAL CORRECT MARKS FOR ALL CHAPTERS							%			

INDEX